High Drama

The Rise, Fall, and Rebirth of American Competition Climbing

John Burgman

TRIUMPH
B O O K S

Library of Congress Cataloging-in-Publication Data available upon request.

This book is available in quantity at special discounts for your group or organization. For further information, contact:
  Triumph Books LLC
  814 North Franklin Street
  Chicago, Illinois 60610
  (312) 337-0747
  www.triumphbooks.com

Printed in U.S.A.
ISBN: 978-1-62937-775-9
Design by Nord Compo

This book is dedicated to those whose names, efforts, and dreams reside in its pages.

From this hour I ordain myself loos'd of limits and imaginary lines,
Going where I list, my own master total and absolute…

Walt Whitman, *Song of the Open Road*

CONTENTS

FOREWORD

WHAT IS COMPETITION CLIMBING TODAY? Where has it been and where is it going? Having been involved with climbing gyms and competitions from the mid-1990s and in places nowhere near real rocks (Florida!), the past couple of decades have shown us how quickly a sport can evolve.

It still seems a little unbelievable, but it is true: the sport of climbing is going to the Olympics!

Will it bring fame and wealth to some incredibly gifted climbing athletes? Absolutely.

Will it spur an incredible amount of growth in the number of people participating in climbing? Absolutely.

Does Olympic inclusion run the risk of further distancing the sport of competition climbing from the sport, or spirit, of rock climbing? Absolutely.

Over the course of my career with USA Climbing, I held out hope that someone would gather the stories about the people (and events) that have given their heart and soul to this sport and shaped the way modern competition climbing looks and functions. As I have seen how quickly things can change and grow, from early competitions in the first-generation climbing gyms to the skyrocketing participation of youth climbers, and now to high-production televised National and World Cup events, this hope was somewhat driven by fear—a fear that history would fade away with our memories and that there would be no chronicle for future generations to read. Kudos to John Burgman for stepping up to ensure that the stories live on: the stories that tell us not only where we are but where we came from.

Like many others, we stand on the shoulders of our predecessors. The list of impactful names is far too long to try to compile here. This history can give us the opportunity to understand where we are now, offer thanks to all of those who stepped up to try to strive for better with our sport, and inspire current and future generations to further shape climbing. We need to recognize the incredibly positive impact that all the folks inside of these pages have made on competition climbing, and that the sport we all enjoy today is a result of a lot of hard work, likely for very little monetary gain. Our cumulative impact is reflected today in both domestic and international climbing competitions, and of this I am extremely proud.

As we look forward to the 2020 Olympics in Tokyo and the 2024 Olympics in Paris, please note the responsibility that we share with every athlete, event organizer, and routesetter: that of staying true to the counterculture roots of the sport of rock climbing while staying open to the possibilities inherent in competition climbing.

"History is a relentless master. It has no present, only the past rushing into the future. To try to hold fast is to be swept aside."—John F. Kennedy

Enjoy the read!

—Kynan Waggoner
November 2019

PREFACE

——————

O NE OF THE MOST EXCITING MOMENTS in the history of American competition climbing took place on February 3, 2018. The Bouldering
National Championship, played out over multiple days and multiple
rounds at the Salt Palace Convention Center in Salt Lake City, Utah,
had culminated in a final boulder. The result of the men's division had already been confirmed, with Nathaniel Coleman besting
all other competitors in a star-making performance in his home
state. It was a historic moment in its own right, but more thrilling
was the result of the women's division, which remained far more
open-ended. In fact, four of the United States' greatest competitors—Brooke Raboutou, Claire Buhrfeind, Ashima Shiraishi, and
Alex Puccio—were in contention to become the women's national
champion. Their respective attempts to climb the last boulder would
determine the outcome.

However, there was more than just a revered championship on
the line. An announcement that climbing was to be included in the

2020 Olympics had recently provided the whole sport with a jolt of energy, and this championship's exhilarating conclusion would give direct insight about the United States' Olympic prospects; indeed, whichever woman won this Bouldering National Championship would be considered one of the early American favorites for a possible invitation to the impending Olympic Games.

On top of that newfound Olympic sheen, indoor climbing was in the midst of a popularity boom in the United States. There were more than 400 climbing gyms around the country, and that number was increasing each year. In congested urban areas, old factories and abandoned warehouses were being purchased by developers and repurposed as climbing gyms. Brooklyn Boulders, First Ascent, Earth Treks, Planet Granite, Momentum Climbing, Mesa Rim, Hangar 18, Hoosier Heights, and other gyms seemed to be constantly expanding with new facilities. With them, new life was being breathed into forsaken real estate, and the sport of climbing was being offered more and more in the American recreational milieu. Students at colleges could now take climbing classes, and children as young as three years old could enroll in climbing gyms' youth clubs. Some American climbers had become veritable celebrities, with lucrative sponsorship arrangements and financial support from companies ranging from Patagonia and The North Face to Polo and Coca-Cola.

Underlying all these extraneous elements at the Salt Palace Convention Center that afternoon was a palpable competitive tension. The event was offering spectators—both inside the facility and watching a livestream online—athletic theater that had long characterized other sports like baseball, football, basketball, and tennis. Specifically, the women's bouldering division was herein presenting a nail-biting finish and proving competition climbing to be exciting, engaging, and unpredictable.

And with that, the first few women competitors—Margo Hayes, Meagan Martin, and Brooke Raboutou—made their respective attempts at climbing the final boulder. It was not an easy task. The boulder's climbing route began beneath a long roof section. Successfully reaching the top for any competitor would entail first crouching below the roof, then moving horizontally over its crowd-facing ledge, and returning to a vertical position to reach the last handhold. Every sequence would require a mix of strength and coordination, as well as a compartmentalization of the fatigue that was reaching its weekend peak.

Hayes, Martin, and Raboutou were undoubtedly three of the best climbers in the entire world; Hayes had successfully climbed famed outdoor routes in countries around the world, such as La Rambla and Biographie in Spain and France, respectively. The ascents, each among the most challenging of all the established climbs, had justifiably made Hayes a climbing icon of her generation. Martin, iconic in her own right, had coupled her decorated competitive climbing career with much-admired appearances on the sports-entertainment television program *American Ninja Warrior*. And Raboutou, whose parents are legendary competitors Didier and Robyn Erbesfield-Raboutou, had become the youngest person ever to climb a route at a difficulty grade of 5.14b when she climbed Spain's Welcome to Tijuana at age 11.

Yet, as Hayes, Martin, and Raboutou attempted to ascend the boulder at the national championship, they each became bested by the climbing route's steep roof section. When it was clear that none of them would be able to successfully climb to the top of the boulder in the allotted time, the crowd began to murmur. The tension continued to mount as the championship's result was undetermined.

The next competitor to make an attempt on the boulder was Buhrfeind. She was noted for being possibly the best American all-around climber; she had dabbled in multiple competitive disciplines over the years and was certainly capable of reaching the top of the boulder's burly sequence. To provide support, the crowd cheered as Buhrfeind began her attempt and worked through the boulder's balance-centric lower section. Reaching the top on this final boulder would be somewhat redemptive for Buhrfeind since she had not reached the top of the previous two boulders in the competition; it was another plotline in the ongoing drama.

Buhrfeind continued to try hard on the boulder. She contorted her body into the requisite sequencing puzzle as her allotted time of four minutes expired. But she, too, was unable to reach the top. The result of the competition was still undecided.

The final two competitors were Puccio and Shiraishi. They epitomized climbing's growth in popularity, with Puccio being a Coloradan who had ruled the national competition scene for more than a decade and Shiraishi being a New Yorker who had only recently entered the adult competition scene.

Puccio climbed first, nudging herself into a nook below the boulder's roof before lunging for an overhanging handhold. Her hands grabbed the correct handhold as her feet swung freely, dangling above the ground. The crowd gasped. As Puccio took a moment to rest in a hanging position on the wall, the clock ticked down— only two minutes remained for her attempt to reach the top of the boulder. She readied herself for a big, methodical reach over the lip section of the roof but fell to the ground amid the movement. The crowd sighed. Puccio was clearly exhausted and there was not much time remaining on the clock; another quick attempt soon proved futile. She did not reach the top either, and now all she could do was wait for Shiraishi's attempt.

Rather than blitz through a series of multiple attempts, Shiraishi's strategy was to assess the boulder's sequencing from the ground and then give a singular effort—an all-or-nothing approach with a calmness that seemed to contradict her teenage years. Like Puccio, Shiraishi began her attempt with a steady climb through the boulder's lower section. Then she advanced to the lip of the boulder's steep roof. But Shiraishi had thus far climbed slower than the previous competitors. The clock had ticked down and she now had only one minute to progress through the boulder's last three handholds.

Shiraishi's pace on the wall quickened. She tried doggedly to lunge for one of the handholds above the lip. When she wasn't successful, rather than fall to the ground, she hung in a horizontal position to recompose herself. The clock ticked down even more—into the final 30 seconds of her attempt. The crowd shouted encouragement. Then Shiraishi sprang once more for the handhold. If she grasped it, she would be on her way to her first national championship.

Shiraishi fell to the ground as the crowd collectively exhaled. It was a valiant effort—worthy of replay and analysis, despite the outcome. And Shiraishi was so talented that a feeling pervaded her performance: she would have many more national championships in her future. Her time would come, someday.

The failed attempt solidified the competition's result: Puccio was once again deemed the national champion. Her performance throughout, particularly on the four boulders in the finals, had been remarkable. She had shown great fortitude as she climbed despite multiple finger injuries. She had also exhibited great veteran savvy, deciphering boulders' routesetting that had been rife with awkward movements and complex handhold series.

As the result was announced, the crowd cheered and gave Puccio a standing ovation. The applause was not only for the winner, but for all the competitors and for the drama of the event itself. Climbing had finally secured its footing as both a participant and spectator sport.

But in the result—in its coupling of athletics and narrative—was a curiosity. As an activity, climbing had its ancestry first in mountaineering and then in outdoor leisure. It had long been a sport of rock and risk. Particularly in the United States, it had been fashioned by grizzled outsiders who derided most activities of the mainstream. Puccio's victory at the 2018 Bouldering National Championship bore little resemblance to such bohemian outdoor recreation. For starters, her victory had taken place *indoors*, and the entire national championship concept had been nourished by a vast network of gyms in all corners of the country that offered climbing indoors. Also, any championship was the pinnacle of a season-long competitive arc, and although a competitive spirit had presumably been present in rock climbing since its inception, organized competitions were not undertakings that had always been embraced and promoted by the climbing community at large.

In other words, Puccio's victory, and the conclusion of the championship, presented a host of intriguing questions: How did American rock climbing evolve so drastically and imaginatively as to no longer include rocks at all? How did it go from being an outdoor niche of insubordinates to the prevalent pastime of people of all ages and backgrounds? And, perhaps most compelling, how did the carefree recreation of climbing become a competitive sport loved by the American masses?

This book is an attempt to answer those questions and tell the fascinating story of American competition climbing. It is a collective story mostly of determined people who were willing to embrace something new, as climbing has long been an activity steeped in tradition and ritual. The history of the United States competition scene is a chronicle of change. Undoubtedly, the advancing competition story will continue to be fashioned in years to come with new people, new circumstances, and fresh ideas. In the meantime, it is worth identifying just how we got to where we are now.

Perhaps the best place to begin is with a couple of buddies who simply wanted to go climbing.

CHAPTER 1

NEW IDEAS

___

ONE HAZY AFTERNOON IN 1987, a young California rock climber named Jim Thornburg met up with a longtime friend, Scott Frye, to carry out an ambitious plan. The first step was to load up the car with an ample supply of the strongest epoxy available on the market. Thornburg and Frye had considered different adhesives before selecting a specific glue that would suit their needs. The epoxy they had chosen, advertised for use in repairing small items like jewelry and ceramics, was the same epoxy California's road construction crews used to adhere small reflectors to the state's asphalt highways.

But in heavy contrast to securing ceramics and road reflectors, Thornburg and Frye needed the epoxy to serve a far more unusual purpose: to hold the full weight of an adult climber.

Upon stocking up on large cans of the adhesive, the pair drove their car away from the mass of homes and retail stores in the heart of Berkeley, in search of a secluded location somewhere on the city's sprawling outskirts. The next phase of their plan entailed holing up someplace that was as architecturally urban as the bustling downtown districts but more nondescript. Thornburg and Frye didn't want anyone to notice what they were about to do.

The spot they decided on was an unexceptional on-ramp located at the back of the Lake Temescal reservoir. At one time, the reservoir had supplied drinking water to a vast grid of California residents. More recently it had served as a haven for ducks and geese, and, fittingly, as a backdrop for a wide array of recreation like boating and fishing. The on-ramp was wedged in between the blandly suburban and mostly residential areas of Oakland's Upper Rockridge to the west and Hiller Highlands to the north. It offered no scenic views of any iconic California vistas; the ocean was miles away, as were trendier parts of Oakland to the south. In fact, in its immediate trajectory the ramp did not lead anywhere of note—it simply served to ease commuters onto Highway 13, which itself only led to more unexceptional spread. It then cut through the blandly suburban, mostly residential Elmwood area.

Hundreds of other cars had likely coasted along this ramp earlier that morning and paid no attention to its load-bearing base. But the concrete base was precisely why Thornburg and Frye were drawn to this particular section of road. Supporting the ramp were a collection of tall concrete pillars that rose up at sheer vertical angles; in a sense, they were not that dissimilar to some of the immense natural rocks of the Sierra Nevada Mountains to the east.

Best of all, the pillars beneath the Highway 13 overpass were wide, which allowed for upward and sideways movement. In fact, Thornburg and Frye had previously been to these on-ramp pillars and scaled the expansion cracks using standard hand jams and layback moves. But today, the end goal of their ambitious plan was to give the pillars entirely new climbable faces. Real mountain cliffs had bulges, depressions, indentations, and protruding chips that climbers could grip, step into, and use for leverage. These pillars possessed no such features aside from a few cracks and small divots, so Thornburg and Frye aimed to create their own handholds and footholds. The epoxy stashed in the car would be used to fasten usable holds directly onto the concrete.

Hoping to remain undetected, Thornburg and Frye quietly set anchors at the top of the on-ramp and rappelled down incrementally, gluing holds onto the pillars as they descended. Their go-to supply of holds was a bag of Tuolumne knobs that Frye had brought back from a recent climbing excursion in Yosemite. The stone knobs were firm and fairly flat—perfect for attaching to the pillars. But Thornburg and Frye were also not averse to collecting small rocks and concrete fragments, globbing them with the epoxy, and attaching those to the pillars, too.

When the two had finished setting a number of holds, they decided to leave and let the epoxy dry. Dutifully, they returned to the on-ramp the following day to continue connecting additional knobs to the upright concrete partitions. Soon, certain sequences and movements could be visualized up the structures, which were now embellished with "artificial" handholds and footholds. Years later, Frye would recall, "We were kind of coursesetting as we'd go. We had names for [the routes]. We were getting into the whole 'artificial' thing, so we had Plastic Surgeon and Artificial Intelligence."

With ingenuity, strong adhesive, and an urban guerilla attitude, the pair successfully established upward routes on the pillars. The practice of buildering—scaling the sides of houses, shops, and other structures—had been embraced by a niche of climbers for decades, but the total creation of new routes and new lines with crude handholds and footholds like this, which Thornburg and Frye had done merely with improvised construction handiwork, was more than innovative. It was revolutionary.

After allowing more time for the epoxy to dry, Frye was ready to test the glued knobs' ability to hold his weight. He slipped his fingertips onto one of the makeshift handholds and applied some pressure. To his delight, the Tuolumne knob seemed to hold just fine. He gripped another glued knob and applied pressure—it also remained secure on the concrete. The ultimate test was stepping onto the footholds to see if his full body weight could be supported.

Again, the glued additions remained firm and secure.

Frye reached for higher handholds and moved his feet higher in conjunction with his body. A longtime climber, he quickly and easily sank into a rhythm on the concrete once he trusted the security of the various knobs. He climbed as high as he could on the makeshift handholds with the cars coasting loudly on the ramp overhead.

The men took turns trading climbs and belays while whomever remained on the ground kept a watchful eye out for police. Although there wasn't a law so specific as to forbid the construction of an artificial climbing wall near the Lake Temescal reservoir, Thornburg and Frye knew that their activity probably wouldn't be seen as normal to bystanders or law enforcement personnel monitoring the freeway.

What Thornburg and Frye were doing by jolting some new urban life into a traditionally rustic pursuit was part of a greater identity expansion that had been going on with American rock climbing for more than a decade. Climbing's Golden Age had been marked by legends such as Royal Robbins, Tom Frost, Warren Harding, Chuck Pratt, Yvon Chouinard, TM Herbert, and others establishing new ascents in Yosemite, the birthplace of American climbing. Yosemite in this Golden Age had been more than a majestic place with world-class mountains—it had become a vortex of creative energy. The antiestablishment climbers had bravely attempted to scale sections of stone that had long been thought to be unclimbable. And they had documented their exploits with photos and guide pamphlets. They had debated outdoors ethics related to bolting, and occasionally engaged in fervent rivalries.

Most importantly, such Yosemite gamesmanship had given American climbing significant forward momentum heading out of the freewheeling 1960s. A group of hardscrabble diehards known as the Stonemasters had pushed the limits of climbing and publicity on real rock even further in California in the 1970s. In the process and in the aftermath, climbers such as John Bachar, John Long, John "Yabo" Yablonski, Henry Barber, Werner Braun, Jim Bridwell, Billy Westbay, Rick Accomazzo, Paul Sibley, and a young woman from Detroit, Michigan, Lynn Hill, had become renowned. Collectively, this group had firmly cemented Yosemite—and the American West—as a supreme climbing destination on par with the Alps in Europe and the Andes in South America.

But by the 1980s, a new climbing subculture had emerged in the United States. Suburban youngsters not unlike Thornburg and Frye, distinctive from the Yosemite vanguard of earlier eras, were increasingly idolizing the chief players of the past and present.

And there were other visionaries as well, ushering in newfangled ideas about what American climbing could be. Foremost among the visionaries was Bob Carmichael, a filmmaker out of the University of Colorado. A former college football standout, Carmichael had been a staff director, writer, and editor for a number of productions with NFL Films, which had subsequently immersed him in network television sports shows and specifically production segments for NBC,

CBS, and ABC. He had also filmed a PGA Championship and the debut of a box lacrosse league.

But Carmichael was an accomplished climber, having climbed famous routes such as Triple Direct and the Salathé Wall in Yosemite, among other big-wall ventures. He had felt that climbing's aesthetic might translate well to television. Specifically, he had observed a malleable American zeitgeist when it came not only to the airing of competitive sports, but also to athletics throughout the 1970s. He had noticed that the public was growing increasingly cognizant of personal fitness—spurred by the widespread popularity of books like *Aerobics* by Kenneth Cooper in 1968 and *The Complete Book of Running* by James Fixx in 1977.

Climbing, Carmichael figured, could be embraced—and swell in popularity—for its inherent fitness rather than merely its risks and thrills. As a way to get in shape, climbing offered heightened awareness—a somewhat spiritual connection to the environment, but also to one's own body.

For the increasingly fitness-conscious American public to embrace climbing as a newfound athletic endeavor along the lines of aerobics and running, climbing needed to be shepherded into the mainstream. To have a hand in that, Carmichael chipped away at an idea to present climbing in a way it never had been—not in book form, like Cooper had done with *Aerobics*, but in films. He sold his truck to finance his idea and hired a Colorado-based film-maker, Leonard Aitken, to shoot a film; Carmichael would produce and direct it. Carmichael also chose two of the best climbers in the region, Roger Briggs and Duncan Ferguson, to star. Ascending the most famous climb in Colorado's Eldorado Canyon, The Naked Edge, would be their objective. In preparing for filming, Carmichael climbed the route himself and spent two and a half days taking notes about camera angles and logistics. Although Aitken, an accomplished athlete, had never climbed, Carmichael felt Aitken could be taught the basics and kept safe with belays as he jumped the fixed routes that a rigging team put in. Together, the small film crew eventually amassed hours of raw climbing footage, along with scenes of nature and of Briggs and Ferguson bouldering—climbing closer to the ground without a rope.

Once Carmichael had a rough cut of film footage that was to his satisfaction, he hitchhiked to New York City to entice potential investors to his idea. One film that resulted from such resolve, ultimately edited and whittled down to a 14-minute tour de force, was *Break on Through*. It distinctively blended nature cinematography with rock music provided by a guitarist, Tommy Bolin. The mixture was appropriate, given the film title's homage to The Doors and nods to some of the more avant-garde aspects of the hippie and consciousness movements. Carmichael would later explain that the film's fundamental idea was that climbing was an "intimate connection to nature for its practitioners"—and that there was a "certain mystical aspect to the keen concentration and physicality of climbing." It all fit with the natural formations of the rock, with climbing's inherent, intense focus lending itself to "visionary experiences."

But beyond the mountain scenery and energetic music, *Break on Through* presented climbing as an intricate kinesthesis, a craft not of death-defying falls and adrenaline rushes but of meticulous physiology. The film's noteworthy camera close-ups of tensed shoulder and bicep muscles, fingers pinching tiny chips of stone, and feet being placed in movement were more akin to dancing than mountaineering. There was even a montage of a climber stretching midway through the film, further connecting climbing to all-purpose exercise.

Unlike how the Yosemite climbing community had often coupled climbing with a dirtbag existence of destitution and social reclusion, Carmichael put climbing in a new context in a decade that was also embracing rowing machines, stationary bikes, Tone-O-Matics, and other products that indicated an openness to new fitness concepts. Suddenly, the stereotypical image of a climber was not necessarily a scraggly, backwoods roisterer, but of a lithe and fitness-conscious enthusiast. Undeniably, *Break on Through* connected climbing overtly with athleticism.

Carmichael showed *Break on Through* to the president of CBS Sports—and the network purchased the film immediately. Sports-caster Brent Musburger introduced the film for its television broadcast, the first time that an American climbing film had ever been shown on network television. In fact, the broadcast presented a kind of vertical athleticism many networks' sport programming executives had never seen before.

Carmichael followed up *Break on Through* with climbing films *Outside the Arena* and *First Ascent. First Ascent* presented climbing as a chiefly athletic endeavor—and a minimalistic one, compared with the conventional mountaineering aesthetic. Whereas mountaineers typically wore bulky outerwear and heavy boots to trudge over snow and ice, *First Ascent* showcased Lynn Hill and another woman, Beth Bennett, climbing in shorts, pullover shirts, and rubber-soled climbing shoes. Hill had been a gymnast and Bennett had dabbled in dancing and running prior to focusing on climbing. At one point in *First Ascent*, Hill and Bennett are shown cycling, jumping rope, and jogging as part of their climbing training. In a voice-over that would prove prescient in the sport's cross-training evolution, Hill explains while lifting weights, "I only know one way to get stronger—hard work."

To produce *First Ascent*, Carmichael had employed a pair of brothers from Ogden, Utah, named Jeff and Greg Lowe. Greg had aided with the film's cinematography, while Jeff had helped with the necessary rigging of cameras.

The partnership between Carmichael and the Lowe brothers would prove to be a landmark union in the coming years of climbing's mainstream media emergence, but *First Ascent* was among the first projects to reveal how the meticulousness of film production could truly augment the meticulousness of climbing. "Because Bob [Carmichael] had filmed other sports, he was aware of the power of the media—getting information out there and getting people interested and just revealing the aspects of a sport that weren't easy to see," Bennett would later recall. "He has an artistic side, and he likes to do special camera shots that show a side of whatever sport it is in a novel way. Sometimes we'd have to do something over and over again until Bob got the shot the way he wanted, but I can appreciate the artistry in that."

For Hill and Bennett, two of the best American climbers of the era, the promotional aftermath of *First Ascent* included an appearance on *Real People*, a television show that profiled the activities and professions of its guests. This marked one of the first instances of American climbers garnering mainstream publicity for an American climb. And Carmichael continued down a diverse career path of filming sports. He earned an Academy Award nomination for the film *Fall Line*, which showcased a combination of alpine climbing and skiing, while an Emmy award for a documentary, *Football in America*, further solidified his status as an influential filmmaker. But he never stopped considering unique ways to present climbing in conventional media.

At the same time, television networks were demonstrably willing to showcase niche sports and present them as easy to digest to a layman consumer, as evidenced by ABC's popular *Wide World of Sports*, featuring everything from alpine skiing to sailing.

All the pieces were in place for American climbing to take a giant leap into the mainstream in 1987 as Thornburg and Frye were rummaging for Tuolumne knobs and attaching them to the pillars of the Highway 13 overpass. After decades on the fringe, climbing finally had a diverse media pedigree—thanks largely to the efforts of Carmichael—which could aid in a vault toward public popularity.

To reach the masses, however, climbing still had to morph from strictly a participatory endeavor to a spectacle that could be watched by enthusiasts and laypersons alike. It needed to become a spectator sport.

Kevin Donald was a Denver-based climbing guide who had founded an instructional facility, the International Alpine School, with Jeff Lowe. Donald had also worked with Carmichael on a number of film projects. During one such project—a Molson beer commercial at a Canadian lodge owned by skier Hans Moser—Carmichael shared with Donald the novel idea of putting together some sort of large-scale climbing competition in the United States. The idea was fueled not only by Carmichael's love of climbing, but also by a feeling that others would love climbing and its inherent drama, too—if only they could see it.

Given the changes in the public's perception of climbing, no longer seen as the fringe activity of a counterculture but as a sport for anyone, such an idea was more than a conversational talking point. Suddenly, it had momentum. So, while still at the lodge with Donald and others, Carmichael penned a letter to Jeff Lowe suggesting they team up on organizing such an event.

A working model for what Carmichael was hypothesizing could be found in Europe, where a rich history of mountaineering dating back centuries was rapidly expanding to include climbing competitions in certain mountain towns. For example, in July 1985, a climbing event called SportRoccia had been held in Bardonecchia, Italy. It had been one of the first of its kind—an international competition that judged competitors' speeds, as well as their climbing styles, up a rock face.

That competition was not without its controversies, particularly with handholds and footholds being chipped into the natural rock wall. But it drew an impressive throng of onlookers nonetheless and included American Russ Clune as a competitor.

The following year Arco, a town 260 miles west of Bardonecchia, was chosen to host a second SportRoccia climbing competition. It amassed approximately 10,000 spectators and featured a pair of European superstars, France's Patrick Edlinger and Catherine Destivelle, claiming victories in the men's and women's divisions, respectively. Lynn Hill, the standout of Carmichael's *First Ascent* film just seven years earlier, also notched a spot on the podium. In doing so, she became one of the first American climbers to place in an international climbing competition. Also in 1986, a speed climbing competition held outdoors in Yalta, a seaside city in the then-USSR, included Clune as well as other Americans Todd Skinner, Dan Michael, and Beth Wald. Together, they composed the first American climbing team to be recognized nationally as well as internationally.

The success and popularity of the events abroad, along with a full-fledged Rock Master festival and competition in Italy in 1987, prompted climbing's international governing body, the France-based Union Internationale des Associations d'Alpinisme (also called the International Climbing and Mountaineering Federation, and more succinctly, the UIAA), to rush to establish a full-on circuit of regional climbing competitions. These events were organized under the auspices of a delegation, the Commission Escalade Competition, which consisted of 19 representatives. UIAA rules for competing solidified and smaller-scale events soon appeared all over the European continent. One climbing competition was even held indoors—a novel idea at the time—in Vaulx en Velin, France.

Along with Edlinger and Destivelle, names such as Jacky Godoffe, Francois Legrand, and Nanette Raybaud (all from France), Susi Good of Switzerland, Jerry Moffat and Ben Moon of Great Britain, and Stefan Glowacz of Germany became common on the big European competitions' podiums. Glowacz even penned an essay for the English magazine *Mountain,* in which he noted that the presence of competitions—and climbing for an audience, in front of officials—signified a new era for climbing. "It can't be ignored that, since competitions became part of climbing, the sport made remarkable progress," Glowacz wrote. "It is now fit for society, presentable to the mass-media, and laymen now have the possibility of judging the standards of performance of different climbers. What some years ago was considered only a pastime for maniacs has become, thanks to competitions, a measurable performance, an accepted new branch of athletics."

The idea of organized climbing competition wasn't totally foreign to the United States either, although it had mostly materialized in smaller versions up to that point. Many of the earliest organized American competitions had been bouldering-themed and had occurred outdoors around Southern California. As far back as 1972, for instance, a modest competition had been held on a boulder at Mission Gorge, northeast of San Diego. Then, beginning in the mid-1970s, an organizer named Werner Landry began holding contests at nearby Mount Woodson. At one point, these competitions were identified extravagantly as the Southern California Bouldering Championships.

Around the same time, other climbers—Kevin Powell, Darrell Hensel, Rob Raker, and Randy Vogel—started a series of similar bouldering contests at Mount Rubidoux, in Riverside, California.

Steadily, aided by word-of-mouth promotion in the close-knit California climbing community, competitions increasingly dotted the region. One of the most notable of these was another series of contests organized by Landry, the Great Western Boulder Championship. One of the first installments was held in Santee, California, in 1981, with the following year's contest taking place in nearby Lakeside.

Ron Gomez was a judge at one of the Santee contests, although scoring was sometimes done less by judges and more on an honor system by the participants themselves. Gomez took part as a competitor in other contests too, such as the ones at Mount Rubidoux. He remembers the lighthearted atmosphere and the amusing anecdotes more than the competitive rigor—such as some participants at one event sleeping in a field that had recently burned by wildfire and waking up the following morning covered in black soot. And Gomez recalls fondly the camaraderie of carousing and bouldering at Pirates Cove Beach, in Corona del Mar, after a contest had finished. "There was a competition, but it was more about helping each other get better," he says. "Sure, we pushed each other, but in friendship and in humor."

Along those lines, at a contest at Mount Woodson, Lynne Leichtfuss and Brenda Bachar tied for first place in a women's division. The judges suggested that the two have a "climb-off" to determine an official winner, but instead, the women chose to arm wrestle for the victory—with Leichtfuss ultimately emerging triumphant.

The carefree nature of the events and the close-knit friendships of the participants did not mean that competitive spirit was totally absent. Lynne's husband, Dan, also found himself in a tie during a contest at Santee and eventually won his own "climb-off" against a young standout named Tony Yaniro by climbing highest on a selected boulder.

The early Southern California bouldering contests were occasionally filmed and even at one point covered by German writer Reinhard Karl in Germany's *Alpinismus* magazine.

Climbing of a competitive nature also received some media treatment as part of an American televised adventure race known as *Survival of the Fittest*. Mike Hoover, an accomplished filmmaker whose credits include an award-winning climbing documentary, *Solo*, helped to organize and produce the multiday contest in Yosemite. Trail running, swimming, and kayaking were the other scored "adventure" events. Lynn Hill placed second in the climbing and rappelling portion behind a talented climber from Washington named Anne Tarver but ended up victorious when scores were tabulated for the competition overall.

Elsewhere, on May 15, 1983, Jim Waugh hosted an outdoor event at Camelback Mountain in Arizona called the Central Arizona Bouldering Contest. Inspired by a festival-style weekend gathering for climbers in Tucson called the Beanfest, Waugh's bouldering competition soon took on the moniker of the Phoenix Bouldering Contest. The roster for that first year listed 35 competitors. When participant Chris Raypole claimed the victory at that inaugural contest, he was awarded a new Edelrid climbing rope as the grand prize.

The same year that Waugh held his first bouldering contest, a California Bouldering Championship at Mount Rubidoux featured 100 different outdoor bouldering climbs for its enrolled competitors.

The boulders' routes had intriguing names like Crank Problem Face, The Overhang, The Beehive Mantle, and Funk-u-Flakes. At the following year's California Bouldering Championships, the number of boulders, some of which were comparable to small houses in size, was expanded to 123—each bouldering problem with its own points designation that ranged from 0 to 20.

Two years later, a two-pronged event emerged in the West that joined the California Bouldering Championship with a contest called the Stone Masters Freeclimbing Competition at Mount Woodson. The former featured separate men's and women's divisions with selected boulders scored on the Yosemite Decimal System and starting at a grade of 5.5. The latter featured an expert division with selected climbable boulders starting at a difficulty grade at 5.11, a men's advanced division with boulders starting at a grade of 5.10, and a women's advanced division with boulders starting at a grade of 5.9.[1]

However subtly, the preamble for the written rules of this two-pronged event at Mount Woodson suggested that the United States possessed a sect of serious climbers who wanted to focus expressly on formalized competition: "The bouldering championship is popular with climbers of all abilities, offering good climbing, friendly competition, fun and prizes. The freeclimbing competition is intended for advanced climbers with well rounded [sic] abilities and good endurance, who desire serious competition."

American climbing's competitive iterations were growing measurably in size and scope and evolving in format. Yet even as word continued to spread about new events, the contestants at any given competition remained mostly local residents. This created an

---

1. The common bouldering grading system that Americans use today, the Hueco ("V") scale, had not yet become the standard at the time of these contests in the mid-1980s— thus the application of the Yosemite Decimal System for assessing boulders.

inherent drawback as participation at these competitions increased to include more out-of-towners: the local climbers were already familiar with the boulders, so they had an empirical advantage over those who were climbing on the stone for the first time. This detail about localism was moot when the atmosphere was mostly relaxed and lighthearted, but it was problematic when substantial winnings were on the line at competitions.

Despite the presence of some outdoor contests in Southern California and Arizona, American competition climbing lacked cohesion and urgency. Moreover, the emergence of a sizable European competition scene was happening largely separate from the development and advancement of outdoor climbing in the United States. The two continents would have likely continued on different trajectories if it had not been for the media connections made by Carmichael through his work in television and film and the ensuing international travels of Jeff Lowe.

By the mid-1980s, Lowe had developed a degree of celebrity for his climbing and mountaineering. This was perhaps epitomized best by a cover feature in *Sports Illustrated*, "Daring Young Man on a Tower of Ice," which chronicled his historic solo ice climbing of Bridal Veil Falls in Telluride, Colorado—an ascent he had previously done with Mike Weis, also to great acclaim. Lowe had also spent more than 20 days attempting to summit the northern ridge of Latok 1 in Karakoram, Pakistan, with an expedition party that had included Michael Kennedy, the editor-in-chief of *Climbing*. Although unsuccessful in its key objective, the expedition was highly publicized, partly because of its direct attachment to the climbing media.

It was in the glow of such fame that Lowe also began attending sports and outdoor industry trade shows. At one such show in

Chicago, Lowe met famed climber Dan Goodwin, well known for having scaled some of the world's tallest skyscrapers. Goodwin was showcasing a homemade overhanging structure designed to train for climbing up cracks on real rocks. At the top of the elaborate structure was a bell that could be rung—to great cheers from a captivated crowd—every time the artificial crack had been successfully climbed. Primitive as it was, Goodwin's "crack climbing machine" was among the earliest artificial climbing wall designs ever constructed, and the bell illustrated how easily competitive accoutrements could be added. Lowe was instantly intrigued and made note to keep in touch with Goodwin for future endeavors.

All the traveling and the adventures, as well as their renown, gave Lowe autonomy to undertake new climbing-themed projects and business endeavors of his choosing. He developed belay devices and other climbing-related gear for Lowe Alpine, a company founded by his brothers. He started his own climbing equipment company as well—Latok Mountain Gear—as a spin-off of his brothers' brand. Among the innovations of Lowe Alpine and Latok were the first internal-frame backpacks for technical climbing and the first port-a-ledge tents for sleeping on the sheer sides of cliffs.

Lowe's famous ascents and climbing accomplishments overseas aided in giving Latok and Lowe Alpine significant global scope. In fact, the Lowe gear companies increasingly looked to expand into Europe and to glean ideas from the mountain-enthusiastic subsections in Great Britain that could be ushered into the American market.

Hired by Lowe to help develop some global business strategies was Rex Wilson, an American marketing expert whose military reserve duties conveniently required European residency. Wilson had moved to Ireland in June of 1984 to split his time between handling international gear sales for Lowe and reporting periodically to an American army base in Germany.

Practically by design, Wilson's modest home in Ireland served as a mock headquarters for Lowe's periodic business visits to Europe. At Wilson's place, sessions discussing clothing fabrics and trekking equipment related to Lowe Alpine often turned to more casual talk of climbing in the Alps. Sometimes the socializing and discussions of mountain ambitions lasted late into the night.

Being climbers, Wilson and Lowe used any downtime between company trade shows as opportunities to travel across the Irish Sea and explore in-depth the bustling European climbing scene. In conjunction with that, once on the European mainland, Wilson, Lowe, and a small cadre of other American businessmen repeatedly sought out those newfangled regional climbing competitions—seen mostly as French, German, and Italian novelties at the time.

As more European events emerged—to the delight of spectators like Lowe and Wilson—the actual climbing contests began to be held on artificial walls in large metropolitan areas rather than remote mountainsides. The artificial climbing walls could be erected in city parks, amphitheaters, parking lots, and any other urban space that was easily accessible to the public. This structural evolution—turning climbing from an endeavor reliant on nature to a competition entirely dictated by human inventiveness—allowed for unique wall placement in major European cities and a degree of freedom for the various events' routesetters. Beyond opening up new possibilities for the competitions' locations, the artificiality of the climbing walls deftly set a stage for an entire event circuit around Europe in the model of a nomadic caravan—or, less glamorously, a traveling circus. Climbing walls could be constructed within a matter of days or hours, play host to a given spectacle, and then get dismantled by a crew much like a transportable circus tent.

"Usually the competitions were in Paris—there was a big one in Grenoble, France, another one was in Munich," Wilson would recall years later, reflecting on the travels around Europe that he and Lowe took in order to watch the various climbing events. "Almost all of the sport climbing walls were being developed in France and Germany, so that's probably what allowed Europe to get ahead of the game, in terms of the competition stuff."

The appeal was not only in the climbing competitions themselves, but how the competitors were respected around Europe. The top European climbers, and particularly Patrick Edlinger, were treated like rock stars in their home countries, where they gained celebrity status. They gave frequent television interviews, appeared in advertisements, and developed throngs of adoring fans. This contrasted greatly with the counterculture roots and rock-bum stigma still associated with climbers in the United States.

Lowe began to wonder whether a caravan of climbing competitions similar to those he was witnessing in France, Germany, and Italy could find success in the United States. Reinforcing that curiosity was the fact that much of the work Lowe and Wilson were doing for Lowe Alpine entailed holding various business meetings and informal consultations related to product endorsements with some of the most famous European climbers—such as Edlinger and Destivelle.

The disparate components fell into place in January 1988, when Lowe returned from business in Europe to attend a conference known as the Mountain Summit at the Snowbird resort in Utah. Snowbird had been co-founded by entrepreneur Dick Bass 17 years earlier—just as another mountain sport, downhill skiing, had begun to gain popularity in America. The success of a skiing movie starring Robert Redford, *Downhill Racer*, as well as the celebrity status of Olympian Suzy Chaffee, had aided in keeping skiing in the public consciousness throughout the 1970s. In the years following the construction of Bass' elaborate Snowbird grounds, the sport, along with several business ventures that Bass had undertaken, had boomed. Bass now possessed substantial capital to invest in any worthy new ventures that piqued his interest.

At the Mountain Summit, the second in an annual series of corporate conferences on how brands could be environmentally conscious in the coming decade, Lowe pitched the idea of putting together a high-profile American climbing competition to Bass.

The conversation about a potential American "artificial-wall competition" was brief, as the Mountain Summit was more centered on expedition-level mountaineering ventures. For example, it featured slide presentations by famed mountaineers Reinhold Messner and Chris Bonington. It also included a comprehensive discussion on the standardization of mountaineering guide certification in the United States. The esteemed panel leading that discussion was Ian Wade, the president of the American Mountain Guides Association; Sharon Wood, the first Canadian woman to summit Mount Everest; and Phil Ershler, a guide with Rainier Mountaineering. Another presentation was simply titled "Sponsorship Support for Expeditions" and included financial advice from various equipment brands.

In attendance at many of these talks were Rainier Mountaineering's founder, Lou Whittaker, and an author of a Mount Rainier guidebook, Dee Molenaar. An American mountaineer who had attempted to climb Mount Everest seven years earlier, Glenn Porzak, was also present, as were Everest guides Karen Fellerhoff and Peter Athans. Perhaps the most notable attendee was Yuichiro Miura, a mountaineer who had traveled all the way from Japan. Miura had gained fame as the subject of the 1975 documentary *The Man Who Skied Down Everest*.

But buried among all the ensuing mountaineering deliberations by such luminaries was another presentation titled "What's Hot in the Mountains." In it, French climber Jean-Claude Droyer described to the attendees how sponsorship opportunities for climbing competitions in Europe had allowed French competitors to pursue climbing full-time. Climbing as a full-time career, Droyer noted, allowed for new feats in the sport as standards were elevated.

The hook for a climbing competition was something Bass gravitated to. Like skiing, climbing was a niche activity, wildly popular overseas, and this was a chance to give it a new identity in the United States. It could also be ushered to a wider audience through competitions and even cross over to the realm of sports spectacle. Also like skiing, climbing's aesthetic seemed ideal for promotion— whereas skiing had blazing speed, climbing had daunting heights; and whereas skiing entailed a race to the bottom of a course, climbing could be contested in an entertaining reversal of that principle—a race to the top of a given route. The basic physics could also help shape the rules for the contestants: don't fall and simply follow the established course.

Best of all, climbing could work as an easy-to-understand contest to any onlookers. The evidence was in the success that Europe was witnessing with its thriving circuit.

If a climbing competition could somehow be put together as a big spectacle in the United States, it could connect various groups and demographics around the country. Moreover, those suburbanites long hungry for climbing to have a presence outside of real rock and mountains could finally be offered a display of the activity in a new, athletic light.

But the elephant in the room was that such a large-scale climbing competition had never been put together on American soil, much less presented to American sports fans. Large questions loomed about whether it could be done and how it should be packaged—or if the whole concept and everyone's grand ambitions would soon come crumbling to the ground.

CHAPTER 2

THIS REVOLUTION
WILL BE TELEVISED

MUCH LIKE 1987 had seen Jim Thornburg and Scott Frye reimagine climbing in a new context, 1988 began with aspirations from two pivotal figures—Bob Carmichael and Jeff Lowe—to see the sport succeed as a form of new entertainment. Carmichael knew from more than a decade of working in the film industry how the sport of climbing could be presented in unique ways to the American public; he also felt that a climbing competition in the European model could garner widespread interest if given a media polish. Lowe had witnessed firsthand the burgeoning success of such competitions in France, Italy, and Germany, and felt that the tour-style template could be applied to the United States.

Also crucial to the formula was Dick Bass, who was unfamiliar with the primarily European concept of "sport climbing," but agreed to sponsor a competition at his famed Snowbird resort in the Wasatch Mountains of northern Utah with a noteworthy caveat: Lowe and Carmichael would have to handle the logistics of the competition's promotion, as well as the resultant visual presentation of the event. As wealthy as Bass was, he was not interested in organizing the event on his own, nor was he familiar enough with the minutiae of the newfangled American competitive sport to do so.

Rather than whittle the competition into a single film—documenting the endeavors of the individual climbers in a documentary style like that of *Break on Through* and *First Ascent*—Carmichael had the idea of broadcasting the competition on American network television. It was a formidable idea. But if the event was going to be contested like any other mainstream sport (with winners and losers, a set of rules, judges, and a crowd of spectators), it made sense to Carmichael that its packaging should be done in the manner of other sports too—chiefly, delivered to the masses through the medium of television, already abundant with athletic programming.

From there, the organization and coordination of the event progressed quickly. Carmichael hired Ed Labowitz, a prominent Los Angeles–based attorney with years of experience in entertainment law, to write up a contract for a working arrangement with Lowe. Carmichael also used contacts at CBS, established years earlier, to run the competition climbing idea up the network's chain of command. CBS had broadcast everything from roller skating championships to skiing earlier in the decade, so a climbing event was not a conceptual stretch.

The pitch eventually reached CBS' programming executive, Rick Gentile, who was intrigued by the idea because the sport was so multifaceted. Case in point: a newspaper article written later that same year would proclaim that a climbing competition "resembles both a gymnastics meet and tryouts for the role of Spider-Man."

Gentile committed CBS to broadcasting the proposed Snowbird competition, eventually going so far as to say it had the potential to be "a hell of a television show." The executive producer of CBS Sports, Ted Shaker, was also sold on the idea. Carmichael was hired to be the director of photography.

The undercurrent in these various business agreements and resultant hirings was the presence of a long-term future for all parties involved. Carmichael felt strongly that a big-time climbing competition in America, packaged for CBS and promoted like any other televised sporting event, would connect with a sizable audience repeatedly if done sparingly, possibly once a year.

With a binding contract in place regarding funding and sponsorship from Bass, it became necessary for the vague television aspirations to solidify into specific objectives within a matter of months. A veteran of television production, David Michaels, was familiar with Carmichael's earlier films and was tapped as the producer for the filming of the Snowbird competition.

Michaels immediately provided the ambitious concept some gravitas, having previously produced niche sporting events for CBS like the Tour de France and triathlons. Among other key logistics—including assigning musician David Arkenstone to compose music that would enhance the drama of a climbing competition—it was Michaels who ultimately convinced CBS executives to greenlight the whole Snowbird project. He would later remember the personnel converging as "a perfect storm," saying, "You had Jeff [Lowe] with the passion, Dick Bass who would do anything for us to make it a good show. I was all fired up, and for Bob [Carmichael] it was something new and different. It was just one of those things that doesn't happen very often, where a group of people are really crazed about trying to make something great."

Equally important as sorting out various media particulars was finalizing obvious aspects of the competition itself. For any promotion and marketing of the event to be effective, it was necessary to have a set roster of climbers who were committed to taking part. The Snowbird competition would be the first large-scale competition of its kind ever held in the United States—and the first one to be broadcast on American network television—so any list of contestants would ideally be composed primarily of American climbers who could then be developed into national sports celebrities.

The idea was optimistic but the reality, given the newness of sport climbing, was that there was not enough depth in the niche to invite solely American competitors. Besides, a vast majority of the best competition climbers in the world at the time were European, like Patrick Edlinger and Catherine Destivelle. Not including them in any American competition risked swathing the entire enterprise as second-rate to those events that were happening in Europe.

Also, attracting any climbers—especially European ones—to a competition was still a tall order in the late 1980s. Climbing on artificial handholds, usually made of clay or resin, was fast becoming the competition standard, yet that notion didn't sit well with some climbers who held firm to a traditional model of rock climbing. Such loyalty to traditionalism would be a figurative burr under the saddle for the sport for years to come, as growth in popularity would inevitably be met with criticism from diehard outdoor dirtbags.

"[Competitions] took a different mind-set, and for some of the traditional climbers, they just didn't go for it," Rex Wilson, Lowe's operational right-hand man, would later recall about trying to entice climbers to competitions. "They wanted to remain true to the traditional roots of climbing, and they didn't think they were doing that if they were sport climbing."

The solution to this dilemma was found in the connections that Lowe had previously made with many European climbers during his work overseas with Lowe Alpine and Latok. Lowe wrote several invitation letters and made numerous long-distance phone calls to Europe, even before the logistics with Bass had been finalized. Gradually, Lowe was able to get multiple foreign climbers to agree to come to the United States for the inaugural competition at Snowbird; they were lured largely by the historic nature of the competition and a $4,000 cash purse for the male and female winners. Sweetening the deal was an agreement to pay consolation prizes to the ten highest-place finishers in each division. The total payout for the event would amount to more than $17,000, a figure unprecedented for climbing events in the United States and a considerable sum by European standards as well. In fact, within just a couple years, the total purse for a comparable American competition would swell to more than $20,000. This would fuel hopes that competing could be a viable, full-time career.

Although a roster steadily filled up with many of Europe's best climbers, the United States was not left wholly without representation for the competition at Snowbird. Most famous of the bunch was Lynn Hill. Hill was one of the few Americans who had prior experience traveling overseas to take part in French and Italian competitions. In addition to a victory in Arco in 1987, she had also won a large-scale competition called the World Indoor Rock Climbing Premier in 1987 in Grenoble, France. And she continued her success the next year, winning the Grand Prix d'Escalade à Bercy on January 30, 1988. Additionally, Hill had garnered recognition and media acclaim since the early 1980s for being the first woman to successfully ascend a number of historic American climbs outdoors—Whiteman in Estes Park, Colorado, in 1980; Hidden Arch in Joshua Tree, California, in 1981; and Yellow Crack Direct in the Shawangunk Mountains of New York in 1984, among others.

Still, Hill's skills as a blue-chip competitive climber had been showcased primarily in Europe. The Snowbird competition would be her chance to finally compete in an international event in her home country.

An added layer of intrigue to Hill's participation was that Destivelle also agreed to climb at the event. The guaranteed presence of both women could allow presenters to spin their rivalry for the entertainment of American audiences: *Tune in to find out which woman is the best climber in the world!*

Another American invited to the event was Ron Kauk, a climber with years of experience in Yosemite and essentially a keystone in joining the rustic Stonemasters scene of a previous era to the burgeoning sport climbing scene of the late 1980s. Kauk had already carved out a place in climbing history, as he, John Long, and John Bachar had established the route Astroman on Yosemite's El Capitan in 1975. Participating at Snowbird, however, would be his chance to make history in the growing competition aspect of climbing.

Christian Griffith, a climber out of Boulder, Colorado; Scott Franklin from North Conway, New Hampshire; and Robyn Erbesfield of Atlanta, Georgia—all also enticed to participate—revealed Snowbird's wide-reaching geographic pull. Like Hill, Griffith and

Franklin were part of a small group of Americans who had previously taken part in competitions abroad.[2] Jason Stern, at 17 years old, was the youngest competitor. Tony Yaniro, Mari Gingery, and Jennifer Cole were among other Americans asked to take part at the Snowbird competition.

One noteworthy American absent from the pending roster was Beth Bennett. Bennett had starred alongside Lynn Hill in *First Ascent* almost a decade prior and affirmed her status as a key figure in the American scene, but she had little interest in competing by 1988. She had been consistently busy with other projects: teaching climbing at Outward Bound, founding a climbing school for women in Boulder, attending graduate school, and starting a family.

But with numerous other Americans agreeing to join, and a roster that was now decidedly international—33 invited climbers, in total—the fast-approaching Snowbird event adopted a supplementary narrative: it would not merely be a big climbing competition, it would be America versus the World.

France boasted the most accomplished team of climbers scheduled to attend, including a 25-year-old star named Jean-Baptiste Tribout, a 26-year-old veteran of France's comp scene named Didier Raboutou, a 21-year-old standout named Marc Le Ménestrel, and another 21-year-old named Isabelle Patissier. Patissier had gained

---

2. A vast majority of the climbers in the eventual Snowbird competition of 1988 were invited during the planning and preproduction stages. They were selected to participate based on past performances in overseas competitions or eminence within the nascent American sport climbing scene. Notable absences were Germany's Wolfgang Güllich, who was one of the best climbers in the world but had no interest in organized competitions, and Stefan Glowacz, who had not yet developed an affinity for climbing on artificial surfaces. Other top competitors who chose not to compete were England's Jerry Moffatt, Italian Luisa Iovane, and Canadian Peter Croft.

notoriety in her hometown of Lyon, France, just two years earlier by winning a competition while climbing barefoot.[3]

As the list of competitors solidified, important procedural components remained—namely, figuring out how to film the competitors as they scaled the wall. At Bass' behest, a decision was made to construct the artificial wall for the competition on the side of the Cliff Lodge at Snowbird. It was a choice that enhanced access as much as adhered to practicality; holding the event on the 115-foot side of the 12-story hotel would allow spectators and resort guests to congregate on the surrounding lawn, and nearly all locations along the periphery of the lodge's grounds would thus have a clear view of the action. Another reason for holding the competition on the side of the Cliff Lodge was likely promotional for Bass. With all onlookers' gazes glued to the competitors scaling the side of the building, the entire event would doubtless proceed like an extended advertisement for the lodge and the impressive Snowbird complex.

Assembling a climbable surface on one side of the lodge, however, would prove to be challenging and expensive. Dan Goodwin, whose artificial crack climbing structure had impressed Lowe years earlier, was the wall's mastermind. Another famous climber, Paul Sibley, was a longtime friend and climbing partner of Lowe's and was given the formidable task of helping to construct Snowbird's

---

3. Even by 1988, Patissier's barefoot win had become an anecdote etched in competition climbing history and lore. The victory occurred at her first-ever competition. She had enjoyed climbing and training without shoes for years, and since she lacked a shoe sponsor at the time, she felt no obligation to don shoes for the event. Even after her victory, some climbing shoe companies had no interest in sponsoring her because she was known as a barefoot climber. Nonetheless, she eventually started competing in shoes and quickly became one of the best competition climbers in the world—and had no problem attracting sponsors as her career progressed.

wall. Sibley was not only a Yosemite veteran and the founder of a climbing hardware business, Colorado Nut Company, but also a contemporary of registered competitors like Kauk and Hill. The wall itself had been swiftly designed by independent architects in concert with Lowe, as the unique overhanging structure attached to the side of the Cliff Lodge needed to be meticulously engineered. Moreover, the architects had imparted an aesthetic implementation of Lowe's ideas about how the climbing wall should be designed, in order to ensure that the finished product Sibley was constructing would be acceptable not only for a single competition, but as a permanent fixture on the side of the building.

Sibley had a keen understanding of what type of structure would elicit a positive response from the competitors at Snowbird. Goodwin joined him in setting routes on the Snowbird wall for the competitors. "It was a real challenge," Goodwin would recall of the routesetting, novel as the concept was at the time. "We hadn't had the opportunity to really test the holds or the panels as much as we wanted to, so we had a lot of breakage happening. That's when we realized that many bolted holds had to have an additional screw in place to keep them from spinning."

With unique routes—solely for the competition—the Snowbird event, once underway, would negate the competitive advantages, familiarities, and predispositions that had beset the smaller local competitions held in the United States up to that point. The perplexing courses set by Sibley and Goodwin would snake up the wall and force the competitors to make jaw-dropping moves; during the climb, each competitor would reach for handholds spread purposefully far apart and step onto foot nubs hardly bigger than a nickel. Wall paneling by Goodwin's own company, Sport Climbing Systems, and a resin made of finely ground rock dust would be layered atop the Cliff Lodge's surface to nod to the stone roots of the sport. The artificial handholds and footholds would be bolted directly into the paneling.

Goodwin was initially given only $10,000 to build the wall, but expenditures and incidentals quickly mounted. "I wasn't even sure if that would cover the cost of materials, but I wanted to be part of it since the wall was my idea," Goodwin would say. "I had some extra money, so I was willing to do whatever it took to make it happen." The cost of constructing the whole face would eventually reach $155,000 once all the routes—"tiny handholds, thin ledges, minute bulges, and daunting overhangs"—had been set and all the rope anchors secured. It ended up being a mammoth expense, but after expedited construction, the wall was deemed climbable.

Next, Carmichael and Michaels had to figure out how to film competitors scaling the remarkable wall, and specifically how to rig video cameras for the event. Carmichael's previous experience filming myriad athletes, from mountaineers to downhill skiers, made him an ideal candidate for figuring out a solution to the impending videography puzzle. Yet despite a flourishing canon of outdoor climbing footage and documentation, there was yet to be an acceptable standard for the way competitions were filmed. The events in Europe, if recorded on video at all, had mostly utilized stationary cameras pointed upward from the ground—zooming in on the competitors climbing from predominantly low angles. Carmichael knew that such fixed camera positioning would be too static and seem too outdated to American sports fans.

In essence, the Snowbird competition would need to capture competition climbing in a way that was more dynamic and fluid, in order to meet the expectations of viewers used to action-packed football and basketball television programming.

Eventually, a determination was made that any climbing at Snowbird would have to be filmed by cameras that could get up close and personal to the athletes who were scaling the wall on the Cliff Lodge, yet also retract at times to capture the structure's full architectural expanse. It would be an extraordinary undertaking. To capture all the drama inherent in each contestant's climb, the cameras would have to oscillate smoothly from the start of each route—when the competitor's feet were firmly planted on the ground—to the very top of the wall, when the climber was potentially high above the spectators. And it would all have to be done with impeccable timing. Michaels, as the producer, would recall, "I told Bob [Carmichael] the kind of shots I wanted to see. I wanted to be able to see fingers holding onto some of those handholds, and close-ups of the feet. We talked about those things and developed some ideas together, but Bob was a little ahead of me because he had done so much filming of climbing in the past. We just figured, 'Let's figure out what would be the most amazing thing to do—and let's figure out how close we can get to it.'"

Carmichael agreed, as he saw sport climbing as a discipline of graceful movement—ropes were used to catch the climbers in any fall, so risk was minimized and precision was maximized. The smallest of handholds were to be accurately *pinched* and *crimped* rather than broadly gripped and grabbed, and such exactness would need to be captured by the event's cameras, just as Michaels had asserted.

On top of that, the competition's date had been set for June—less than six months from the time the contract had been signed and Carmichael had first been hired. The looming date expedited the planning and made extensive testing of camera equipment and videography ideas nearly impossible. The event finally had a name, too: the International Sport Climbing Championship.

Now under a significant time crunch, Carmichael brainstormed more ideas for the camerawork mechanics. Operating the cameras for the Snowbird competition would be Tommy Rowe, a veteran cameraman who had worked with Carmichael on several additional *Survival of the Fittest* television broadcasts. Carmichael was confident that Rowe would expertly capture all the nuance and drama of the climbing if he had some sort of complex dolly system—a system that would not be perfectly stabilized but would nonetheless allow for maneuverability up and down the wide expanse of the great wall.

The mechanical apparatus eventually devised was a large winch system, whereby Rowe could operate the camera firsthand like an extensive maneuvering steel tentacle. A vertical dolly on the side of the Cliff Lodge would allow for a cameraman to get raised or lowered with the aid of good riggers and constant radio communication. It was an innovative system that would capture competition climbing like never before.

The final component was coordinating a large public relations push heading into summer. From a network perspective, the historic nature of any event at Snowbird and its elite athletes from around the world would only be pertinent if it could translate to significant viewership. And so, promotion for the International Sport Climbing Championship ramped into high gear beginning in April. An article at the end of the month by Gary Langer ran across the Associated Press, proclaiming, "Sport Climbing Gains a Tenuous Handhold in the States."

Langer's article heralded the forthcoming competition, but it also deftly posed a point that would be applicable to competitions for years to come: "The question: Whether sport climbing can hang on long enough to gain an audience here as sizable and loyal as it has won in Europe—or whether it will take a 'screamer,' in climbing parlance, and plummet from the scene."

There were indications, as Langer noted, that sport climbing was on a secure upward trajectory. Michael Kennedy, the editor of *Climbing* at the time, noted in the same article that the magazine's circulation had doubled since 1985.

Also, by the spring of 1988, Lynn Hill's status as a world-class athlete was increasingly well known to non-climbing media around the United States. Her climbing exploits had been referenced in national magazines and she had officially turned professional. The year before, she had taken part in the Rock Master festival overseas and pioneered several first ascents domestically at New York's Shawangunks. In April 1988, she was even present at a media press conference in New York City to formally announce the Snowbird competition that was scheduled to take place in Utah in just three months.

As one of the most accomplished American climbers in history, Hill was widely billed as the best climber in the world—and certainly the star of the forthcoming International Sport Climbing Championship. One final big effort was made to promote the event by having climbers and crew members appear on television morning shows to demonstrate climbing skills and explain the concept of competing on an artificial wall as Snowbird's start date approached.

By June 6, the eve of the competition's official start, many of the participants had arrived at Snowbird's Cliff Lodge, ready for the upcoming weekend's spectacle of cameras, crowds, and markedly hard climbing. Would-be competitors arrived from Italy, Germany, Spain, and Canada. The diversity made the inside of the Cliff Lodge akin to an Olympic Village with so many foreign languages being spoken amid casual socializing and focused stretching. A rowdy precompetition banquet—with alcoholic drinks fueling the revelry—jump-started the historic event.

For Carmichael, Lowe, Michaels, and others, the whole bustling scene of Snowbird was a realization of a quest that had blended countries and sport cultures, media and creative zeal. It was indisputable that the result after multiple decades of progress and evolution would feature some of the best climbing the world had ever seen. However, there were hopes and expectations that surpassed merely the athletics. This was the video age, and to be deemed a true success, the event would have to also produce some of the best *television* the world had ever seen.

CHAPTER 3

THE THRILL OF VICTORY

———

ALTHOUGH THE PREPARATION in the spring of 1988 had been a blitz to make the International Sport Climbing Championship at Snowbird a reality, the start was more subdued. For some competitors, hangovers from the eclectic dinner banquet the previous night had to be nursed. For others, jetlag lingered after the long flight from their European homes. For practically everyone involved—from the athletes to the crew working on the television production—the whole event had to be undertaken in steady segments that would not build to an apex until five days later. It was going to be a long week.

To systematically pare down the robust field of competitors, the event's chief organizer, Jeff Lowe, decided to divide the multiple days of competition into various rounds. The first round—the qualifying portion—would last two days. A semifinal round in the early part of the weekend would follow, and a final round would conclude the event. The format would provide a logical, easy-to-follow narrative for any viewers who watched the event live on the lawn at Snowbird or later on CBS' television broadcast. It would also adhere to the format standards of competition climbing's global governing body, the UIAA. The president of the American Alpine Club—essentially the American conduit for the UIAA's competition standards—was a legendary Shawangunks climber named Jim McCarthy, and he would be in attendance.

Various exhibitions would divide the rounds of exciting climbing competition. These would include a speed climbing segment, interviews with the competitors, and demonstrative roped falls by Dan Goodwin filmed for the television broadcast. Goodwin would also provide color commentary on the television broadcast with a play-by-play sportscaster, James Brown.

But as a way of adding to the competition's allure, the opening rounds were uniquely designed. The two days of qualification were open to all comers at a fee of $50 per participant. This meant that any amateur climber willing to pay the amount could enter the competition, potentially progress through the rounds, and eventually win the grand prize. The underdog characters that this decision would allow for could make great drama for an audience. Additionally, it could give some of the United States' unsung climbers a chance to get noticed on a grand stage.

The route on the side of the Cliff Lodge for the ensuing qualifying round was a sheer line with a difficulty rating that hovered around 5.12b/c—certainly not easygoing for the climbing standards of the late 1980s.

As expected, more than 40 climbers paid the entry fee for an attempt to scale the route, with most ultimately falling shortly after progressing through the lowest moves. By the numbers it was a solid turnout, but such limited upward progress on the wall was a harbinger of stymied climbing that would continue in later rounds.

Another aspect that would remain as the competition progressed was the intermixing of genders, with men and women competitors alternating and attempting the same route. This refreshing production decision allowed viewers and competitors alike to see just how the top American climbers of the day, such as Lynn Hill and Ron Kauk, compared with each other.

As the qualification round ended, four men and two women emerged as the competitors earning advancement into subsequent rounds—which were loaded with the world's elite. Of the qualifiers, Dan Michael had come closest to topping the route, with Pat Adams, David Lanman, and Merrill Bitter behind him in the scores. Bitter, a resident of nearby Salt Lake City, was the only participant with decidedly local ties to earn a berth into the event's later stages. In the women's division, Lieija Painkiner and Melissa Quigley were the only women to advance.

The difficulty of the route notwithstanding, the first few days of the Snowbird competition went splendidly. Bob Carmichael and the production crew continued to film footage from the mechanical winch system through Friday, which was a rest day for some competitors and optional speed climbing practice for others.

At times, Carmichael positioned himself on a seat suspended from a vertical dolly, video camera in hand, filming just a couple feet from the competitors dangling off the side of the Cliff Lodge's wall. Competition climbing was being successfully captured in the television age; the viewer could travel up the wall alongside the climbers—indisputably one of the greatest media innovations the activity of "sport climbing" had ever seen.

Although the sleekness of the production would remain paramount in the coming days, the competition itself would be rattled by problems that nobody saw coming in the preproduction stages.

As Saturday, June 11, dawned at Snowbird to begin the much-anticipated semifinal round, the competitors who had not been eliminated from contention migrated to the base of a new route on the side of the Cliff Lodge. The angles of the wall's paneling and their artificial handholds, mostly in the shape of dimpled finger pockets, caught the morning sun. A cadre of photographers on the lawn around the lodge tilted cameras and tripods upward in preparation for a full day of action. As entertaining as the early days had been, this was the true start of the elite portion of the competition, and everyone in attendance knew it. The best climbers in the world were now set to begin a weekend-long cutthroat contest for prize money, national pride, and publicity. Waiting in the wings were television executives who were hoping for a good show, and Carmichael and the crew who had thus far proved fully capable of shooting it.

Like the week's qualification round that had trimmed the roster of amateur participants with a surprisingly stiff route, the semifinal round started with a string of competitors getting bested by the requisite reachy moves on the wall's 5.12d route. Unlike the early round, however, many competitors in the semifinal round progressed high on the wall and fell nearer to the Cliff Lodge's roof. Such frequent, long falls translated to great theatrics through the lens of Carmichael's video camera.

Ron Kauk was among the competitors to take the biggest "whipper" of the semifinal round, falling nearly 50 feet from the upper lip of the Cliff Lodge paneling before being caught safely by his belayer, Ed Barry.

More than half a dozen ropes were retired as additional men and women competitors neared the wall's upper ledge—the lip—then lunged for a handhold and fell downward in elaborate swoops.

In the women's division, Americans Quigley and Painkiner, along with Alison Osius, Rosie Andrews, Bobbi Bensman, and Robyn Erbesfield, had solid showings but did not advance to the final round. Hill and Jennifer Cole, however, managed to reach holds that were high enough for advancement.

In the men's division, Christian Griffith reached the 72nd hold—the highest of any American man—with his compatriots Jason Stern and Scott Franklin also coasting into the final round.

Paralleling the impressive climbs by the Americans were those of the French. Marc Le Ménestrel reached the top of the route, as did Patrick Edlinger, in impressive fashion. Other French stars such as Jean-Baptiste Tribout, Corinne LaBrune, and Isabelle Patissier climbed high enough to ease into the final round. Even Alex Duboc, who reached a highpoint of six centimeters above the 71st hold to tie with Australia's Geoff Weigand, squeaked into the final round. It was an extraordinary run for the French and proved why France was famous for competitive climbing. It also provided a goal for the Americans to push toward: someday possessing an abundance of international elites, along with a national community ready and willing to support their competitive ambitions.

The semifinal round was not without controversy, and it came with a peculiar blend of American and French elements. The storm began when Didier Raboutou, one of France's most renowned competitors and a candidate to win the entire Snowbird competition, flagged his left foot far out to counterbalance an outstretched hand. As he continued upward, he smeared his left toe ever-so-slightly against the wall paneling's surface before stepping into a subsequent foothold and eventually reaching the top of the Cliff Lodge. Raboutou waved to the cheering crowd below—even though the audience was mostly American, they appreciated the fluidity and grace with which Raboutou had scaled the route.

Once Raboutou was lowered to the ground, however, a judgment came that he had been disqualified. His left foot, in that moment of calm and pause on the route, had flagged out of bounds, beyond a thin red line that designated the wall's vertical field of play. By all analysis, the red line was a poorly designated boundary that had never been adjusted once the wall's construction was completed. Nonetheless, for the competition to be legitimate, the judgment had to be upheld.

Adhering to the rules, in principle, was not difficult. But Raboutou's controversy in the men's division was quickly coupled with a similar issue by American Mari Gingery in the women's division. Gingery also went out of bounds in the same place during her attempt, with a brief tap of her left hand beyond the makeshift red border. But unlike Raboutou, Gingery was not initially disqualified.

Needing to bring some order to the chaos, American Alpine Club President Jim McCarthy agreed to further analyze both competitors' fouls that evening to make a final judgment. Complicating matters was a lack of footage and instant replay capabilities for the analysis. The production crew led by Carmichael had filmed the competitors' attempts, but the reels of raw footage for CBS were not ready to be played or used as materials for arbitration.

In a lucky break, McCarthy was able to locate footage that had been recorded from the lawn by a spectator taping the event. It was not an ideal recording for close analysis; it was grainy, amateur-level footage shot from a low, faraway angle. But at least it provided some reference from which McCarthy could base a decision.

The judges for the competition—Americans Neil Cannon and Alan Watts, along with France's Jean-Claude Droyer and Jean-Marc

Trossier and Australia's Kim Carrigan—were split about what to do with the ruling; a competition ruleset by the UIAA had only been codified three months before the start of the Snowbird competition. It was conceivable a particular movement could fall into a gray area not yet itemized given the newness of the rules.

At the heart of the controversy was the phrasing of various articles in the rules and how that phrasing pertained to Gingery's and Raboutou's individual attempts. The UIAA ruleset asserted that Gingery should have been halted at the time of her left-hand infraction and her highest point on the wall up to that foul deemed her score. However, since none of the judges had recorded her high-point at the time, McCarthy was left to do some guesswork from the shoddy film footage.

As for Raboutou, had he merely flagged his foot, or had he pressed his toe on the paneling? The difference between flagging the foot and putting weight on it, minor as it might have seemed to any spectators, was significant, as the rules stated: *In case a part of the body goes beyond the lines, the judges will establish whether this was for support or only for balance.* Again, the lack of high-quality replay footage made such a firm establishment more challenging.

In the end, McCarthy upheld Raboutou's disqualification. Gingery, who had not used her left hand for support while out of bounds, was allowed to advance to the final round.

In a change to the previous scores, Gingery was now ruled as having tied in the semifinal round with Catherine Destivelle at four centimeters above the 45th hold. The retroactive ruling was not popular with all competitors, some of whom felt it to be a dishonorable and surreptitious attempt at creating a showdown in the final round between Hill and Destivelle. Talk began to circulate around the Cliff Lodge that having a climax of the America versus the World storyline, which had existed since the competition's preformation, had perhaps superseded the spirit of competition at Snowbird.

Although the ruling hung in the air as Sunday's final round began under a pall of overcast gray, competitors and an audience of approximately 2,000 spectators had little time to dwell on the controversial judgment.

Lowe and Carmichael continued to make subtle adjustments to the event in format and in presentation. Such changes included announcing that the final round's standings would also be the final standings for the entire event. This was quite different from the initial plan, which was far more cumulative, of having the final standings be a summation of every round from the entire week. Although a small modification at the time, this change hinted that different scoring and formatting styles could be considered by other event organizers in the future who might be willing to toy with the preconceived contest designs.

Another adjustment was the extension of a competitor's allotted time for a given attempt, from 15 minutes to 20 minutes. This was an effort to give the competitors more time to progress through the difficult sections of the final route without worrying about the added factor of timing out. In theory, the extra five minutes would allow for more competitors to reach the top of the Cliff Lodge. But as the initial competitors proceeded through the start of the final round, it was evident that spectators were in for yet another offering of arduous climbing and frequent falls.

Of the American men who had advanced thus far, Jason Stern reached seven centimeters higher than Christian Griffith in the final round. Both concluded the 1988 Snowbird extravaganza with notable finishes of fifth and sixth place, respectively. Scott Franklin was right behind them in the standings, too. Ron Kauk finished in 10th place and Pat Adams, though not a finalist, finished in 11th place.

The American women, on the whole, had an impressive showing as well. Lynn Hill and Mari Gingery got the crowd cheering with tying highpoints at the 31st hold. Jennifer Cole finished several places lower, having almost secured a grip on the 19th hold.

Despite the enjoyable patriotic euphoria from the Americans, the crowd began to grow restless at the lack of anyone reaching the top of the final route. Termed the Lacerator and rated at 5.13a/b, the long route of sparse holds was the handiwork of judge Kim Carrigan. It stretched upward along a gray path of paneling before a concave upper section curved into the lip of the headwall. It was an undeniably difficult course for the competitors. With requisite hand-foot matches and foot switches, it had done a perfect job of showing spectators just how technical and nuanced climbing movement could be.

Eventually the field of competitors was whittled down to two, all other participants having been bested by the Lacerator. With such exposition, France's Patrick Edlinger strolled to the wall, calmly removed his music headphones, acknowledged his friend and belayer, Paul Sibley, and began his attempt. With each upward movement, as Edlinger advanced beyond previous competitors' highpoints, the crowd on the lawn below grew more enthusiastic.

Beyond the 47th hold, where his compatriots Ménestrel and Tribout had faultered, Edlinger clinched into a lockoff position with one arm and dug the fingers of his other hand into a mono-pocket handhold. He had officially reached a point beyond that of any previous competitor, and the crowd cheered loudly.

Edlinger continued climbing even higher on the route, moving over the lip of the wall just as the gray sky above started to clear. The sun, shining through a seam of clouds, captured Edlinger in perfect calm. Recaps of the competition would later cite Edlinger's figure climbing there in the momentary golden glimmer as the perfect television moment. It was immediately etched in competition climbing history. "No one could have written a better script," *Climbing* would later report.

Already having clinched the victory then, Edlinger found a position on the wall that allowed him to rest as onlookers far below clamored for a better view. He soon continued up the headwall's slab portion and clipped into the top anchor. Not only had he won—and reached the top of the Cliff Lodge—he had made the whole process look graceful and effortless.

It was unlikely that the last climber in the women's division—Catherine Destivelle—would match the audience fanfare that Edlinger had garnered. Judges and spectators could sense that Edlinger's performance was something that would quickly become legendary—particularly when enhanced by a touch of expert editing for television. Nonetheless, Destivelle ambled to the base of the Lacerator, ready to try for the victory and carve her own fascinating storyline. In the scores, Hill and Gingery were tied for first place. In order to beat them and claim the win, Destivelle would have to progress beyond a difficult two-finger pocket high up the route.

The audience remained mostly silent as Destivelle worked through the low pockets on the wall but steadily came alive as Destivelle neared the previous competitors' highpoints. Moving beyond the 27th hold, she surpassed Corrine LaBrune in the scoring. Then, by reaching higher than the 28th hold, she surpassed Isabelle Patissier's highpoint. As Destivelle proceeded and latched her fingers into the 31st hold, the crowd grew nervously hushed. Destivelle set her feet wide and crouched, then she reached up—latching the 32nd hold and thus claiming the victory. Destivelle progressed through two more holds before falling. The dominance of the French, having won both the men's and women's division, was the fundamental takeaway of the weekend's climbing at Snowbird. Additional victories in a speed climbing portion—by Jacky Godoffe for the men and Destivelle for the women—confirmed France's supremacy. One subheading in a review of the Snowbird festivities would read, THE FRENCH FRY THE COMPETITION AT THE FIRST AMERICAN INTERNATIONAL CLIMBING CHAMPIONSHIP.

Above all else, the Snowbird competition affirmed that competition climbing on an international scale could find a home with an American audience. Despite some of the sensational headlines that followed, American competitors had proved they were capable of contending with the greatest athletes from France and elsewhere. "Organized contests are healthy and can provide deserved recognition and support for talented climbers," wrote George Bracksieck in *Rock and Ice*, adding about the event, "This was an excellent first effort, especially given the short amount of time to pull it together. Sport climbing is here to stay."

For competitors and organizers, the future of climbing in the United States looked bright. The question, though, was how the rest of the country would respond to this newfound competition form.

CHAPTER 4

TOO BIG TO FAIL

———

AROUND THE TIME the International Sport Climbing Championship at Snowbird was sending the American climbing community into a euphoric buzz, Thornburg and Frye arrived at their hallowed Highway 13 on-ramp one day to discover something heartbreaking. For months the two climbers had continued to carry out their vision of crafting their own routes at the structural base of the busy overpass. They had used the hoarded supply of epoxy to attach more Tuolumne knobs and concrete fragments of assorted sizes and shapes in snaking upward trajectories. Some of these makeshift routes had nearly reached the cars high overhead. In fact, the methodology of gluing the fragments hadn't been all that dissimilar from that of the formal climbing competition routesetting at Snowbird. At times, other climbers around the Bay Area such as Marc Jensen and a blond-haired climber at California Polytechnic State University in San Luis Obispo named Hans Florine had even joined Thornburg and Frye in the urban climbing exploits, epoxying new holds and scaling the side of the on-ramp.

But even with a devoted crew of friends, Thornburg and Frye's craftsmanship had remained low-key by necessity. What had resulted from repeated secret sessions of making the "glue-ups" was an array of climbing opportunities with a wide range of difficulty. The men figured their easiest on-ramp route was rated 5.11, and the hardest route up one of the 40-foot pillars was 5.13.

All totaled, the glue-ups had provided hours of training for Thornburg, Frye, and the few friends who admittedly didn't have the money or the means to drive from Berkeley to Yosemite every weekend like other climbers in the area.

Still, everyone knew from the onset that they were, at best, bending the rules of recreation allowed by the Lake Temescal park authorities. At worst, all involved were breaking the law and could face fines or incarceration.

So, it was not surprising when Thornburg and Frye showed up one day, ready and anxious to climb, only to find that the California Department of Transportation had discovered their guerilla climbing enclave and removed all the makeshift handholds and footholds beneath the on-ramp.

The sight of the barren pillars was crushing given how climbing in suburban America was just starting to gain traction as a viable discipline outside the rugged mountains. Thornburg and Frye knew that the sport was gaining popularity; a competition scene was gathering momentum around the country, and climbing routes—of plastic, concrete fragments, wood, or other materials—could now exist on surfaces beyond real stone. The Snowbird competition on the side of a lodge, as well as the Highway 13 glue-ups, had proved that climbing was booming with creative possibilities. Other versions of glue-ups had even begun to appear beneath highway overpasses in other cities and suburbs. One California newspaper reported outright that the

California Department of Transportation was seeking "to destroy all climbing walls." But the article also noted that such destruction was a long-term objective: "Walls are carefully guarded secrets, passed by word of mouth in a very small circle."

If Thornburg's climbing fix could no longer be satiated by frequent trips to the highway concrete near Lake Temescal, he had to find another outlet. Back in Berkeley, he soon took a job teaching weekly climbing classes to beginners at Cal Adventures, the University of California's department that offered instruction for a variety of recreational activities. But he quickly found the climbing options at the Recreational Sport Facility—commonly called the RSF building—extremely limited. With no substantial climbable surface, no real rock to be found, and no array of artificial handholds or footholds on any large face, Thornburg was tasked with teaching his Cal Adventures students how to climb in theory more so than in practice. A sole rope hung from an anchor on the RSF building's ceiling for practicing and drilling the mechanics of belaying, but there were no walls or routes on which to actually belay a climber.

One night, Thornburg pitched an idea to his Cal Adventures boss, Rick Spittler: to build an artificial climbing wall on the back side of the RSF building. It was a novel concept—constructing a scaled-down version of what had been done on the massive Cliff Lodge in Snowbird. The allure was two-fold. First, a climbable wall on the back of the university building would enhance the breadth of instruction that could take place in Thornburg's weekly classes. Second, it would focus on the sport climbing craze that California college students, known for being among the first to embrace trends and fads, would undoubtedly be anxious to try.

Spittler was not sold on the idea, but he did not see the harm in improving Cal Adventures' climbing instruction by utilizing a side of a nondescript wall that was otherwise serving no purpose.

Over the next few weeks, Thornburg and a handful of other Cal Adventures employees worked to construct a climbable surface on the RSF's back wall. They brainstormed sequences, drilled holes for T-nuts into the paneling, and set up ropes. They ordered handholds and footholds from Europe, where there was a growing market for the items due to the increased frequency of climbing competitions there.

Once enough holds had arrived in the mail and been attached to the building to create some routes of varying difficulty, Thornburg began utilizing the new climbable wall for his instructional courses.

Word quickly spread around the university as students weary from studying took notice. Soon students who had not enrolled in Thornburg's classes were also wanting to climb on the artificial surface. Climbers in Berkeley who weren't part of the university wanted to climb on it, too.

A decision was made to open the Cal Adventures climbing wall to the general public, and the response was immediately positive. On a given weeknight, the RSF building would fill up with experienced climbers and people new to the sport, all anxious to try out the routes on the wall. On a weekend, there would be as many as 30 people waiting for a turn to climb.

For Thornburg, it was like a dream—getting paid to play a part in climbing's sport evolution. He was making $100 per day to teach students how to climb on the artificial wall, and when he wanted a break from giving instructions, he could dig into the storage crates of spare handholds and footholds and bolt up new routes.

The increasing size of the crowds prompted another idea for Thornburg: Why not hold a competition on the RSF wall in addition to the instructional classes? With nearly 25 routes set at any time, the logistics would be relatively easy—adhere to an all-comers format, with the winner being whomever could climb the highest on the hardest routes. The draw for the students would be that this was the university's version of the scene that was thriving in Europe. It would be climbing tailored to the niche of sport-loving California twentysomethings.

Flyers were posted around campus to advertise the first-ever Cal Crank, as the competition was named. To Thornburg's surprise, 106 people showed up to compete—far exceeding the expectations of everyone involved.

The surprisingly large turnout meant that another competition was warranted. For the next Cal Crank event, a local architect and builder named Wayne Campbell fashioned a large prism-shaped feature out of steel and coated it with paneling and climbable holds. Campbell's creation, nearly 10 feet tall and 5 feet wide, was bolted to the top of the RSF wall to add a slight overhang to one of the routes. It would be an edifice way ahead of its time—resembling the large volume holds that would come into vogue for routesetters nearly 30 years later.

The number of participants for that second Cal Crank—122—surpassed expectations as well. Climbing competitions now held an exceptional place in the public consciousness: they were events that most American climbers had heard about by that point, but they also felt decidedly new, still malleable and brimming with conceptual potential.

Such immediate interest in the Cal Crank competitions was illustrative of more widespread intrigue happening around the United

States. Sport climbing was reaching into nearly all aspects of culture, and with that, competition climbing was materializing as a sports entity that would be well-suited for the upcoming flashy 1990s.

Shortly after the International Sport Climbing Championship at Snowbird, *The New York Times* published an article by Marlene Werner titled "How the Times Are Changing: Climbing A Wall Is Fun Now." Werner noted how sport climbing had been born in Europe but recently crossed over to the United States. All that was required for a layman to participate, Werner pointed out, were the bare essentials like climbing shoes, a harness, and a rope.

Buried deeper in Werner's assessment of wall climbing (as opposed to rock climbing) and its physical necessity of "strength, balance, flexibility, power and grace," was an assertion of its over-all accessibility. She wrote, "The beauty of the sport, according to enthusiasts, is that anyone can do it…."

Climbing was given another mainstream platform, albeit far-ther afield than a newspaper write-up, in the opening scene of *Star Trek V: The Final Frontier* in 1989. Hollywood had taken notice of climbing in the 1970s, as evidenced by Bob Carmichael's films and a Clint Eastwood thriller, *The Eiger Sanction*. But climbing had more cinematic momentum now than ever before.

For *Star Trek V: The Final Frontier*, producers turned to familiar experts in the field to portray Captain James Kirk (William Shatner) climbing El Capitan in "Yosemite National Park, Planet Earth" on "Stardate 8454.1." Carmichael was hired to rig the cameras for the scene, utilizing many of the videography techniques he had perfected just a year prior at the Snowbird competition. He and a crew filmed the on-location climbing on a feature known as Boot Flake on the Nose of El Capitan, among other spots, and a portrayal of Captain Kirk's fall amid conversation with Spock (Leonard Nimoy) was shot on the seventh pitch of a route called Tangerine Trip on El Capitan's southeast face.

The scene's filming and the movie's eventual release epitomized a noteworthy interest in climbing by Hollywood producers. It was evident by 1989 that many people in the movie industry were beginning to recognize the sport's blockbuster potential—if given the right story and the right actor.

There were other indications of a sport climbing boom born from or amid the competitions, particularly in the equipment market. Tom Jones had founded a company, Jrat, in 1985 in Boulder, Colorado, and by the late 1980s, the brand's spandex tights and t-shirts were practically the uniforms for many competitors. "Comps were an opportunity for small, new companies to get splash at minimal cost," Jones would later recall. "We could sponsor climbers (with gear) because we were dirtbag climbers just like them, so they did not expect much from us. As in, they did not expect money. My deal with sponsored climbers was always, 'If you can get a better deal, take it!'"

Christian Griffith, who had placed sixth at the International Sport Climbing Championship at Snowbird, started his own company, Verve, out of his bedroom in Colorado. He had noticed European climbers at various competitions wearing European brands and felt that American climbers would respond similarly to a homegrown label. He sold 40 hand-sewn chalkbags at a modest competition in Idaho in Verve's first year, 1988, and from there, he quickly established the brand as a hot new clothing and equipment supplier.

Also in 1988, an artificial climbing wall manufacturer based in France, Entre-Prises, opened an American headquarters in Bend, Oregon. The company had started modestly when a Parisian engineering student, Francois Savigny, used a loan from his grandmother to create hexagonal climbing wall panels made of resin. But business and demand for more climbing wall paneling had exploded since those humble beginnings due to sport climbing's global popularity. A year after the unveiling of Entre-Prises' American satellite office headed up by climbers Alan Watts and Chris Grover, the company built a 60-foot climbing wall for The Sporting Club in Atlanta, Georgia, at a hefty cost of $92,500. This was soon followed by the construction of a climbing wall inside The Sporting Club of Chicago, branded in advertisements as "the world's tallest indoor climbing structure."

Elsewhere, Jeff Lowe was turning his promotional notions about competition climbing into a full-fledged business: the Sport Climbing Championships (SCC). In early 1989, he set out to implement his plan of creating an American circuit in the European model he had observed years before. In fact, the American Alpine Club even awarded Lowe with exclusivity rights to organize sanctioned American climbing competitions. Lowe promptly began working with a French architect, Jean-Marc Blanche, to create mobile climbing walls that could be erected for competitions and then dismantled and transported in trucks to subsequent stops on a hypothetical cross-country event tour.

JMB Sport Climbing Designs, as Lowe's partnership with Blanche was called, opened an office in Broomfield, Colorado, in 1989 to begin the long process of creating and constructing state-of-the-art walls—part of "The Next Generation of Climbing Walls"—that could be unveiled to big fanfare the following year. The first advertisement for JMB Sport Climbing Designs in *Climbing* asserted: "The physical and mental challenges of climbing, combined with the improved safety of modern climbing systems, has made climbing the fastest growing segment of the outdoor/sporting industry over the past five years."

Amid the expansion into various American market tiers, competitions in the United States began to flourish. A multiround sport climbing contest at Sports Chalet, an athletic supply store in the La Cañada Flintridge section of Southern California, was one example. At the competition, resin holds were screwed into the building's outside brick wall. Climbing equipment was sold on the premises in conjunction with the festivities, and a large crowd of spectators gathered in the parking lot to watch the competitors scale the side of the building.

Most significant among the proliferation of competitions was another International Sport Climbing Championship, which took place again at the Snowbird resort beginning on Friday, August 11, 1989.

The second annual championship was organized largely in the same vein as the 1988 event, with some notable differences. The wall on the side of the Cliff Lodge was again used as the structural base for the routes, even though the company that had produced the panels, Dan Goodwin's Sport Climbing Systems, was in the midst of closing under pressure from the Environmental Protection Agency, the Occupational Safety and Health Administration, and other entities. In fact, many regulatory agencies at the time could not yet grasp the concept and logistics of an artificial climbing wall industry and slapped pioneering companies—like Sport Climbing Systems—with exorbitant fines and penalties that proved to be ruinous. And unlike the first Snowbird championship, the 1989 event began with an initial round deemed the North American Open. In this round, American climbers who had been invited by the American Alpine Club competed for a chance to progress to a final round that was populated by international competitors. Christian Griffith set the routes on the Cliff Lodge wall for the Open, while the finals' routes were set by French routesetters Fabrice Guillot and Antoine Le Ménestrel (the older brother of Marc Le Ménestrel, who had competed in the previous year's championship at Snowbird).

The final round featured 15 competitors—many of whom were returning to Snowbird from the previous year, such as Ron Kauk, Didier Raboutou, Jean-Baptiste Tribout, Catherine Destivelle, and Isabelle Patissier.[4] Most significant from an organizational standpoint was that Jeff Lowe had returned to oversee the competition.

Lowe continually worked to improve the spectacle aspect of his SCC creation. For instance, the 1989 event cost approximately $250,000 to produce and spanned two weekends rather than just one, with the final round given a World Cup designation. In total, 4,500 spectators descended on the lawn at Snowbird throughout the week. Some people camped out in tents and tailgated from cars; others packed the hotel rooms of the resort complex. A showcase of clothing, gear, and meet-and-greets called the Sports Expo was held on the grounds to provide added entertainment for those in attendance. And throughout the various rounds of climbing, rock music blared through loudspeakers as the competitors scaled the routes.

The 1989 event also maintained a strict isolation stipulation. Climbers were not allowed to mingle with spectators or watch each other's attempts on the routes. This contributed to the larger spectacle too, as the competitors emerged from their sequestration

---

4. Conspicuously absent for the 1989 competition at Snowbird was Patrick Edlinger, the winner of the event in 1988. Famed European climbers Stefan Glowacz (of Germany) and Jerry Moffatt (of England) also did not attend the event—to the surprise of many spectators and journalists covering the event at the time.

one-by-one to cheers from an adoring crowd. There was added drama when Jennifer Cole, a competitor from Chattanooga, Tennessee, was disqualified for failing to sequester herself—ultimately due to a miscommunication with the event handlers. It was a shaky adjustment to the isolation format that would become standard in years to come.

By all measures, the 1989 event at Snowbird was a more ostentatious version than the previous year's championship, but it was lacking a key figure. Bob Carmichael, who had been a seminal figure in making the event a success on CBS in 1988—and had shared a 50/50 partnership with Lowe in the SCC—was not involved at all by the time the second annual International Sport Climbing Championship rolled around.

Carmichael still felt that such large-scale climbing events were best as once-a-year spectacles. Lowe, in contrast, was beginning to conjure up notions of holding competitions far more frequently. In a magazine interview about the first competition at Snowbird, Lowe had not even mentioned Carmichael's name or his key involvement. This glaring omission would later be chalked up to forgetfulness by Lowe, but such a blunder revealed the rift that had emerged between the SCC's two key players.

Realizing that the television networks were perhaps not ready to embrace climbing competitions with great frequency, Carmichael had asked attorney Ed Labowitz to draft a memo that dissolved Carmichael's partnership with Lowe. With a simple signature, all rights and financial responsibility—and liabilities—had become exclusively Jeff Lowe's.

Carmichael's ability to unite the two disparate worlds of sport climbing and network television proved even more valuable in retrospect; the 1989 Snowbird competition had all the raw action and dramatic content necessary to create a compelling video presentation, but it no longer had such mainstream television network interest.

Particularly captivating at the competition was the rise of an American contingent in the women's division. Lynn Hill had suffered a devastating fall six weeks prior to the 1989 Snowbird extravaganza, dislocating her elbow and breaking a foot in the process. The fact that she was even climbing at all—much less vying for competition victory at Snowbird—so soon after her accident was a remarkable storyline underpinning the event.

Also, 1989 had thus far proved to be a banner year for Robyn Erbesfield. Prior to Snowbird, Erbesfield had traveled to Europe and won a World Cup event in Leeds, England, and a Master's competition in Paris, France. Her activity on Europe's circuit had earned her a spot on a budding American national team—a somewhat dubious designation, as there was also an "Alaskan Team" partaking in various competitions at the same time. Such disparity spoke to the utter novelty of the team concept for most climbers in the United States in the late 1980s.

By the end of the glitzy 1989 competition week at Snowbird, the French had again proved their dominance. In the men's division, Didier Raboutou had won and, in doing so, redeemed himself of the surprising disqualification from the year prior. Simon Nadine of England, who had recently turned professional and would eventually beat out Raboutou to claim the overall World Cup for 1989, had claimed second place.

Victory in the women's division of the 1989 Snowbird event had gone to Nanette Raybaud, with Hill, still recovering from the effects of her accident, taking second place. The previous year's winner, Destivelle, had taken third.

Despite Europe's continued competition supremacy, strong placings by a number of Americans attested to a viable group of climbers around the country now fully ensconced in the competition milieu. Ron Kauk had taken third place in the men's division, and Jim Karn had taken seventh place; Erbesfield had ultimately placed fourth in the women's final. Other Americans—Pat Adams, Dale Goddard, Kristen Druheller, Bobbi Bensman, and others—had placed in the semifinal round. The event had also featured a speed climbing portion won by French climbers (Jacky Godoffe and Catherine Destivelle in the men's and women's categories, respectively), but Americans had proved to be adept there too: Christian Griffith had placed second in the men's speed climbing division, and fifth and sixth place in the women's speed climbing division had gone to Jennifer Cole and Meg Hall, respectively.

Hans Florine, who had first heard about the Snowbird competitions in a climbing magazine and sent Lowe a resume in hopes of gaining an invitation, took 10th place in an early portion of the week's festivities at Snowbird known as the North American Open. Much of Florine's training to prepare for the vertical face of the Cliff Lodge had been done on the Highway 13 glue-ups prior to their removal. Despite an aptitude for methodical, difficult climbing outdoors, Florine would come to rule the American speed climbing discipline within a year and eventually become one of the country's most decorated competitors.

Florine, Kauk, Goddard, Erbesfield, Bensman, and the multitude of other American participants were situated to be the driving forces behind the continued success of competitions around the country. But the climbers' collective influence was contingent on the existence of a competition surplus in years to come beyond a Utah ski resort.

Whether more competitions could flourish in the same spectacular vein of Snowbird remained to be seen.

Two other Americans at the 1989 Snowbird event who would prove to be pivotal in the evolution of competition climbing had been working behind the scenes rather than competing on the wall.

One of these, Steve Gabel, had recently completed graduate school work at the University of Colorado and handled a complex surveying device called a theodolite for the event's scoring. That scoring process had involved the reflection of competitors' highpoints down to the ground, where readings of each competitor's precise height could then be computed.

It was innovative work, using a combination of the theodolite and a computer at a time when calculations and scrupulous assessments in all athletics were generally done manually. But Gabel, holding an MBA, also had business acumen that was applicable to Lowe's ideas about frequent competitions. It would be Gabel who would help Lowe organize a particular business plan for the coming year.

Also working behind the scenes at Snowbird was California native Roy McClenahan. Like so many others connected to the championships, McClenahan had old ties to Yosemite's Stonemasters era. He had climbed with Hill and others in the 1970s—and, in 1980, repeated the free ascent of the Astroman route originally done by John Bachar, Ron Kauk, and John Long. He had also worked as a climbing guide, plying his craft at famed California climbing crags such as Tahquitz, Suicide Rocks, and Joshua Tree National Park. The experience had culminated in McClenahan leading Yosemite Mountaineering School's first guided ascents of the Nose and the Salathé Wall on El Capitan.

By the summer of 1989, McClenahan had carved his name into the sport climbing niche by helping another climber, Peter Mayfield, a noted Yosemite wunderkind and Jim Bridwell protégé, get a climbing gym called CityRock off the ground in Emeryville, California. In the lead-up to CityRock's grand opening, McClenahan and Mayfield even took a portable wall—with paneling by French manufacturer Entre-Prises and some utilitarian scaffolding for support—to a convention center and a municipal park in Berkeley to promote the idea of rock climbing on an artificial surface to the general public.

It was an astute publicity move. Climbing on anything but real rock was considered an odd pursuit. Overseas, a physical education teacher had built a brick climbing wall for winter training purposes at the University of Leeds in England, and in the United States, the University of Washington had a comparable outdoor climbing wall for training and conditioning. But climbing gyms of any sort were rare—although there were a few. In 1987, climbers Rich Johnston and Dan Cauthorn had started Vertical Club in Seattle. It featured graveled flooring and rock handholds glued to the indoor walls. Around that time, a concrete wall on the campus of Southern Illinois University was regularly drawing crowds, too. Although not technically a gym, the campus wall featured permanent wooden holds and played host to its own climbing contest, the Arm Blaster Competition, in 1988 spearheaded by local climber Eric Ulner and another collegian, Rene Keyzer-Andre.

That same year, Portland Rock Gym was founded in Oregon and offered approximately 2,000 square feet of climbing space with 22-foot walls. It had an exercise corner with pegboards and pullup bars and an adjustable wall crack machine. The following year, 1989, a climbing competition called the Idaho Open at City of Rocks, Idaho, was organized outdoors on private property and included several graspable artificial features being screwed into the natural rock face.

The idea of climbing indoors was still unusual to much of the United States' recreation-seeking public. One outdoor equipment store in Pacific Beach, California, called A Striving After Wind had long housed an indoor section of vertical surface that was technically climbable, although the wall offered little more than undulations carved into the brickwork. Another outdoor equipment store in New Hampshire, International Mountain Equipment, boasted "demonstration walls" for gear testing, but details regarding what an indoor climbing facility could—and should—provide to its patrons were still unrefined. One article in Salt Lake City's *Deseret News* espoused of the new climbing gyms: "Climbers can hit the wall during their lunch hour, not unlike jogging or bicycling." California's CityRock, and particularly its plethora of holds securely attached to artificial walls, was largely inspired by the European competitions at Arco in the mid-1980s. CityRock's owner Mayfield envisioned his gym as being a full-on "climbing institute," in essence an indoor "interactive sculpture garden" on which people could climb and have "transformational experiences." Mayfield would later reflect, "I was wanting to change people's lives with this amazing mind, body, and spirit-connecting activity of rock climbing. My gym's target market wasn't going to be people who already went climbing outdoors. I was making a much bigger play, to people who would otherwise never try climbing."

As it materialized, Mayfield's indoor facility nodded to the fitness montage that Carmichael had put in *First Ascent* ten years prior—climbers jogging, jumping rope, and getting fit to supplement their climbing—and the guerilla urbanism that climbers had enacted with their concrete handholds beneath a highway overpass. "Back then, [exercise] was all about pumping iron—and it was this really objectifying scene: people were working out to look good in bathing suits," Mayfield would say. "There was no Pilates. There was no yoga. 'Wellness' wasn't a word. So in a way, CityRock was part of the early trend of functional fitness. Climbing at the gym wasn't objectifying. It was good for people. It was functional fitness."

But Mayfield embraced another groundbreaking idea. A climbing gym could be utilized for more than just training; it could be used to actually host competitions, too. And to illustrate the growing popularity and scope of climbing competitions, Mayfield played a Betamax tape of CBS' broadcast of Snowbird as part of his pitch to potential CityRock investors. He also pointed out to would-be backers that climbing might even be part of the Olympics someday; CityRock could become a stronghold for that global competition ethos.

Coinciding with this vision, Mayfield's business wingman, McClenahan, eagerly headed to Utah to assist Jeff Lowe in managing the organizational and administrative minutiae of the second annual Snowbird competition. McClenahan quickly became Lowe's aide, of sorts, with an outward objective of helping him run the event.

However, an underlying aim for McClenahan, much broader in scope, was to shadow Lowe as much as possible and, in doing so, informally learn how to be a competition organizer. Such newly acquired knowledge could be taken to Emeryville, California, where McClenahan would leverage his enhanced resources to expand his contribution to comparable programs and events at CityRock.

Such intentions signified how competition climbing was gaining in complexities and even allegiances—or at least assorted social circles and employers. There were elements that organizers at all levels could draw from and harness into their own visions; competitions could exist in innumerable forms in states around the country. There were enthusiastic audiences and participant rosters for the events.

The diverging competitive incarnations in the United States seemed to be set for steady growth and development, and possibly the realization of a viable circuit if given time to evolve.

At the end of 1989, nobody could have predicted how one particular competition in the coming year, bigger than anything that had come before it, would single-handedly take the lively American "comp scene" to an unimaginable level of achievement—and, in the end, destroy the entire circuit altogether.

CHAPTER 5

SETTING THE STANDARD

WITH LOWE'S SCC BRAND THRIVING and several gyms opening, it became clear that some standards were needed to give any forthcoming climbing competitions around the country a degree of consistency and fairness. Many of the local bouldering contests that had been held on real rock in the 1970s and 1980s had stuck to an honor system for arbitration, or at least entailed climbers monitoring each other when it came to adherence to any specified rules. Even when more formal mediation had been present at those smaller events, judgment calls or squabbles among competitors had usually resolved quickly via a convivial esprit de corps. Beers were often toasted, prizes were frequently shared, and most climbers always went away happy—and often contentedly buzzed.

The rise of the Snowbird era did a lot to change that relaxed norm. Such an abundance of international climbers now willing to travel to the United States to take part meant that any aura of localism and fellowship among competitors at the venue was lessened; if loyalty existed, it was to one's country more so than to the climbing tribe as a whole. Also, with multiple rounds of climbs being vehicles for athletes to win prize money and get noticed by potential sponsors, it became more imperative that specific judging criteria would be put in place, so as to avoid controversy or dissent when scores were calculated and money awarded. There was also a growing band of American climbers separating from the old dirtbag ethos. While many had previously relished the seclusion of the wilderness crags, they were now interested in taking part in big events like the ones at Snowbird. Being a professional climber, or at least a sponsored one, by way of traveling and winning competitions was now an attainable vocation.

In theory, the adoption of widely known standards would allow all climbers to train more specifically and know precisely how rock climbing outdoors differentiated from competing on artificial climbing walls. And by 1989, rules and regulations for competitive climbing had already been cemented in Europe, crafted for the most part by the UIAA and utilized at the various competitions that had formed a circuit around that continent for years. Following the success of Snowbird in the United States, Lowe was positioned as the person spearheading the United States competition climbing scene, so an onus of establishing a reliable system of judging comparable to the international one fell on his shoulders.

Lowe was already quite familiar with Europe's procedural rules due to his time traveling and watching competitions there. However, his duties of organizing his own competitions—and conjuring up some soon-to-be-unveiled plans for an extraordinary 1990—did not allow him the time or resources to dive deep into the intricacies of rules and pen his own judging manual. Instead, he needed to find someone who could wade through the detailed UIAA standards, garner useful concepts and relevant data, and mastermind a similar system of judging that could be the standard for American competitions going forward.

The scribe Lowe turned to for help was a longtime climber from New York named Peter Darmi. Darmi had been educated in the UIAA's international standards in 1988 through sponsorship by the American Alpine Club. Shortly thereafter, he had been introduced to Lowe through a mutual friend—American Alpine Club President Jim McCarthy. Appropriate for Lowe's needs, Darmi's knowledge and official certification as a UIAA judge for international competitions allowed him to gain experience by officiating some of the World Cup events—in Japan, Germany, France, and elsewhere. Moreover, Darmi and Lowe had a mutual interest in wanting to standardize subsequent competitions in the United States.

Darmi's background interested Lowe, as well. Darmi was a music engineer by trade, having worked on albums for a number of famous artists, including Dionne Warwick and B.B. King. Thus, Darmi was already deeply immersed in the ways of the entertainment industry.

Darmi was forthcoming in telling Lowe that any climbing competitions absolutely had to be embraced foremost as *entertainment* if they were to be successful with sponsors, advertisers, and spectators. The first International Sport Climbing Championship at Snowbird had been given an extraordinary theatrical gloss because of its CBS television broadcast. But entertainment had to be the anchor for all future competitions too, regardless of whether they received network exposure. In fact, Lowe's need for internationally accepted judging criteria within an entertaining exterior seemed to be the perfect blend of Darmi's interest, experience, and skillset.

The zenith of Darmi's knowledge and his connection to the competition facet was a book, *The Sport Climbing Championships Competitors' Guide*, which he wrote and published in 1989. The book drew on

the UIAA standards—most of which Darmi translated from French—
and established an American benchmark that could aid climbers and
organizers for years to come—whether at competitions as big as the
ones at Snowbird or as local as the Cal Cranks at the RSF in Berkeley.

"Sport climbing competitions have suddenly become hot, both
here and especially in Europe," Darmi wrote in the book's introduction. "Top competition climbers are now international celebrities."

With chapters devoted to climber eligibility, the protest and
appeals process, and ideal climbable surfaces, Darmi's book instantly
became the chief ruleset and compendium for the SCC. Not only did
it provide scrupulous formulas for scoring competitions and calcu-
lating competitor rankings ("B = 50[(T min ÷ Tx) + Hx ÷ Hv)]"),
but it also delved into the nuance that made competition climbing
unique from outdoor rock climbing: "The technology is still evolving,
but at present most walls consist of molded fiberglass or laminate
panels which have a grainy texture for friction, and rocklike features
which can be used as intermediate holds."

At one point, Darmi even mitigated the physiological transition
from real rock to man-made paneling for any nervous participants,
writing:

> The first-time competitor on an artificial wall may find it
> alien and disconcerting. The panels have a hollow sound
> to them and considerably more 'give' than real rock. Since
> they are mounted on a scaffolding, the entire structure may
> vibrate a little. Also, the holds and their placements are not
> nature's design, but are from the mind of a route designer
> whose mission it is to create problems of route finding and
> difficulty of execution. The whole 'feel' of the route will be
> different for that reason.

Darmi was looped in to help Lowe with mediating future competitions, but Darmi also knew that more had to be done from an educational standpoint. A guide for competitors was not sufficient for giving the American competition scene a degree of depth that could last for generations. An entire workforce of judges was needed, rather than just Darmi himself acting exclusively. These judges could, in turn, train additional judges; and through such exponential advancement, a ruleset would become universal.

Over several brainstorming sessions, Darmi conceptualized a personnel model that resembled that of the UIAA but was modified to work within the United States: organizers and judges residing in all regions of the country would be promptly trained and made capable of presiding over events whenever and wherever called upon.

With that ambitious goal, Darmi hit the road to build a roster of qualified judges. He traveled to Berkelcy, Phoenix, and Seattle, among other cities, to hold seminars and training courses. Nearly all the potential trainees were devoted climbers who had an interest in learning the formal UIAA rules and becoming the fundamental regulatory core of competition climbing in the United States. Darmi would arrive approximately one week prior to a local competition, train the personnel, and serve as the Jury President, which was the UIAA's term for the chief judge.

In a given stretch, Darmi would spend 10 days on the road before returning to his home in the Northeast to network, make phone calls, and schedule more appointments for judging instructions. Then he would hit the road again to conduct more training. "I'd been a touring musician for years, so road tripping to set up the judging network was easy," Darmi would recall. "I was motivated by the vision of building something I believed in." Further fueling the endeavor was the fact that Darmi was actually getting paid, albeit modestly, by those aspirant judges who took his courses. Within a matter of months, Darmi had dozens of certified competition judges.

The benefit of having so many capable judges was not limited to the United States. Such depth meant that the United States could now be increasingly represented on judges' panels at competitions in Europe too. This was particularly important to Darmi because he had long noticed a nationality bias from certain European judges. In one event, a French competitor had slipped away from the isolation section near the climbing wall for a quick dalliance with a fan at a nearby hotel room—an obvious violation of the clear-cut rule that competitors were not to leave the confines of isolation. And yet, upon discovery of the incident, one of the French judges at the competition had deemed the violation acceptable and the competitor was inexplicably not disqualified. It rankled Darmi less as an isolated incident and more as a representation of the favoritism that was rampant in competition judging. He knew that having American judges in Europe wouldn't completely squelch all such cases of bias, but at least it would level the playing field—and show the world that the United States was fully embracing competition climbing, too.

Around this time, Darmi and his workforce of new American judges also started hearing rumblings from overseas about the upcoming 1992 Winter Olympics. The Games were still several years away, but preparations had already begun, and the rumor was that competition climbing would be introduced as an Olympic sport. Supporting this was the fact that the Games would be held in Albertville, France—and as the host country, France would be permitted to include any sport of its choosing in the Games. That country's longstanding connection to competitions, not to mention its general embrace of mountaineering culture around the Alps, meant that climbing's inclusion was all but guaranteed. The American Alpine

Club even released an advertisement authored by its president, Jim McCarthy, with the headline BEYOND SNOWBIRD. "Now we all have to look to the future," the advertisement read. "Climbing will most likely appear as a demonstration event at the 1992 Winter Olympic Games in Albertville."

A natural extension of the sport's bright future and such new-found depth of American judges was the creation of some sort of governing body for competitors and organizers. As successful as the UIAA had been in overseeing various competitions in the 1980s, it was a European organization and had never attempted to establish an American branch. Darmi figured the best way to keep the United States in the fold of the faraway UIAA but also cement its own homegrown identity was to create a hierarchical feeder system: autonomous climbing competitions around the United States could contribute to a ranking system of exclusively American climbers, ultimately providing a pathway for those ranked competitors to advance to international competitions sanctioned by the UIAA.

Aiding Darmi in this vision was Ralph Erenzo, another certified competition judge who had been stationed at the top slab of the Cliff Lodge wall at the 1989 Snowbird event. Together, with little more than a phone and a fax machine, Erenzo and Darmi conjured up an idea for the American Sport Climbers Federation (ASCF), an ad hoc organization that would be geared toward meeting the needs of the United States' competition climbers.[5]

Issues discussed for Darmi and Erenzo's federation included its ability to sanction competitions, provide insurance and long-term care for competitors, cover the travel and hotel expenses for

---

5. In past documents and interviews this organization is sometimes referred to alternatively as the American Sport Climbing Federation.

all those involved in any event, attain sponsors, accredit facilities, and offer consistent messaging to the entire American sport climbing community. Darmi could conduct most of the logistics required to get the organization off the ground from his music engineering office in New Paltz, New York, and Erenzo could be the point man for correspondence with other organizations such as the UIAA. The model for the ASCF's scoring system was the weighted system used in cross-country skiing events. Jed Williamson, who would eventually coach American cross-country skiers in the biathlon at the Olympic level, helped Darmi and Erenzo learn the scoring structure and administer it in a uniquely climbing context.

Despite budgetary limitations, Darmi and Erenzo devised the rough outline for a monumental, albeit embryonic, system. In a revised edition of Darmi's book, retitled *The Sport Climbing Competition Handbook*, Ralph Erenzo—acting as the Executive Director of the ASCF—wrote that there were more than 200 climbing walls ("in schools, gyms, recreation centers, universities, silos, barns, etc.") and that competitions were "taking place almost daily." The need for an American standard of organization was thus more urgent than ever. Erenzo wrote, "When you join the ASCF, you become a party to the birth of sport climbing in the United States."

The desire to put together an American governing body solely for competition climbing would continue to manifest and gain support in years to come. For the time being, any arc toward legitimacy was considered a considerable step toward the United States' eventual participation in the all-but-certain Albertville Winter Olympic Games. Best of all, it also dovetailed with the equally extraordinary plans that Lowe had for the American competition climbing scene.

CHAPTER 6

GREATER THAN EVER

D URING THE HOLIDAYS in the winter of 1989–90, Roy McClenahan took a train from Jeff Lowe's JMB headquarters in Broomfield, Colorado, to his parents' home in Arcadia, California. The initial plan, arching back to the 1989 competition at Snowbird six months before, was for McClenahan to impart the wisdom that he had acquired from Lowe about conducting climbing competitions directly to Peter Mayfield. Mayfield could then use the information to host independent, small-scale events at CityRock. The CityRock competitions would be totally separate from the competition empire that Lowe was piecing together in Colorado.

It was an idea that had originally suited McClenahan's hopes of transitioning out of the hand-to-mouth lifestyle he had assumed as an itinerant climber and guide. Helping Mayfield eventually hold competitions at CityRock, outside of Berkeley, could provide McClenahan with a management and development stake in Mayfield's gym enterprise. After all, McClenahan was now in his late twenties, perhaps cresting beyond the age where self-imposed destitution and vagrancy seemed romantic and admirable. Increasingly he found himself wanting to belong to something, somewhere—and even with extensive big-wall guiding to his credit, the remuneration available to a guide was desperately low in comparison with other trades and professions.

But something had happened to alter that initial plan. Lowe had been so appreciative and impressed with the organizational zeal that McClenahan had lent to the 1989 Snowbird competition that Lowe was now asking McClenahan if he'd move to Colorado; Lowe wanted McClenahan to be part of a crew to help run future Lowe-based competitions. Lowe had big plans for future events all over the country—not just in the summer at the Snowbird resort, but throughout the year as well.

McClenahan knew that Lowe's idea of rolling out a touring circuit of competitions in various American cities was ambitious. The concept was also something that no event organizer had ever done before in the United States. The thought of being part of a requisite crew, committed to a venerable cause, gave McClenahan a feeling of connecting with something important. Best of all, if successful, Lowe's plan would blaze a new path in the world of climbing. How could anyone who loved the sport turn down a chance to take part in that?

As the train chugged along, over the rocky undulations of a Utah backdrop and past the Nevada drylands, McClenahan read a comprehensive business plan that Lowe had given to him back in Colorado. The booklet was meant to be a corporate pitch to McClenahan—an enticement to join Lowe's competition organizational team instead of settling down in California. And while the content of the business plan was instantly alluring, it ultimately indicated tenuous ideas that, unbeknownst to McClenahan, would eventually prove destructive to the entire American climbing scene.

Lowe's grand ambition, as explained in his business plan, had two tiers. First, his wall company with Jean-Marc Blanche—JMB Sport Climbing Designs—would construct elaborate artificial climbing walls that could be sold or leased to other event planners, competition organizers, and facilities in the years to come. One such wall had recently been built in an outdoor gear store, Adventure 16, in Orange, California.

The JMB walls were not mere panels attached to the sides of buildings like those at the Cliff Lodge at Snowbird; they were immense freestanding structures complete with foundational supports, steel frames, wires, and scaffolding. Going forward, the walls would also include cutting-edge prototypes of artificial handholds and footholds, and they would be, essentially, "beautiful, futuristic wall designs," according to one advertisement. With sport climbing's popularity increasing and JMB's business prospects looking good for additional clients, the construction and erection of these self-supporting walls would require an entire crew of laborers, not unlike a team required to build houses or, more accurately, miniature vertical skyscrapers.

Notably for McClenahan, working as an independent contractor for Lowe for a number of fixed engagements throughout the year could bring cash and some freedom to take trips to places like Yosemite—unencumbered by long-term employment commitments or a daily office grind at a climbing gym such as CityRock. Competitions, after all, could be held at facilities intermittently, and in between, McClenahan could fill the downtime with the vagabonding so ubiquitous to the climbing life.

By itself, that construction tier of Lowe's remarkable plan entailed innumerable logistics, and the second tier was to significantly increase the number of climbing competitions held throughout the year—all overseen by Lowe as well. Under a moniker named for Lowe and his wife, Janie, the J&J Lowe Sport Climbing Championships would traverse the country, supplying the artificial walls for all the respective competitions. By default, this touring would promote the JMB wall company and bolster the recognition of the climbers. In some ways, it was comparable to what a concert promoter in San Diego, Bill Silva, had done in 1988 by producing a nation-wide, 35-date tour of professional skateboarders called the Swatch Impact Tour.

But holding climbing competitions on a semi-regular basis was a formidable proposal. It would require Lowe to frequently correspond with potential competitors, coordinate promotional schedules, communicate with municipalities in multiple states, and court prospective sponsors. There would also be challenging specifics for each event—such as supervising the routesetters and athletes, communicating with the judges, and controlling the audience.

Lowe's business plan hit the perfect note with McClenahan. It was inspiring, but it did not touch on any more details than it had to at such an early juncture, particularly when it came to finances and funding. McClenahan was aware of how successful Lowe's first large-scale competitions had been at Snowbird—he had even watched the first one as it aired on CBS. And if this business plan was the way for Lowe to continue his vision, it was worth jumping on board. The JMB walls would foster interest in the competitions, and the competitions would foster interest in the JMB walls. It was an enticingly cyclical business model. Besides, Mayfield's CityRock enterprise was not yet up and running, while Lowe's endeavor was already staffed.

By the time McClenahan's train arrived in California, he had made a decision to fully commit to Lowe's tour of competitions. The booklet with the two-tiered business plan had sold him on the reciprocal concept. He would soon find himself taking a train back to the Broomfield, Colorado, headquarters to meet up with the rest of the crew that Lowe had assembled. It promised to be a year of vibrant events with enormous artificial walls. And, if everything went as planned, 1990 would end up being the greatest year in the history of American competition climbing.

Notwithstanding underlying good intentions to grow the sport, uncertainties about large spectacle-style competitions' financial viability would loom over Lowe's two-tiered endeavor practically from its inception.

Shortly after settling down in Colorado and committing wholly to Lowe's ambitious enterprise, McClenahan and a few close colleagues—including Paul Sibley, who had worked with Lowe to build the wall for the inaugural competition at Snowbird—were given a schedule of climbing competitions for the remainder of the year that revealed Lowe's cross-country climbing competition tour in greater detail. Specifics about wages had still not been specified to everyone, but the scope of Lowe's schedule was nonetheless exciting to all.

The Sport Climbing Championships tour would begin with a big competition at the Community Theater in Berkeley in March 1990. Approximately one month later, the tour would continue with a competition at the Hec Edmundson Pavilion on the University of Washington campus in Seattle. Together, these two competitions in California and Washington would be held under their own branded banner: the North American Rockmaster Series. They would serve to hype a competition scheduled for the summer that Lowe was also separately branding: the United States Championships.

The United States Championships would be Lowe's celebrated return to Snowbird for the third year in a row, penciled in for July 4 weekend, 1990. In a letter penned that same year, Lowe would write, "Due to Snowbird's reputation as a great venue for Sport Climbing competitions, increasing public interest in the sport, and this year's free admission in conjunction with the U.S. Climbing Team fund raising efforts, we should see the largest audience to date for a climbing competition…at Snowbird."

The event was slated to include all the glitz and expo festivities of the previous year's competitions at the resort—but even bigger and more grandiose.

According to the schedule, the circuit would culminate with a North American Continental Championship in September. This competition would be modeled after the ones that had occurred previously at the Snowbird resort, but instead it would be held at the extravagant Mount Cranmore Mountain Resort in North Conway, New Hampshire. The resort had recently erected a 40-foot artificial wall at its Cranmore Recreation Center, which would serve as an isolation zone and warmup area for the competitors, while the competition itself would take place on a larger wall at Cranmore's 5,700-seat outdoor stadium. By early estimate, this Continental Championship was set to be another colossal undertaking, both administratively and logistically. And the jaunt to New Hampshire would also be the Sport Climbing Championships' official entry into the East Coast market. If the preceding Rockmaster and World Cup promotion had been successful, this Continental Championship was sure to draw a hyped crowd from the hubs of Boston, New York City, Philadelphia, and elsewhere.

The competitions loomed on the schedule. To make his group of workers as efficient as possible, Lowe divided his personnel into separate, smaller crews. Tasked with carrying out the two-tiered business plan, all of these crew members played multiple roles to meet deadlines or accelerate productivity.

Sibley acted as the leader and taskmaster for the workforce. McClenahan slipped into a role—informally, Deputy Director of Operations—which he ostensibly took over from the author of *The Sport Climbing Championships Competitors' Guide*, Peter Darmi. Functionally, the role meant that McClenahan was Sibley's right-hand man. McClenahan organized the construction and implementation of the walls on-site, figuratively trying to wear two hats: Lowe needed McClenahan to oversee operational aspects of the overall project, but Sibley needed McClenahan to apply those same skills directly to making sure a functional climbing wall was delivered to the competitions. Sibley's motivating argument was simple: without a wall, there would be no competitions to manage.

Together, Sibley and McClenahan would be responsible for making Jean-Marc Blanche's artistic designs into tangible structures that could stand alone and support the weight of the competition climbers. Most of the welding for the structural bases of the walls was done by a metalworker and longtime friend of Sibley's named Karl Arndt in Denver. Presiding over various fiberglass-related responsibilities was Billy Roos. Roos was a well-respected Outward Bound instructor who had been a childhood friend of Sibley's and a pivotal figure in the creation of the Colorado Nut Company. He had also been a member of the rigging crew for Bob Carmichael's landmark film, *Break on Through*.

Roos' leadership background made him adept as the de facto manager for the scraggly-but-devoted squad working on Lowe's competition circuit. With this, over the next several months, Blanche, Sibley, Roos, McClenahan, and others would single-handedly set the aesthetic for American competitions of the era.

A transportation crew consisting of a talented Yosemite climber named Kurt Smith, a former ski jumper named Mike Pont, and McClenahan were slated to drive the unwieldy walls to the assorted cities for the events, with necessary scaffolding erection done by an entrepreneur named Sasha Montagu, as well as other workers. Additional crew members filled in as needed—including a doctor named Rosemary Augustini, tending to any injuries that arose from construction mishaps—and various routesetters (Sean Miles, Geoff Wiegand, Scott Franklin, Gia Phipps, Christian Griffith, and Antoine Le Ménestrel) were hired to work at the events.

Administratively, Lowe and his wife were also aided by a sizable and, at times, rotating staff. Acting as Lowe's secretary was Chris Farquhar. The touring competitions had an acting chief financial officer, John Gallo. Many of the marketing duties for such an ambitious circuit were handled by just two men—Jeff Gillis and Steve Holmes. Sponsorship deals were negotiated by a businessman, Bart Fay, and his partner, Tracy. Dan McConnell dealt with much of the obligatory public relations. Don Barnes worked as an office coordinator. The voice of the competitions was an announcer named Darrell Luebbe. Matters of event judging were at times overseen by Peter Darmi and Ralph Erenzo, given the work they continued to do to establish formal competition guidelines in the United States, with Colin Zacharias, Keith Haberl, and a UIAA-certified judge from

Yugoslavia named Ivika "Johnny" Pilcheck also aiding in competition mediation.

To create a unique artistic identity for the circuit, Lowe turned to a local duo, Susan X. Billings and Caroline Quine. Billings Quine Design Group, as the pair's graphic design firm was known, had an office on the corner of Spruce Street and Broadway in downtown Boulder, and the location was serendipitously where Lowe was also choosing to rent office space for his competition venture. It was a logical union; Billings herself was a climber and a skier, and she promptly created a logo that suited Lowe's vision. Lowe wanted an iconic representation that was "loose, fresh, and a little unpredictable." The resulting design of a multicolored stick-figured climber on a stark black background was soon emblazoned on shirts, posters, and other merchandise.

Jim Waugh was eventually appointed as the technical director and general organizer for events; he brought to the position significant expertise that he had gathered from previous years of running his own annual competition—the Phoenix Bouldering Contest. Eventually, Lowe's old friend in Europe, Rex Wilson, also came onboard to act as a bookkeeper and general manager of the JMB tier of wall construction. And when results and statistics needed to be compiled on a computer or relayed to the press, the job fell upon the shoulders of Steve Gabel, who had helped Lowe organize a business plan in the first place.

With so many people involved, and such an interwoven network of responsibilities in the multifaceted endeavor, a key issue quickly became a topic of gossip among all the crews: Lowe had to pay *everyone*. And as the crews met up in various facilities around Broomfield and Denver to complete their respective tasks on a daily basis, questions arose about just how Lowe was going to meet his hefty financial obligations. Those questions soon turned into major concerns.

Anxiety about pay from all crew members probably would have resulted in collective action if it had not been for two key factors. First, practically everyone involved, including McClenahan and Sibley, were competent climbers. Thus, they were motivated by an altruistic concept of seeing just how much they could grow this unique competition angle of the sport. Plus, carrying out Lowe's business plan was a labor of love for most because Lowe was such a charismatic leader. Lowe genuinely believed in the viability of his two-tiered business plan. When misgivings did arise, everyone was already exhausted from the demands of each task; any energy that remained at the end of an average workday was best spent on relaxation (or climbing in the mountains nearby) rather than acrimonious dialogues with Lowe about money or recompense.

At times, construction of the artificial walls would have to be continued throughout the night in frenzied preparation for a competition. Those tasked with driving trucks would have to wake up and hit the road early, racking up hundreds of miles transporting disassembled walls and delivering materials on a tight schedule. McClenahan would later recall nights of delirium on the road—and colleagues being punch-drunk from lack of sleep.

In the Colorado facilities, productivity for Lowe's devotees was fueled by everything from coffee and doughnuts to nicotine. McClenahan, in particular, was given credit by baristas at the local coffee shops for single-handedly inventing the ultra-potent quad espresso.

Enacting an ever-expanding climbing road tour from scratch was an uncharted initiative in the United States, complicated even more by competition dates quickly approaching on the schedule. Given such a tremendous work pace, on-the-job hazards were abundant. Furthermore, there was no template for safely building gigantic artificial climbing walls.

Lowe was shouldering his own multitude of responsibilities too, balancing executive duties with sponsorship meetings. He was often unaware of the risks his workers were taking; crews would precariously climb scaffolding to see if enormous panels could be joined. They would sometimes laminate and cut fiberglass without wearing the shielding respirator masks. Helmets were rarely used. If nerves could be calmed and respite found, it was through a joint smoked behind the buildings for some; for others it was through climbing-themed daydreams as they stared at the mountains on the horizon.

Any temporary reprieve, however, could not mask the growing frustration that paychecks from the J&J Lowe Sport Climbing Championships were already few and far between. Among themselves, the crew members were beginning to discuss whether they could do anything to ensure that they got paid for their work.

"Rockmaster 1," as the competition at the Berkeley Community Theater was denoted on the schedule, was held March 17 and 18, 1990. It was not a completely newfangled endeavor, though. A smaller competition, also under the tutelage of Lowe, had taken place on October 11 and 12, 1989, at Seattle's Union Station. It was named the North American Open, but more often referred to informally as the Seattle Open. On the heels of that, an intracontinental competition, the North American Continental Championship, was held December 1 through 3, 1989, at the University of Colorado's Event Center. Coinciding with the American Alpine Club's annual dinner, it drew an impressive audience of nearly 1,500 people and even received coverage on Denver's evening news.

Although these earlier events acted largely as formative exercises for Lowe's workers, they were nonetheless rife with problems. For example, at Seattle's Union Station, the artificial wall's four-foot square surface paneling proved to be heavier than preferred for ease of assembly. More problematic was that the wall's surface coating was a mixture of sand and adhesive that crumbled too easily—much to the consternation of those on the crew tasked with cleaning up the debris. From a visual perspective, the highlight of the competition at Colorado's Event Center ended up being a protruding orange-colored feature below the wall's overhanging upper section. Nicknamed "the blob," the feature's use indicated how artificial climbing walls could have an aesthetic and a routesetting methodology wholly separate from those of established outdoor climbs. But the blob was cumbersome and difficult to reuse on walls in ensuing competitions.

In a mostly positive recap of that Event Center competition, *Climbing* reported, "There were no squabbles, and the massive logistical operation was admirably coordinated by [Lowe's] hard-working staff. However, some things can still be improved, such as organization and spectator appeal."

In hopes of making the Rockmaster competition at Berkeley an all-around smoother operation than those two preceding events, Lowe made the call to use mostly the same materials and build basically a replicate wall from the North American Continental Championship. It was a surprising choice, but following many of the previous construction methods and means—however troublesome they might have been—ensured that further complications would not arise due to the crews' unfamiliarity with any new structural designs. Simply put, there just wasn't enough time or manpower to risk additional complications.

Despite the strategy, as the structure came together, there were issues with the wall's surface veneer crumbling and sloughing off prematurely.

To complicate matters of wall assembly, McClenahan and Sibley decided to take action regarding their lack of pay. They went on strike for the duration of the Berkeley Rockmaster, refusing to work unless Lowe agreed to pay them in advance going forward—something that Sibley negotiated for them both, based on his personal knowledge of Lowe's prior business outcomes. Sibley and McClenahan used the break to get to know each other and climb many of the classic test pieces in Eldorado Canyon. This left the head foreman-like duties for the competition to a worker of Lowe's named John Cook. It was an all but insurmountable task for Cook to remedy the problems left over from the previous competition on such short notice—and head up the already overextended wall crew for a new event.

McClenahan and Sibley's strike revealed early cracks in Lowe's competition business aspirations for the year, but it did not stop the momentum of the rest of the workforce. Steve Gabel, manning the computers, was also constantly busy. He would recall, "We flew out [to Berkeley] and had all these boxes and boxes of stuff— programs and equipment. We tipped a skycap some money and he let it all go through. Then we got to a hotel room and we were sleeping two-to-a-bed, some people had to sleep on the floor, and Jeff doled out money for food."

A bright spot amid the grind was that Lowe had managed to secure non-endemic sponsorship for his Rockmaster competitions from Danskin. Known for making activewear leotards, Danskin was a perfect financier of climbing competitions given the standard apparel for climbers. This was the age of Lycra and spandex, sleek neon tights that differed wildly from the raggedy t-shirts and jeans that had been pervasive on climbers in erstwhile decades. And since the United States was still in the midst of an aerobics boom in 1990, Danskin was an optimistically lucrative association for Lowe to establish for his tour.

Other major sponsors had been looped in by Lowe too, such as REI and PowerBar, as well as magazines like *Climbing*, *Rock and Ice*, and *Outside*. Lowe's familial brand, Lowe Alpine, also provided some funding. The multitude of sponsors was an indication that the dual-tiered business plan, at least financially, was off to a positive start as the competing climbers finally took to the walls of Berkeley's Community Theater to kick off the first Danskin Rockmaster event. The Berkeley Community Theater happened to be part of the Berkeley High School's campus, which gave the Berkeley Rockmaster added gravitas. Other sports such as football, basketball, and soccer had consistently drawn frenzied young crowds to the school. The climbing competition was well-suited to do much the same and hold climbing to a similarly prescribed athletic standard with rules, time limits, and overall sportsmanship.

Many of the competitors at the Berkeley Rockmaster were returnees from the previous championships at Snowbird in 1988 and 1989, but there were new names on the roster as well. Most notably, Jim Thornburg, his climbing skills honed from the glue-ups and the Cal Crank competitions nearby, climbed strong and eventually took fifth place. His counterpart from the glue-ups, Scott Frye, also participated, but later recalled the event's scattered procedural nature. In fact, as the competition progressed, there were glaring indications that the technical proceedings of the whole Rockmaster format were problematic. "The comps early on were terrible," Frye would recall. "You might be in isolation for eight hours with no idea when you might climb, and all of a sudden they'd say, 'Okay, you're up!' They were so disorganized. It really wasn't that much fun."

Other competitors who endured the isolation agony and scattered nature of the events included Peter Mayfield, still active at the time in getting his CityRock gym off the ground. He eventually placed 25th at the Berkeley Rockmaster. Famed Stonemaster John Yablonski placed just behind him in 26th place. Despite a close mid-tier field, the competition standout was clearly Jim Karn, already a veteran of competitions due to time spent in Europe in the late 1980s—which had included a victory at a World Cup event in La Riba, Spain, in 1988. Karn easily took first place at the Berkeley Rockmaster, scaling nearly 10 meters higher on the wall than any other competitor.

The women's division offered a much closer finish, as Bobbi Bensman edged out Alison Osius on the wall; less than one meter separated the two competitors, and their scores were deemed a tie. Such a slim margin of separation launched an intense-yet-cordial rivalry between Bensman and Osius that would prove to be one of the defining narratives of Lowe's Sport Climbing Championships in 1990. With other strong climbers such as Laura Lonowski, Susan Price, Amy Irvine, and Nancy Prichard also in the mix, American competition climbing officially had a roster of adversaries that equaled those of the French and Italian women's teams. It also helped lay the groundwork for an intriguing circuit of events.

Yet, the excitement of the competitive action aside, it was clear at the close of the Rockmaster in Berkeley that significant changes had to be made for the following competitions. Sasha Montagu had been in the vicinity of the of the Berkeley Community Theater as the competition portion had been in full swing. He would later remember stopping in to say hello to his friends on the crew who were working the event: "I went inside the venue and within minutes realized that there was a very high level of tension. Everybody I came in contact with was so up to their eyeballs in stress, it looked like they couldn't breathe. It was a situation I wanted nothing to do with, and I got the hell out of there."

Montagu's observations were valid. The next Rockmaster was to be held at the Hec Edmundson Pavilion in Seattle the following month, and the issues with faulty surface veneer and imperfect operations had to be fixed. To that point, Lowe agreed to pay McClenahan and Sibley up front, which ended the duo's strike and ushered them back into the fray of trying to remedy some of the woes.

To create a wall for the impending Seattle Rockmaster (listed as "Rockmaster Finals" on the schedule) comparable to the earlier formative exercise at Seattle's Union Station, Lowe directed Sibley and his crew to again construct the wall panels on-site—this time at the campus of the University of Washington. The upside of the directive was that it reduced the chance of the wall disintegrating or breaking during its long commute from Colorado to Washington. The downside was that McClenahan was tasked with leading an even larger transportation convoy with thousands of small pieces of material—plywood, paint, nuts, bolts, steel frames—in trucks over a distance of nearly 1,500 miles.

Exhausted and sleep deprived by the time they reached Seattle, McClenahan and his drivers unloaded the myriad pieces with little time to spare. It took everyone pitching in to construct a wall from scratch in just a 24-hour period. As in the previous competitions, a highly engineered setup of wires and scaffolding was used to support the wall, which also featured a surface coating of anti-slip paint.

The Rockmaster Finals at Seattle, held over a two-day period of April 21 and 22, again featured Jim Karn winning the men's event and Bobbi Bensman and Alison Osius finishing neck-and-neck in the finals of the women's division amid a plethora of other close scores. Jim Thornburg again climbed well at the competition, as did his old glue-ups partner, Scott Frye—they took 31st and 21st place, respectively. Tony Yaniro, by this time a cunning veteran from events dating back to the local bouldering contests around Southern California in the early 1980s, also participated.

But by the conclusion of the Seattle's Rockmaster Finals at the Hec Edmundson Pavilion, as the crews disassembled the structures, loaded up the trucks, and began the long haul back to the Broomfield headquarters, it was undeniable that Lowe's North American Rockmaster Series had been a challenging mix of highs and lows. The field of American competitors now had more depth than ever before and captivating rivalries had emerged. Spectators had flocked to watch the competitions. However, keeping the tour going required a dizzying mix of construction logistics and organizational coordination. Workers' morale was wavering due to fatigue and a dubious pay schedule.

Continuing operations would be a challenge. But Lowe, ever the visionary, had his sights set on going even bigger for the rest of 1990. Specifically, as his workers in Colorado would soon realize, he was striving to create the most entertaining international climbing competition ever held on American soil, and for that, he wanted to showcase an extraordinary artificial wall unlike anything the world had ever seen.

CHAPTER 7

ON THE BRINK

I N THE SPRING OF 1990, with the North American Rockmaster Series finished and Jeff Lowe's Sport Climbing Championships surging ahead for a summer of even grander spectacles, peculiar construction plans began to circulate around Lowe's Colorado headquarters. The sketches detailed an immense configuration labeled the Twin Towers. The completed structure would measure 54 feet high and, befitting its name, feature two identical wall sections. Upon assembly, each of these sections would have multiple mid-height hinges adjustable to alter the overhanging angle of the respective wall. And each of these climbable "towers" would also feature a prominent overhanging headwall labeled the "horse section." Nodding to the stately World Trade Center skyscrapers, Lowe's Twin Towers would be unabashedly "the best walls ever used in international competition."[6]

---

6. This quotation comes from a write-up about the Twin Towers that was penned by Billy Roos for insurance purposes. As a primary source, Roos' text provides insight into the scope of Lowe's vision for the structure: "It was designed to be portable and easily assembled on site to provide a competition wall that could be used for a variety of local, regional, and international competitions, as well as demonstrations, special events, or a fixed installation in a municipal recreational center or gym."

Even as basic drawings on drafting paper, these Twin Towers were spectacular—not only in scale and design, but also in the uniformity of their proposed walls. No artificial climbing structure had ever been built that featured identical climbable faces side-by-side; and in proposing the venture, Lowe and Jean-Marc Blanche, as JMB Sport Climbing Designs, were redefining what sport climbing competitions would be.

Practically all contests that had been held up to this point—from the homegrown ones at Mount Woodson in the 1970s to the large-scale international ones at Snowbird in the 1980s—had been showcases for the climbers and displays of elite skills. Artificial walls in America and Europe had always been background dressing to a given exhibition—flaunted at times, but solely in the context of particular climbs or, like the first Snowbird competition, spectacular falls.

JMB Sport Climbing Designs' plans for the Twin Towers deviated from that more so than any competition construct in history. For the first time, the structures, by themselves, would become the main characters in a competition. The identical towers' mere existence, enormous and awe-inspiring to spectators, would be the entertaining story rather than any world-class climbers invited to climb on them. As much as audiences had flocked to watch spectacular, competitive climbing, crowds would now gather just to gape up at the walls.

To make the ambitious Twin Towers sketches come to life, Lowe decided to utilize the concept of small construction crews that had proved successful at his previous Rockmaster competitions. Again, Roy McClenahan and Paul Sibley would collaborate to carry out Blanche's artistic visions with raw materials. Billy Roos would manage the woven roving fiberglass work, aided by Mike Pont, Mike Pelletier, Stephen Hadik, Al Levy, and a 20-year-old Michigan native,

Bobbi Bensman works her way up a boulder en route to winning the 1987 Phoenix Bouldering Contest. As the 1980s came to a close, Bensman became one of the biggest names on the American competition climbing scene. And the annual outdoor contests in Arizona became among the most prestigious and popular in the whole country. (Beth Wald)

Russ Clune (left), Beth Wald (center), and Todd Skinner (right), part of the American team (along with Dan Michael, not pictured) that traveled to the Soviet Union
for a speed climbing competition in 1986. This team, recognized at the time by the
American Alpine Club after much rumination and correspondence, thus became
the first-ever national climbing team for the United States. (Note the uniform jackets
that read AMERICAN SPEED CLIMBING TEAM.) (Beth Wald)

France's Patrick Edlinger climbs over the lip of the wall at the inaugural Snowbird competition in 1988. The gray clouds would soon dissipate, the overcast sky would turn sunny, and Edlinger would reach the top to earn his famous victory. (Beth Wald)

France's Didier Raboutou scales the side of the Cliff Lodge at the second annual Snowbird competition in 1989. Raboutou would eventually win the international portion of the event, much like his compatriot Patrick Edlinger had done the year prior. In victory, Raboutou beat out Simon Nadin, Ron Kauk, Jim Karn, and others—all legends of the sport in their own right. (Beth Wald)

Roy McClenahan (left) and Mike Pont (right) as part of the cross-country transportation crew for the climbing competitions in the late 1980s and leading up to the Berkeley World Cup in 1990. Hauling all the components required for constructing climbing walls from scratch at various locations was an incredibly ambitious undertaking, but it was necessitated by a dearth of preexisting climbing walls—and climbing gyms—around the country at the time. (Roy McClenahan)

The Twin Towers, among the most famous competition climbing walls ever constructed, are unveiled at the Berkeley World Cup in the Greek Theater in 1990. The venue's iconic columns and colorful banners added to the grandeur. (Beth Wald)

Robyn Erbesfield climbs the walls of one of the Twin Towers at the Berkeley World Cup. Erbesfield was one of the top stars in the 1990s and on the shortlist of likely Olympians—if climbing was to become an Olympic sport at the time. (Beth Wald)

Steve Schneider (far left), Mike Pont (hat), Christian Griffith (long pants), and Tony Yaniro (far right) attend a routesetting training course at Colorado's Paradise Rock Gym in the early 1990s. This course was led by UIAA representative Hans Peter Seigrist (white shirt, pictured next to his wife). The hands-on clinic would result in the formation of the American League of Forerunners, thus jumpstarting American routesetting as a learnable and teachable craft. (Hans Florine)

Speed climbing extraordinaire Hans Florine drinks from a World Cup trophy in 1991. Florine, a pioneer of the speed climbing discipline, was one of the most decorated American competitors in that decade. (Hans Florine)

Tim Steele works his way out of a roof section of the climbing wall at Miami University during the final round of the Mideast Indoor Climbing Competition in 1994. Steele was one of the big names on the competition scene, along with Tony and Todd Berlier, Tiffany Levine, Ben Ditto, Kadi Johnston, Margarita Martinez, and others. In addition to competing, Steele became an influential routesetter and honed his craft on the walls of Miami University, his alma mater. (Tim Steele)

Guy Kenny; Kenny was not a climber but had previous experience working with fiberglass because his father owned a plastics manufacturing plant in Detroit. Kenny could apply his invaluable knowledge of plastics to the Twin Towers' unique surface angles and curves as the summer portion of Lowe's touring circuit rapidly approached.

A Denver-based company called Waco Scaffolding and Equipment, and an engineer named John McQuarrie, were contracted to configure the necessary framework for the towers; a local climber named Deanne Gray would help put together the elaborate scaffolding. Gray would thus find herself to be one of the few women in a devoted crew that was composed mostly of men. That dynamic, however, did not bother Gray. A native of the Bay Area, she had spent extensive time climbing in Yosemite and working as a cocktail waitress at the Mountain Room bar in the Yosemite Valley Lodge before relocating to Colorado. She quickly found the close-knit workforce for the Twin Towers to be "definitely a boys' club," but also inclusive in its camaraderie. Gray would note, "I was absolutely used to that [dynamic] and enjoyed the bullshitting. I never felt out of place or uncomfortable."

With duties solidified and everyone buckling down to construct the Twin Towers practically from scratch in Colorado, Lowe searched outward for a suitable venue for the great structure's unveiling. At times, McClenahan was pulled from the grunt work to research—and visit—potential host venues around the country.

Lowe eventually deemed California, with its burgeoning embrace of climbing on artificial surfaces, to be the optimal state, but McClenahan had an arduous assignment: find a locale somewhere that was willing to take a chance on this newfangled towers concept—within a niche of climbing that was still somewhat new and different as a spectacle that people would pay to see.

Some potential venue hosts were intrigued by McClenahan's pitch and Lowe's vision that underscored it. Others dismissed the concept outright on the grounds that a competition wouldn't recoup the costs required to host it.

Finally, Berkeley was pinpointed as the optimal city for the Twin Towers official unveiling, given how popular Rockmaster 1 had been in the city back in March. In contrast to Rockmaster 1, however, the ensuing competition for Lowe's Sport Climbing Championships would not be held at the Berkeley Community Theater. McClenahan scouted a handful of alternate venues of greater scope, and eventually Lowe agreed to hold the event at the much larger Greek Theater, part of the University of California's sprawling Berkeley campus. The theater had been previously considered but deemed too expensive, yet its renown for holding big concerts and large-scale theatrical productions was undeniable. Lowe, McClenahan, and others understood implicitly that the unveiling of the JMB walls, in order to be a success in the eyes of the public and sponsors, required such a grand stage.

The Greek Theater was a historic scheduling choice. President Theodore Roosevelt had spoken there in 1903, and the theater had hosted the first Berkeley Jazz Festival in the 1960s. Throughout the 1980s, the Grateful Dead had played at the theater too. And there, on August 17, 1990, the venue would house the Twin Towers structure as the official centerpiece for an American World Cup climbing event, the third stop on the UIAA's seven-stop World Cup tour at points around the world in 1990. The uniqueness of the magnificent Twin Towers would accentuate the significant occasion. The semicircle-shaped Greek Theater could hold more than 8,000 spectators, which would rightly give the whole weekend a festive tone.

Although logistics gradually fell into place for the venue in California, the Twin Towers' construction crews worked increasingly grueling shifts back in Colorado. To maximize productivity and output, labor was often done at odd hours, and wearisome tasks had to be accepted without complaint.

McClenahan single-handedly cut and bent the steel studs that would become the frames of the 36 differently sized external panels for the towers and their articulating headwalls. At one point, taking a break from working with a steel cut-off saw in Karl Arndt's metalworking space, McClenahan stared out a window. He could see across the railroad tracks. Mount Evans rose up in the distance. In the moment of repose, McClenahan was struck with a realization: he had to accept the reality that he was working for *free*, at least until a paycheck for his organizational functions and manual labor came through and proved him wrong. And that didn't sit well with him—or Sibley.

Nonetheless, acting as foreman for the road crew, McClenahan began to make arrangements for transporting the massive wall components to Berkeley. He meticulously documented everything that was progressing to make the World Cup an operational triumph—from materials on hand to components still needed, and from vendors' contact information to construction specifications—in a notebook deemed the "janal," which was shorthand for *anal-retentive journal.* The euphemism became a running joke among the crew members.

While McClenahan juggled his duties, Roos, Kenny, and the rest of the crew tasked with making the climbing wall's surface texture continued work with a pungent and toxic resin, rich in volatile organic compounds, to create new wall paneling. "Jean-Marc Blanche would carve what he wanted the final product to look like out of foam, and on top of that we would pour silicone to create a mold—and that was the mold we'd use to create the wall template," Kenny would say in describing the painstaking process. "We would take a combination of sand, silica, resin, and Catalyst, mix it with a big paddle mixer, and then spread it around the silicone mold. Then we would let that cure—which was about a day—and put fiberglass across the back of it, pull the whole piece off of the silicone mold and install steel frames on the back."

This procedure was done repeatedly to create numerous replicate wall panels. The fiberglass reinforced the resinous concrete mixture to make a remarkably durable structure, but the result was the need to work longer hours in order to finish the whole project.

Sibley continued to keep everyone on task in Colorado as the schedule supervisor. Lowe knew he could count on Sibley to physically deliver the construct of the wall, and do it on time. And Sibley depended on McClenahan to keep such a critical function on target in an organizational sense.

The crews worked efficiently but were getting burned out. There were no happy hour breaks or evening partying. The only leisurely releases of any sort were occasional breakfast outings prior to starting a workday, but even those were frequently just morning extensions of the night's laboring. McClenahan would later say, "There was literally no social scene attached to the competition push. Absolutely zero. Except that the whole thing was a tremendous bonding experience for all of us. We never had any time to drink at night. Christ, there was no 'night' where off-time was concerned, unless it involved sleeping. We worked 12- to 16-hour days, and during the events themselves, often considerably longer."

Amid the slog, the Twin Towers' development progressed piece by piece, groggy day by groggy day. Subtle changes were occasionally made to the design and solutions were often crafted on the fly. For instance, small openings in the artificial walls were crafted, to be fit with special circular inserts. These disc-like inserts were to become handholds and footholds that could be rotated on the wall—and they signified a distinctive, modular aspect of the Twin Towers that had not been present on walls of previous competitions. A climber named Katie Cassidy was in charge of painting the backing panels of the discs in the vacuous space of the Broomfield headquarters. But these small circular openings, inventive as they were, also caused entire panels of the wall to crack during the necessary curing process. Guy Kenny solved the nagging issue by eventually eliminating many of the circular openings altogether. It was meticulous work, as were all tasks on the makeshift assembly line developed for the various crew members.

As the workers toiled away, Lowe, his general manager Rex Wilson, and others kept their own hectic schedules of administrative and clerical responsibilities. A venue and a wall were only parts of the formula for success. Competitors also had to be contacted and invited, and sponsors had to be enticed prior to the August 17 start date. In total, the event was to cost $250,000 with all aspects pieced together. The competitors' prize money, alone, was to total $20,500, and renting the Greek Theater for a weekend would cost $7,000. So, securing substantial backing as soon as possible was crucial.

In a whirlwind to garner funds, organizers undertook a series of sponsorship-seeking phone calls and meetings. Diligent executive efforts culminated in a connection made by Lowe with representatives Sally McCoy and Ann Krcik from The North Face, the San Francisco–based equipment company that had subsidized previous festive events related to outdoors-themed adventure. The North Face agreed to sponsor the forthcoming event at Berkeley's Greek Theater.

Outwardly, this meant that the World Cup would be identified by The North Face moniker, much like the previous Rockmasters had been linked with Danskin. On a more insular level, it meant that The North Face would provide $45,000 to fund the competition, with an understanding that such a hefty loan would be reimbursed at the competition's end.

In a publicity windfall spearheaded by Krcik and CityRock's Peter Mayfield, famous concert promoter Bill Graham was also attached to the climbing event. Graham had organized live shows for many of the world's most famous music acts—from the Grateful Dead to Led Zeppelin—and now he was officially involved in promoting one of the world's most famous climbing competitions.

The deals that were struck on a promotional level gave the upcoming World Cup in Berkeley a lot of momentum by the summer of 1990. There was much focus on getting the Twin Towers built and the necessary sponsorship secured in time, but the United States Championship was still scheduled to be held at the Snowbird resort on the Fourth of July weekend and, as such, officially conclude the multievent Danskin series.

Previous years' competitions at Snowbird set a lofty precedent; in fact, Snowbird was now the preeminent competition in the country, so there was a standard of promotional and competitive excellence that had to be upheld.

Yet, from the onset, it was clear that Snowbird 1990 would be somewhat different from those events from 1988 and 1989 of the same name. For starters, Jim Waugh—rather than Jeff Lowe—was to be employed as Snowbird's organizational and managerial architect on-site. A team of routesetters would include Scott Franklin, Gia Phipps, Chris Hill, and Jimmy Surrette. Judging would be overseen by Colin Zacharias, and although the competition had its roots in network television innovation, the focus would be almost exclusively the live show from the lawn. Waugh was now eight years into his masterminding of the annual Phoenix Boulder Contest, so he knew how to host a climbing competition that prospered both as a challenge for the contestants and a spectacle for the onlookers.

In fact, as the competition got underway, the onlookers became more of a focal point than perhaps originally intended. An errant lawn sprinkler doused a sizable segment of spectators and caused brief pandemonium in the crowd. "Almost 200 nicely-settled observers instantly transform into a stampede reminiscent of a good Who concert," wrote author Drew Bedford in an observation of the event. "The horde seeks cover, dragging blankets, power-loungers and offspring. Yes, indeed, it's a perfect day for a climbing contest."

A storm later in the weekend would further soak the spectators on the lawn at Snowbird and ultimately cause the men's portion of the event to be truncated.

Still, Waugh quickly proved adroit at managing and crafting a successful Snowbird event without the presence of Lowe—and all of this despite the fact that the World Cup, certain to be historic, loomed so soon on everyone's schedule.

In terms of the specific divisions at Snowbird 1990, Bobbi Bensman won the women's climbing event with a narrow victory over Alison Osius in a superfinal round (necessary after both women successfully climbed to the top of the finals route). Dale Goddard, leading the men's field after the semifinals, became the default winner upon the aforementioned storm's development. And while Sally Bartunek won the women's speed climbing portion, the most phenomenal accomplishment of the weekend was a win by Hans Florine in the men's speed climbing event. With the victory, Florine completed a speed sweep for the entire Danskin series of competitions.

There might have been brief respites and a few climbing outings afterward on the part of the Snowbird 1990 crew, but everyone—especially those involved in the Twin Towers' construction—soon found themselves returning to Lowe's Colorado headquarters, their collective focus once more sharpened on Berkeley by late July.

However, as August arrived, changes to the group's dynamic quickly occurred. First, following the competition at Snowbird, Peter Darmi decided to leave Lowe's employ. The reason Darmi gave for his departure was a familiar one—lack of pay on the part of Lowe. And while Darmi was leaving Lowe's circuit without any ill will and proud of the part he had played in solidifying a ruleset for American sport climbing with Lowe, the truth was that he was being pulled elsewhere in the competitive climbing milieu. The Albertville Winter Olympics were continuing to take shape in Europe, as was the prospect of American climbers being featured in them. Darmi wanted to be in the midst of any progress being made on that front. There was still work that needed to be done in New Paltz to jump-start and formalize the American Sport Climbers Federation (ASCF) as a governing body for the United States' competition climbing scene with Ralph Erenzo. In the end, Darmi decided to pursue his objectives without any further occupational connection to Lowe's Sport Climbing Championships.

Likewise, Steve Gabel, an important figure in organizing Lowe's initial ideas into a formal business strategy, had also decided to leave Lowe's crew by this point. "Jeff [Lowe] owed me money, and my wife and I had a new baby—I had to work to put food on the table," Gabel would remember. "I couldn't continue working and hanging out just for the fun of it. It was matter-of-fact when it ended. Jeff and I shook hands. There weren't any hard feelings—it was just business."

Even those workers who opted to stay on Lowe's tour and committed to working at the upcoming World Cup were growing doubtful of any long-term success for the two-tiered business plan. Lowe had made it known that paying all crews up front prior to the Berkeley World Cup was not possible. Lowe and Wilson had even gathered their whole workforce together for a fiscal meeting at one point—a conference in which all the workers were told bluntly about the financial risks inherent in choosing to go forward as part of the Sport Climbing Championships.

Once the Twin Towers' construction was finally completed in the weeks following the United States Championship in Snowbird, Utah, Lowe's devoted road crew led by McClenahan set out on an 18-hour drive from Colorado to Berkeley's famed Greek Theater— but the future felt very unpredictable. Sibley and McClenahan, in particular, knew the economic perils, having been apprised of them by Lowe himself in the meeting. Nonetheless, they were trying to stay optimistic. Issues still remained regarding Lowe's whole business venture. In reality, it was proving to be fascinating in theory but thus far unsustainable in practice. Everyone was hoping that a wildly successful World Cup event—with The North Face sponsorship for publicity, a fervent college crowd for support, and a much-needed profit for all—would prove to be the turning point toward a more lucrative future.

As scheduled, the competition at the University of California's Greek Theater began on Friday, August 17, 1990. Adhering to the joint arrangement that Lowe had made months earlier with the UIAA, the event was an official stop for the UIAA's globetrotting World Cup circuit, on the heels of previous events that had been held that year in Vienna, Austria, and Madonna, Italy.

Despite the high hopes from those who had worked tirelessly under Lowe's direction to make the American World Cup competition a reality during the spring and summer, the event at the Greek Theater had problems practically from the onset.

In the morning, a thick fog blanketed the east side of the Bay Area. The murkiness limited visibility of the Twin Towers as they loomed, fully constructed after an arduous 72-hour on-site assembly session, in the outdoor arena space. Attendance was noticeably sparse as well, with many of the spectators trickling in to learn of a higher-than-expected admission price—$27 to watch both the men's and women's divisions.

Although multiple Americans competed in that morning's qualifying round—Steve Schneider, Scott Frye, Doug McDonald, Drew Bedford, Kurt Smith, Ed Barry, Colin Lantz, and Doug Englekirk among them—the standout was undeniably Francois LeGrand, a former French junior champion. To the surprise of the spectators, LeGrand topped one of the tower's routes, which had been set by Christian Griffith and Fabrice Guillot at a difficulty grade of 5.12d.

In total, the men's round boasted nearly two dozen total entrants, but the women's division did not have enough independent competitors to merit a qualifying round at all. It was a dearth that was symbolic of further ills that were to come as the competition ensued.[7]

Saturday morning dawned with clearer weather, but less-than-ideal separation for the competitors as the women's semifinal round proceeded.

---

7. The qualifying rounds for the event were reserved for those competitors who did not have any formal attachment to their respective country's national team.

The round's designated route on the Twin Towers started with a slab portion and progressed to an overhanging dyno move in which the competitors jumped dramatically to a higher handhold. The slab section, in particular, was a choice that perplexed competitors who had anticipated a route that would demand full-body movement to electrify the crowd. "I remember we were in isolation and somehow word got out that it was a slab," recalls Frye. "Everyone just immediately thought, 'Are you kidding?' I got so distracted by it, I climbed terribly. I love slab climbing, but there was nothing interesting to watch about people slab climbing."

The slab demanded emphatically difficult and slow, technical movement on the wall. When the round finished and the scores were tabulated, far more women earned berths into the forthcoming finals than had been anticipated. Among them were a strong roster of Americans—Lynn Hill, Robyn Erbesfield, Bobbi Bensman, Alison Osius, Jennifer Cole, and others—along with the stalwart French standouts Isabelle Patissier and Nanette Raybaud.

A "Celebrity Competition" followed the women's semifinals and preceded the women's finals. It featured Michael Kennedy of *Climbing* beating renowned photographer Galen Rowell and Sally Moser of *Rock and Ice*. The lighthearted tone of the spectacle could not mask the serious fact that overall attendance numbers for the event were still disappointing. By the time the women's final round got underway late Saturday, the typical rivalry of the Americans against the Europeans was played up, but the audience's enthusiasm was noticeably subdued.

Patissier's attempt on the finals route was thwarted by a technicality, as a loose handhold caused her to fall. Her French compatriot Raybaud climbed higher than she had, falling just a few feet shy of the top. Hill provided the event with a temporary jolt of patriotic excitement as she neared the highpoint on the wall. But she also fell short of the top and took second place behind Raybaud.

Other Americans were scattered in the results: Erbesfield placed fourth, Osius fifth, Cole eighth, and Bensman thirteenth. By its end, the day had showcased some impressive depth for the United States, but many spectators had hoped that the Berkeley World Cup would actually provide the backdrop for a breakout win by an American woman. A French victory at yet another American-hosted international competition tainted the overall mood in the crowd of mostly Californians, and cast a pall over whatever remained for the weekend's festivities.

The men's division did not fare much better as it progressed through its respective semifinal round the following day. Although the dual nature of the Twin Towers was intended to accommodate identical routes for simultaneous competitors, the blistering sun shone through clear skies and heated the eastern-facing wall to a ruthless temperature. Those men selected to climb on the hot paneling in the morning were at a disadvantage to those competitors assigned to the same route on the much more comfortable adjacent wall. Such disparity was precisely the sort of technicality that Darmi had worked so diligently to mitigate with the formulation of regulations and a push for overall event consistency months prior.

Worst of all, the oppressive summer heat and an irritating sunny glare made it unlikely that the competition would see any late surge in ticket sales. In fact, attendance had already dropped to less than 1,000, leaving most of the theater starkly empty.

Only one American man progressed through to the finals—Jim Karn, who had dominated at the Danskin Rockmaster competitions months earlier. Adding to the letdown for the last remaining round was a surprising early fall by Didier Raboutou, a perennial favorite and winner of the 1989 Snowbird event.

The climax of the competition and the pinnacle of the Twin Towers-as-spectacle was a showdown for the World Cup win between England's Simon Nadin and France's LeGrand—with Nadin ultimately emerging as the victor. He climbed eloquently and swiftly, falling just shy of one of the towers' tops. Karn, also impressive, ended up in fifth place.

The event concluded with a speed climbing competition held at dusk. There, America finally claimed a victory with Hans Florine beating LeGrand. Florine's personal triumph, inspiring as it was, could do little to alter the shroud of overall disappointment for the event. The fraction of the audience that remained steadily trickled out of the Greek Theater on Sunday night as Lowe's crew went to work dismantling the wall paneling. A requirement to disassemble the Twin Towers alongside construction union workers—who had no connection to sport climbing—added to the frustration for the various crews. Although much time and effort had gone into the structural arrangements dating back to the inception of JMB Sport Climbing Designs, the Berkeley World Cup had failed to transcend its smaller niche. The total weekend spectator count was approximately 2,500—a respectable turnout but not a number that validated a six-figure cross-country tour or ensured continued success of the two-tiered business plan.

McClenahan, as head of the road crew, was in charge of getting the disassembled Twin Towers back to the Broomfield headquarters in the aftermath of the competition. The past several months had been a whirlwind of toil and exhaustion. As McClenahan sat in the passenger seat of the convoy's lead truck, he realized there was little he could do to correct the hitches inherent in the American competition model.

Seated next to McClenahan was Sasha Montagu. Montagu had bags under his eyes from exhaustion. The two men traded humorous quips, both totally worn out but embracing some levity. McClenahan knew he had to muster some energy for the long drive that lay ahead and the unclear competition future that backdropped it. He joked to Montagu, "Lead on, Charlemagne."

And with that, McClenahan closed his eyes. He would later recall, "Across the inside of my eyelids danced a conflagration of toy climbers bouncing between floating plastic holds in a kind of Brownian motion, like the Cowboys, six shooters, Winchester rifles, bows and arrows which adorned the curtains in my childhood bedroom of the early 1960s."

McClenahan's associations with such Wild West iconography were apropos. There had never before been an American competition that had required as much preparation as the Berkeley World Cup had, and now that it was over, all those involved were free to forge their own paths—and demand answers. The close-knit group that had been so devoted to Lowe's Sport Climbing Championships was already fragmenting, pursuing different destinies. And now the only reality that was clear was that everything was about to change.

CHAPTER 8

TRIALS AND
TRIBULATIONS

FOLLOWING THE BERKELEY WORLD CUP, Jim Thornburg, by then working as a journalist and photographer, wrote an article for *Climbing* that recapped the event and hinted at the precarious future that the American competition climbing scene was facing. Thornburg's authorship on the topic was appropriate given how innovative his epoxied constructs beneath the Highway 13 overpass had been a few years prior. But more so, his Cal Crank competitions, held mere blocks from where the World Cup competition had taken place at the Greek Theater in August 1990, were continuing to harness a combustible enthusiasm of the young, primarily suburban and city-based climbing sect of California on a regular basis. The much larger and extravagant Berkeley competition had represented the pinnacle of possibilities for that same demographic of climbing enthusiasts at the dawn of the new decade.

"Overall, the future of competitive sport climbing in this country is in a state of flux," Thornburg noted in his *Climbing* article. He went on to say that grassroots events, which were the antithesis of the expensive, big-scale productions that Jeff Lowe's Sport Climbing Championships tour had birthed in the United States, might become more prevalent and prominent around the country in the future.

Although prescient, Thornburg's assessment padded what swiftly amounted to a total crumbling of the United States' premier competition climbing model. In large part, the demise began immediately following the Berkeley World Cup event. Indeed, that competition proved to be such a financial letdown that the entire American competition industry was soon drawn down in its whirlpool.

"Unfortunately, the 2,500 fans and enthusiastic sponsors that showed up at Berkeley were not enough to put the competition in the black," Thornburg wrote of the World Cup event's earnings in his *Climbing* recap.

The overall aesthetic of the Berkeley World Cup had been extraordinary, but the competition's spectacle and the awe for its immense climbable structure—the remarkable Twin Towers—could not make up for the irreparable pecuniary problems. "Owing to the venue and wall-installation costs, and deals cut with local promoters and concessions, the well-run event was a financial disaster," Ralph Erenzo would assert in an article for *Rock and Ice*.

In an interview years later, Jeff Lowe would cite international socio-political influences, saying of his climbing competition tour's disappointing revenue, "I saw it would be another year or two before we made money—what you'd expect for any business to break even. And then Iraq invaded Kuwait and my bank pulled all their peripheral loans."

Iraq's invasion of Kuwait also forced Lowe's bookkeeper, Rex Wilson—still active as a Special Forces officer in the military throughout the summer of 1990—to abruptly leave the Sport Climbing Championships altogether and report for service duty at the Pentagon just days after the Berkeley World Cup had wrapped up.

Lowe himself soon became enmeshed in new undertakings of his own. He had surprised many of his employees by not being present in Berkeley for the World Cup competition; he had opted instead to travel to Pakistan and take part in a film about a mountaineering expedition on Nameless Tower, a 20,510-foot peak in the Himalayas.[8] The elaborate mountaineering trip had roots dating back to the year before, when ESPN had contacted Lowe during the 1989 competition at Snowbird about making an alpine-centric program as part of an "adventure series" of shows. More detailed discussions between Lowe and ESPN had quickly developed, eventually looping in a film company, Adventure World Productions, headed by producer John Wilcox.

In addition to Lowe, the expedition team that was eventually put together and sent to Pakistan for ESPN featured Catherine Destivelle, winner of the first Snowbird competition, as well as a veteran of the Yosemite scene, Jim Bridwell, along with David Breashears, Kim Lowe, Paul Sharp, Lucien Abbet, Veronique Choa, James Brundage, and more than one hundred porters. For all intents and purposes, Lowe and Destivelle were to be the film's stars, as Lowe's concept of the expedition from a storytelling standpoint was to feature "an American man and a French woman—a retired alpinist paired with a famous competitive climber—a great combination for both the climb and the viewing public."

---

8. Nameless Tower is sometimes alternatively referred to as Trango Tower.

Although talented and esteemed in terms of personnel, the mountaineering team quickly encountered problems once on Nameless Tower. The initial objective had been for ESPN to capture the team completing the first free ascent of the Kurtyka-Lorentan route on the peak's south face. Such a landmark climb would have meant that the route was done for the first time without the use of any equipment to aid in the team's upward progress. However, the accumulation of substantial ice made climbing the Kurtyka-Lorentan route in that manner impossible. The team was forced to switch to a different course, the Yugoslavian route, instead.

Like Kurtyka-Lorentan, the Yugoslavian route up Nameless Tower was long and technical—30 pitches in total with a difficulty grade that exceeded 5.12—but it had already seen a first free ascent two years prior to Lowe's arrival by the German team of Kurt Albert and Wolfgang Güllich. As a result, the pioneering angle of the ESPN film project was somewhat nullified.

Even with the altered plans, Lowe's team continued to be hindered by the ice throughout their expedition. At one point, Lowe was forced to scale a 60-foot crack in an exhausting layback position because the upward crack he was following had been awash with draining water and massive chunks of ice from the mountaintop.

Breashears, Destivelle, and Lowe successfully climbed the final 15 pitches on Nameless Tower, and the whole extravagant endeavor was captured on video as planned. Though impressive in achievement, Lowe's foray with ESPN had been hindered by unforeseeable circumstances to the point where the end result was quite different than what had originally been envisaged. Summarizing the expedition, *Rock and Ice* wrote:

The quality of climbing, combined with the spectacular location make it a free-climbing classic. However, the pair [of Lowe and Destivelle] had looked forward to climbing more difficult pitches—to have to push themselves to the limit and actually work out moves. A future trip, in better weather with less icy conditions, may find Jeff and Catherine once again on Nameless Tower, combining their technical prowess and alpine experience to explore the potential of adventure climbing.

The Nameless Tower expedition was broadcast on ESPN in November 1990. An article in *Men's Journal* asserted years later that the film was a means for Lowe to obtain a "quick infusion of cash" to pay off his mounting competition-related invoices, but did not turn out to be the saving grace for all the tribulations:

> The film was broadcast on ESPN, but several European sponsors had backed out at the last minute. The upshot was that Lowe came home from Pakistan deeper in debt than ever, owing money even to close friends and fellow climbers who had worked as his support party. For decades Lowe had been one of the most admired figures in the tight-knit fraternity of American climbers; now, around certain campfires, in various climbers' bars, his name began to elicit bitter oaths and tales of fiscal irresponsibility.

Furthering and fueling the notoriety surrounding the film were eventual allegations of infidelity on Lowe's part, his relationship with Destivelle having become personal amid their professional time mountaineering in Pakistan.

Lowe and his wife, Janie, divorced in 1991. In response to a question about Destivelle in *Rock and Ice*, Lowe clarified: "Catherine and I are not mates. We're lovers and best friends and we're quite involved with each other, but we're both dealing with our own things, too. We're not together in the sense of being mates, although both of us think there's that possibility." He added, "Although we're very supportive of each other, she lives in France and I live here. I'm not planning to move there, she's not planning to move here. She won't limit herself to just seeing me, I won't limit myself to just seeing her. We'll do our own climbs, we'll do our climbs together."

Even with multiple extraneous factors having contributed to the woes of the Berkeley World Cup competition in hindsight—such as Lowe's complete absence due to his Nameless Tower endeavor, poor spectator turnout due to the heat, unenticingly high ticket prices, and a changing global economic patina due to the Middle East conflicts—the fallout meant that The North Face was shouldered after the fact with footing the entirety of the Berkeley World Cup bill without recompense.

As a result, Lowe returned from his international expedition and declared bankruptcy for his Sport Climbing Championships tour just weeks after the competition at Berkeley had concluded. Bobbi Bensman, who had tied Alison Osius to win the Danskin Rockmaster events, would later note that all her winners' checks for Lowe's events bounced, although Lowe always remedied the situation eventually. Other competitors experienced similar woes regarding prize money owed. The American Alpine Club was forced to remunerate outstanding payments owed to judges and the UIAA, which computed to approximately $4,000. All totaled, the financial hole was nearly $75,000.

Perhaps more detrimental to the growth of the American climbing scene on the whole, Lowe canceled all events that remained on the Sport Climbing Championships' tour schedule. Hopes for possibly holding a World Cup competition the following year—in 1991—were quickly dashed as well.

Thus, instead of the United States' World Cup event heralding a big eastward push for Lowe's circuit in the fall of 1990—first to the International Invitational in Colorado and then to the North American Continental Championship in New Hampshire—it marked an inglorious and unexpected end of an era that had begun so spiritedly in 1988 with the first international competition at Snowbird.

As much as Lowe's tour had been pioneering in its original vision, its quick dissolution and lack of any comparable organizations proved problematic for the personnel who had been involved in all the preceding events' successes.

Still, a few other competitions, unaffiliated with Lowe's grandiose national tour and mostly lacking international luminaries, did follow. For example, a San Diego Indoor Climbing Championship, held at the San Diego County Fairgrounds, became an annual event and a showcase for established American stars like Bensman and Jade Chun, Kurt Smith, and Boone Speed, as well as youngsters Chris Lindner and Tyson Schoene in a 14 & Under category.

Nearly a thousand miles east, at an outdoor crag in White Rock, New Mexico, climbers gathered for the inaugural White Rock Meltdown, which included a unique format: competitors attempted as many toproped routes—with the ropes already looped through fixed anchors at the top of the cliff—as possible within a 90-minute allotment. The day of toproping was followed by a day of lead climbing, in which the competitors clipped a rope into bolted protection on the rock as they ascended. For the lead climbing portion,

each competitor was given four hours to attempt to climb nine
routes. A local New Mexico climber named Matt Samet, who would
become an editor at *Climbing* years later, dominated the other
entrants, while Jim Walseth of Boulder, Colorado, won the division of non-locals.

Further afield from sport climbing contests and standard competition formats was an ice climbing get-together by four climbers from
Kalamazoo, Michigan. Their objective was to climb the immense
frozen waterfalls on the cliffs along the shores of Lake Superior.
Over time, the regular meetup swelled with additional participants
to become a renowned annual ice climbing tradition, the Michigan
Ice Fest.

The most well-known American climbing competition was still
the annual summer event at Snowbird, but it scaled down significantly following the sudden disbanding of Lowe's network. Going
forward, the Snowbird competitions operated on much smaller bud-
gets and were run by a competition staff of only a handful of workers.
Also, the successive events were given only regional designations
by the American Sport Climbers Federation (ASCF); gone were the
days when Snowbird was synonymous with international competition, and the Cliff Lodge no longer bustled with foreigners in an
atmosphere similar to that at an Olympic Village.

Future years' offerings at Snowbird were important, but for other
reasons. An exciting plotline of Bensman and Osius battling annually
for first place became an exhilarating part of the event's legacy; it
was an extension of the rivalry the two competitors had had during
the Sport Climbing Championships in 1990. "It was through comps
that we became real friends," Osius would recall of her frequent
competitive connection to Bensman. "We would hang out in isolation. Bobbi is a lot of fun, and we were just simpatico. We did go

back and forth a lot of times in results, finishing one-two one way or another. There were times where we tied in finals and went into a superfinal, and people would laugh and say, 'As usual.'"

The Snowbird competitions would also mark climbing's alignment with social causes. Utah's adoption of a stringent anti-abortion law prompted most women competitors to wear pro-choice stickers at one Snowbird event. An NBC-affiliated television station in Salt Lake City, KUTV, even ran a news segment about the climbers' collective political action.

As noteworthy as Snowbird and the other competitions were, they were scaled-down versions of the circuit that Lowe had briefly brought to life. No other American climbing entity developed a complex business plan like Lowe had done for his two-tiered system. By extension, no other administrator had attempted to manage all aspects of a competition circuit with such a dedicated crew.

As a result of the dearth, Lowe's employees found themselves taking divergent paths. Susan X. Billings and Caroline Quine, the artists for Lowe's complex enterprise, parted ways with Lowe after his bankruptcy. They moved out of the graphic design office that had been serendipitously located next to Lowe's in downtown Boulder and into a roomier workplace on Pearl Street. They successfully continued their firm for years, but never again with a client attempting to reshape and reimagine competition climbing in such a unique way. Billings eventually moved to the Telluride area and focused entirely on her own painting and fine art. She would recall, "In hindsight it was always obvious that [Lowe] was working with a house of cards. Clues were everywhere—his car floor was littered with scratched out lottery tickets…should have known then. But Jeff never flagged. He just kept on keeping on. So we did too."

In that same vein, Deanne Gray kept moving too. Following the World Cup, she left the Colorado home base, returned to California, and resumed working at the Mountain Room bar in the Yosemite Valley Lodge. She also climbed a lot herself, and eventually moved northward to Bend, Oregon.

Other employees, particularly those who had diligently built the competitions' splendid walls and logged countless miles on the road, found themselves marooned without any alternative employment options. Roy McClenahan would later recall, "We all had to find something else to do. The ship went down and it fell to the bottom of the ocean. There was no longer an organization. If employees had wanted to hang on, what would they have hung on to? A sinking Titanic? There was nothing to do in terms of continuing the vector of the charted course, and it was time to swim away in search of terra firma."

In fact, amid all the construction demands—transporting and erecting the Twin Towers, in particular—and the long hours of committed working partnership with Paul Sibley, McClenahan had never actually learned the details of running a competition. Ironically, that objective had been ostensibly why Peter Mayfield had introduced McClenahan to Lowe in the first place, in a past that now seemed quite distant.

As the remnants of Lowe's business fragmented, McClenahan and Sibley were deemed custodians of the Twin Towers. In a last-ditch effort to receive due payment for their past labor from Lowe, McClenahan, Sibley, Billy Roos, and Guy Kenny contacted a lawyer, Julianne McCabe, and decided to keep the Twin Towers as part of a mechanic's lien. The Twin Towers, with all the design originality and requisite logistics for construction, had been the most important and highly priced tangible aspects of Lowe's competition tour—and now the whole disassembled structure was being held as legal leverage by the close-knit group of Lowe's former laborers who had built the towers in the Broomfield headquarters months earlier from scratch.

"That isn't exactly what I would call moving forward or picking up any pieces," McClenahan would note of the decision to file the mechanic's lien for the towers. "That's rooting through the ashes trying to retain something of token value."

Sibley and McClenahan soon had the Twin Towers' value assessed by a Boulder-based wall company, Climbing Arts, Resources & Productions (CARP). The assessment was a long, extensive process that scrutinized the towers' 44 total panels, counting and observing everything from their 149 four-inch external movable holds to their 244 six-inch external movable holds and the "weathered feel" of the wall paneling's surface texture.

The structure's full official appraisal was finally released by Ramsay Thomas, CARP's chief assessor, on September 16, 1991—more than a year after the Berkeley World Cup event had concluded. In his appraisal, Thomas noted the Twin Towers' craftsmanship and versatility. "The wall is excellent for World Cup or other competition," Thomas said.

However, the distinctiveness of the structure was pointed out as being potentially problematic in matters of repurpose or reuse. Thomas wrote, "The panels could be reconfigured such that they could be installed other than in the twin tower configuration to vary the climbing experience and/or accommodate a wide variety of facilities," but, "replacement parts would be hard, if not impossible, to obtain."

Although the lien acted as leverage, promises regarding payments owed resulted in negligible payouts for Sibley, McClenahan, Roos, and others who had been part of Lowe's competition ventures.

McClenahan would later say, "All totaled, there were something like 13 of us who were listed as lien holders. We all got pennies on the dollar. I think I was owed something like $1800 in wages, for which I received $300. Sibley and Roos were in for several thousand each, and received the same ratio of payout for their efforts. And yet again, even to secure that meager funding for Paul [Sibley], Billy [Roos], and the rest of the crew, I ended up spending many, many hours on the phone with lawyer Julianne McCabe, who did the work pro bono—yet another person drawn into the labor sucking maelstrom of J&J Lowe Sport Climbing Championships."

Following the appraisal, the Twin Towers were sold separately by their lien proprietors, and the numerous wall components were dispersed piece by piece to various businesses over time; one of the towers was reacquired by Lowe and sold to entities in Japan, and some of the panels of the other tower were sold to Colorado's Breckenridge Outdoor Education Center. Other pieces were utilized by Colorado's Outward Bound School thanks to Roos' previous connection with the organization. A few leftover pieces were kept by Sibley as notable relics for his personal workshop in Colorado.

Despite continued utility of the Twin Towers' paneling, handholds, and footholds in various iterations around the state in the years that would follow, the incredible climbing walls would never again be assembled in full, nor would a completed version of the Twin Towers be used for an international climbing competition at such a prestigious level ever again.

The competition at Berkeley's Greek Theater continued to reverberate with debt, restructuring, anger, a permanently dismantled set of unique towers, and ultimately unemployment for many of those involved in the Sport Climbing Championships. Yet, the irony was that 1990, the year that Lowe's circuit fell apart, was a positive year for American competition climbing by several other metrics—and particularly for competitions that resided outside of the Sport Climbing Championships sphere.

A primary showcase of success was the Southeastern Regional Sport Climbing Championships, which had been held at the Sporting Club in Atlanta, Georgia, on June 30 and July 1—roughly one month before the final preparations for the Berkeley World Cup were being made. The massive event in Atlanta was the first of its kind in the southeastern region of the United States and was patented largely after competitions like Lowe's that were more common in the Western United States up to that point.

The Atlanta competition featured approximately $10,000 in prizes—easily among the largest payouts of the year for an American climbing event. Equally as notable as the prize money was that the championships attracted nearly 125 competitors, all of whom were amateurs. Such a substantial turnout signified a healthy feeder network of competition climbers around the United States and a general swell in popularity of the whole competition paradigm—beyond the nucleus of the West and the traditional go-to host locales that Lowe had frequented like Snowbird, Seattle, and Boulder. Nancy Prichard, who had participated in Lowe's Danskin Rockmaster competitions earlier in the same year, won the women's division at the Atlanta event. A local climber, Penny Jordan, placed second, and Paula Benrich placed third. In the men's division, Porter Jarrard of North Carolina placed first, followed by Harrison Dekker and Shane Rymer in second and third place, respectively.

Another large, successful competition around the same time was hosted by the Colorado Athletic Training School in Boulder and titled the First Annual Rocky Mountain Open. It featured a mix of bouldering, speed, traverse, and lead climbing disciplines on clever route names like Baryshnikov, Popeye, and Arc-de-try-umpff. Pat Adams won the men's division, followed by Kurt Smith and Dale Goddard, who placed second and third, respectively. Sarah Spaulding won the women's division, Nancy Prichard placed second, and Sue Wint finished in third place.

A fitness complex with an indoor wall in Fort Collins, Colorado, called the Healthworks even hosted a competition that featured a children's portion; the youngest participant was a five-year-old named Shawn Beck-Gifford. The routesetter for the event was a local climber, Tom Henry, and several of the sponsors—*Climbing*, Power-Bar, and Lowe Alpine—had also sponsored Lowe's Sport Climbing Championships.

Yet the most unusual competition to take shape was the Tour De Hyalite at the Grotto Falls in Bozeman, Montana. The event, a unique biathlon, combined 15 miles of jogging to the summit of Hyalite Peak with climbing of numerous toproped routes.

Another significant occurrence of 1990 was the announcement of an American climbing team by the national governing body, the ASCF. The original roster for the men's national team was: Jim Karn, Dale Goddard, Chris Hill, and Ron Kauk. Doug Englekirk, Jason Stern, Scott Franklin, Tom Herbert, Pat Adams, Hans Florine, Peter Mayfield, and Scott Frye (one of the innovators of the Highway 13 "glue-ups") were alternates. The women's team, much smaller in membership, consisted of Lynn Hill and Robyn Erbesfield. Bobbi Bensman, Jennifer Cole, Alison Osius, Melissa Quigley, Shelley Presson, and Aimee Barnes were deemed the women's alternates.

Despite other successful events such as Springstone '90 in Washington, D.C., which attracted nearly 300 spectators, competition climbing in the United States was soon further marred by administrative decisions that were taking place in Europe.

First, considerations for climbing to be included in the 1992 Winter Olympics stalled, stymying any visions of the American standouts like Hill, Erbesfield, Bensman and Osius claiming Olympic victory over their European rivals on the biggest international stage. Eventually a "Pre-Olympics" climbing competition was held in Chambéry, France, a week prior to the start of the Olympics in Albertville. However, the climbing competition was only a shell of what the American climbing community had long envisioned. Erbesfield climbed well and took third place behind Switzerland's Susi Good and the victor, France's Isabelle Patissier. But other famous Americans like Hill and Jim Karn had opted not to participate at all, citing fatigue from previous international competitions at the time.

Furthermore, the UIAA, still the governing body for all major international climbing events, issued a decree for future World Cups: competition judges must hail from the host continent of a given competition. This meant that only European judges could preside over competitions held in Europe, and competitions in Asia were to only be officiated by judges from Asia.

The prevailing reason for the decision was logistical, as localizing all judging reduced the UIAA's travel costs and expenses for its international officials. But speculation also emerged within American circles that the UIAA—and specifically those within the association who clung to the hallowed European climbing tradition—might be feeling threatened by the United States' thriving and ever-growing competition profile.

Regardless of the exact motives for the decree, the United States' turn at hosting a World Cup had proved economically problematic in Berkeley, so it grew increasingly unlikely that the country would be given another opportunity to host a major international competition again. This left the qualified American judges that Darmi had worked tirelessly to teach without any global competitions to judge—and effectively cut the American competition scene off from the rest of the world in matters of event arbitration.

Darmi would recall, "Because there were no viable World Cup organizers in the United States after [Lowe's] enterprise failed, it meant all the U.S. and Canadian judges were landlocked."

Lacking administrative support from the international community, and with the most esteemed touring circuit of competitions around the United States defunct, the country became the rogue outsider; it had quickly grown to be a stronghold of competition climbing, yet it was now without any cohesive competition identity.

The only embers that glowed were the climbing gyms that had begun to appear with greater frequency by the early 1990s; a network had arisen and spread since the founding of CityRock in Emeryville, California, and Vertical Club in Seattle. It was unclear if—and how—the newer gyms might aid in repairing the broken American competition framework, but it was evident that indoor climbing was becoming a popular fitness activity.

By mid-1991, there were multiple gyms in the West, such as Cornerstone Climbing Gym in Long Beach, California, and SolidRock Gym in San Diego. But there were also gyms out east— Boston Rock Gym in Somerville, Massachusetts; City Climbing Club in New York City; and Basecamp and Exkursion in Pennsylvania. Middle America had gyms too, with Inside Moves opening in Grand Rapids, Michigan, and Dakota Rok Gym opening in Rapid City, South Dakota.

Canada also had its own emergent network, jump-started by the construction of a climbing wall at the University of Alberta in Edmonton and the opening of a gym, Joe Rockhead's Indoor Rock Climbing, in Toronto, Ontario.

The appeal of gym climbing in North America drew from the same allure as the ASCF competitions. Gym routes on artificial walls could be created, climbed, and dismantled in a short allotment of time—a far cry from the sanctity and permanence that epitomized routes on real stone outdoors. A 1991 advertisement for Denver's new 4,800-square-foot facility, Paradise Rock Gym, even boasted, "Over 35 routes set and changed weekly." That same year, the Paradise Rock Gym hosted its first annual competition, Pumpfest in Paradise. Another competition at the gym within the year, Showdown at Paradise, drew 140 participants—a record at the time for the most competitors at an indoor climbing competition.

For gyms, the necessity of frequently changing the routes to keep customers and competitors returning to the facility quickly gave rise to a vocation, that of the head routesetter. It was a role that several former employees of Lowe's, including Mike Pont and Kurt Smith, found themselves gravitating to following the end of the Sport Climbing Championships. Smith and Pont began routesetting at Paradise Rock Gym—first on a nightly volunteer basis while they worked full-time at a restaurant during the day, but more frequently and formally with time. Together, the pair adopted and invented procedures that quickly became commonplace at other gyms, such as the ways in which routes on a wall were grouped and identified. "Right next door to Paradise Rock Gym was this supply house distributor company," Pont would recall. "I don't know why we even went in there—Kurt and I—but the place sold colored duct tape. And I have to give all the credit to Kurt. I think he was the one who said, 'We could mark different routes with different colors of tape—and then we could have more than one route on a wall; we could use different colored holds, and the route would be marked by the tape, not the holds.' And I remember thinking that was brilliant."

Even with some progressive routesetting and a rising gym culture, as well as the onset of an official World Championship in lead climbing and speed climbing on the faraway European continent, American competition climbing in the post–Berkeley World Cup period became unfocused and subsisted at first on the fumes of events' previous eminence. Doubts arose in the whole climbing community that a homegrown competition network would ever again develop in the United States. And even if it did, who would lead the charge?

CHAPTER 9

DAZED AND CONFUSED

O N MAY 28, 1993, as American competitions found new footing and the elite competitors relied mostly on World Cup events overseas for subsistence, *Cliffhanger* hit movie theaters and gave climbing an unexpected injection of mainstream interest and layperson curiosity. The film, a high-octane thriller about a criminal heist gone awry in the mountains, had nothing to do with the competitive or sporting elements of climbing—and showcased mostly an egregious exaggeration of the climbing aesthetic. But unbeknownst to viewers, its production had close ties to the lineage that had also fashioned the Sport Climbing Championships, the 1990 World Cup event at Berkeley, and even the American Sport Climbers Federation (ASCF), still advancing into a role as the principal authority for organized events in the United States.

Casting the Dolomites of Italy as the Rocky Mountains of Colorado, *Cliffhanger* featured cinematography by David Breashears. In the mid-1980s, Breashears had summited Everest with Snowbird's entrepreneurial founder, Dick Bass. Much of the rigging for *Cliff-hanger's* elaborate climbing scenes was handled by Paul Sibley, Kevin Donald, and others who also possessed longtime connections to Bass and Jeff Lowe's competition ventures. In Sibley's case, the drawn-out narrative with Lowe related to the Twin Towers' mechanic's lien had only recently concluded.

Even the filmic techniques in *Cliffhanger* were largely adapted from the camerawork that Bob Carmichael had developed for Bass and Lowe at the first Snowbird competition six years prior.

Throughout *Cliffhanger's* filming, accomplished climbers like Ron Kauk, Wolfgang Güllich, David Walling, and Georgia Phipps stood in for the movie's stars—Sylvester Stallone, Janine Turner, John Lithgow, and others. In some cases, hired climbers had worked for longer than four months on the project. In fact, the filming of *Cliffhanger* had involved a total of 30 accomplished climbers working through a number of highly technical stunts "on the rocks and dangling in the air, doing aerial rigging, hoisting big cranes up and bolting them to the cliffs, riding around in helicopters and hopping out of them as they landed on single skids on high skinny towers."

From a physical standpoint, filming had entailed 100-hour workweeks at times, padded by "lavish catered meals," "five-star hotels," and other amenities for those involved in the production. Monetarily, the film had been backed by the TriStar Pictures movie studio and had racked up a massive $73 million budget by production's end.

But one of the most impressive aspects of the movie's filming had not been the outward lavishness for certain members of the crew, but the innermost mechanical nuance of rigging and all the preparation that went into conveying certain emotive effects with the climbing. For instance, at one point, a crew headed up by *Cliffhanger's* technical advisor, Mike Weis—who had previously worked on *Break on*

Through, as well as the Yosemite showcase of *Star Trek V: The Final Frontier*—meticulously painted belay cables and bolts to camouflage with the stone. Characters in the film could thus be perceived as free-soloing while actually being safely on belay behind the scenes.

Another *Cliffhanger* scene entailed hanging a replica helicopter from an 800-foot-tall wall of stone. The emotive climax of the setup was a jump made by Stallone's character over a 60-foot chasm. Although a nod to an actual smaller jump made by climber Dave Schultz in Czechoslovakia and filmed for ESPN, the exaggerated version for *Cliffhanger* utilized an "overhead traveling belay."

At one point following the completion of many of the film's climbing stunts outside in the Dolomites, Schultz, Weis, and Brooke Sandahl even traveled to Cinnecittà Studios in Rome to work on the construction of artificial walls for use in the movie. These immense walls, made of fiberglass to mirror outdoor stone structures and rock features, would be used in additional camera shots of the characters climbing the "Rocky Mountains." It amounted to nearly a year of work for some of those involved in the intricacies of the film's climbing scenes. The fact that none of the parties involved—actors, stunt performers, or climbers—were injured at all during all the labor in the mountains (aside from several encounters with lightning) spoke to the talent and wisdom possessed by the film's entire climbing crew.

In the end, *Cliffhanger* was a success in every sense. It grossed more than $80,000,000 in the United States following its release. It had been directed by Renny Harlin, most famous at the time for working on installments of the blockbuster franchises *Die Hard* and *A Nightmare on Elm Street*. The film became a vehicle for separating Stallone from his well-worn 1980s characters like Rocky Balboa and John Rambo, while conversely elevating the rock climber archetype to comparable fame. And as a "visual rollercoaster of stunts, scenery, exposure, violence and more stunts," the film succeeded in presenting climbing as an entertaining endeavor for the masses.

Of course, the glaring caveat was in most matters of climbing authenticity. "You have to realize this isn't a real climbing movie," wrote Susan E.B. Schwartz in a 1993 review of the film for *Rock and Ice*. "Instead of belays and placing pro, it's all soloing roofs, exposed faces and bat-infested chimneys' novice-clumsy lunges, bull-in-rut grunts, swelling biceps and two-person pendulums on strands of 100-year-old hemp."

Schwartz's insight was accurate and emblematic of the direction climbing, on the whole, was taking in the early 1990s. The unforeseen end of Lowe's Sport Climbing Championships narrowed the upward mobility for climbers on American soil and left them embracing mostly smaller-scale events. The result was a lateral expansion: climbing increasingly made inroads in other monetary areas, tangential to competitions, that were unprecedented in the decades before.

Cliffhanger, as an inroad into the realm of Hollywood's summer blockbusters and all the inherent publicity, was just one iteration. Another example of climbing's outward growth was the work of Hans Florine, winner of numerous speed climbing competitions in the late 1980s and early 1990s. Florine began collaborating with Project Bandaloop, a modern dance group in California that was the brainchild of choreographer Amelia Rudolph and CityRock founder Peter Mayfield. The theatrical troupe blended aspects of dance with climbing and required carefully choreographed routines on rigged ropes. In addition to climbing sequences facilitated by Florine, Project Bandaloop's performances incorporated pendulum swings and artistic shadows on the walls.

But Florine continued to compete as well throughout his foray into other climbing-related projects. As he got Project Bandaloop up and running, he also won the CityRock National Championship in Emeryville, California. A recap of the competition noted the duality, saying, "Hans employs a bizarre training regime: while other competitors are busy dieting and climbing on plastic, Hans is either practicing for his Project Bandaloop performance or racing up long routes in Yosemite." Such success—outdoors on famous climbs and indoors for competition—was even chronicled in segments of a video called *Painted Spider*.

Florine also received publicity for setting a number of speed climbing records outdoors, particularly on the Nose of El Capitan in Yosemite. His first noteworthy achievement on the route had been done with climber Steve Schneider. The pair climbed the Nose in a record-setting time of 8 hours and 6 minutes in 1990, besting the previous record held by climbers Peter Croft and John Bachar by almost two hours. As the decade progressed, a number of other pairs traded record-setting ascents at a breakneck pace. Florine, with climbing partner Andy Puhvel, again established the Nose's speed climbing record in 1991 (in 6 hours, 1 minute), and yet again in 1992 with Croft (in 4 hours, 22 minutes). The frequency at which the outdoor climbing records were broken in the early 1990s, along with the renown that the Nose held in all climbing circles, made the speed climbing that was taking place in Yosemite among the most famous competitive endeavors happening in the sport at the time.

Other indoor climbing competitions began to take on slightly altered forms, too. A prevailing thought in the past had been that large-scale climbing events should aim for the exhibitive nature of team sports: draw large crowds, offer large payouts, and be contested on whatever grand staging that exciting climbing necessitated. Lowe's earlier Danskin Rockmaster competitions at Seattle's Hec Edmundson Pavilion and Berkeley's Community Theater had epitomized this and proved that there was value in the ideal. Lowe's World Cup at Berkeley had embraced the large-scale staging as well, complete with concert-like promotion and a festival aura.

More than any other competition organization, Lowe's Sport Climbing Championships had enticed crowds and utilized immense artificial surfaces to present contests as extravaganzas. The marketing of other events embraced pageantry too, with many branding themselves as *championships* dating back to the mid-1980s, despite nebulous justifications for the label.

With a spate of climbing gyms and artificial climbing walls in the early 1990s came an increasing appearance of smaller-scale competitions too. These did not demand such extravagant production or promotion. Florine would later remember the hardscrabble nature of early ASCF-sanctioned competitions of all sizes: competitors working together in warehouses to construct makeshift warmup walls out of plywood prior to a competition at a nearby gym and finding discarded carpets to use in walling off enclosed isolation zones at competitions that lacked secluded rooms.

In a sense, the gym-based competitions and the do-it-yourself preparations by the competitors harkened back to the bouldering contests of Southern California in the 1970s, when organizers and participants were content to compete in contests of a less assuming manner.

The ASCF's competitions had great breadth and ranged considerably in their levels of staging and publicity. One competition series in 1993—the Tour de Pump—scheduled a succession of sizable events sponsored by La Sportiva, Five Ten, and other brands; the series culminated with a well-publicized ASCF National Championship at Denver's Paradise Rock Gym on April 3 and 4 that year.

Contrastingly, another competition that was contested at Miami University in Oxford, Ohio, was also sanctioned by the ASCF but only modestly branded and promoted. In fact, in title and description, the event was plainly marketed as the Mideast Indoor Climbing Competition.

Many of the small-scale competitions wrestled with issues of formatting, particularly because an industry-wide standard for rules was slow to take hold after the disappearance of Lowe's circuit. *The Sport Climbing Championships Competitors' Guide* that Peter Darmi had authored made a case for having events at the local, state, regional, and even national level sanctioned by the ASCF to generate a healthy feeder system for competitor rankings. But the reality was that the new climbing gyms were also attracting new audiences—people simply interested in giving the sport and its competitions a try after watching *Cliffhanger,* or seeing an appearance by Lynn Hill on *Late Night with David Letterman,* or catching an eventual segment on *The Tonight Show with Jay Leno* that featured a portable climbing wall in midtown Manhattan supervised by Ralph Erenzo. Beginners did not possess ASCF memberships or official licenses to compete; they were just intrigued by the vertical athletic aesthetic that was growing more prevalent.

Gyms were increasingly providing such people with their very first climbing experience. Nowhere was this more evident than at CityRock. From the outset, a main focus of the California climbing gym was that of the figurative first-time climber. "What we created, nobody had done in the world at that point—a clean, well-lit place to climb, with a professional front desk," founder Mayfield would explain. "We invented the safety-check, the belay-test. We had a nice little North Face retail shop. There was a place around the corner to get coffee. We made it so on the opening day a dad could bring his two daughters in, sit in a nice chair and read *The New York Times* while we did kids-belay with the kids."

Coupled with an increased number of casual gym members was the question of whether the format of elite competitions was applicable in smaller settings, and specifically whether it was best for more amateur clientele. In a 1991 article titled "How to Build a Better Competition," Dale Goddard wrote, "Many local-level events copy the World Cup format. With this scheme, each stage of the competition (qualifier, semifinal and final), involves one route designed to spread out the field of competitors. But since the walls, competitors and audiences are so different from those in the world-class competitions, it's worth asking whether this format is really best for climbing gyms."

Goddard concluded, "Our sport is young, and competitive formats are still an open issue. By sharing ideas which bring competitions more into line with the actual sport rather than the other way around, competitions will provide a more legitimate test of a climber's ability."

A willingness to develop a unique format for a given event appeared the following year at a 1992 CityRock National Championship. Although Florine had won the competition previously, he chose to organize the event, albeit out of necessity. He would recall, "I felt like I still had many years of competition left in me—I could have easily waited until I retired. But here was CityRock, which was the number one newfangled gym in the country—if not the world—and there wasn't going to be a Nationals because [the ASCF] didn't have much money. I thought, 'Wait a minute—I don't know how, but let's make it happen!'

In those days, there were maybe two dozen or three dozen competitors, and all of them were the reps for Petzl, Blue Water, Black Diamond, La Sportiva. And everybody knew everybody in the industry, and I knew them. I knew that [the comps] were good because they kept people climbing and kept people buying shoes and harnesses and ropes, so I asked the companies if they could help us keep [the comps] going. It wasn't like they gave us $10,000 or $20,000; it was $500 here, $1,000 there. But it was enough to help the sport grow."

Florine's efforts were successful even if the ensuing 1992 City-Rock National Championship was to be run on an admittedly shoe-string budget by the ASCF. Florine also created a unique scoring system for the event. While most other competitions nationally and abroad had long embraced scoring that corresponded to the highest point reached on a wall or rock face, this CityRock National Championship designated specific point values to individual holds as well. For instance, one of the event's rounds deemed every hold on the wall worth 10 points; another round increased each hold's point value to 20.

The novel concept of scoring each hold added viewing excitement as climbers progressed through lower sections of the wall—and secured, for points, lower holds that would have otherwise been mundane from the spectators' perspective.

In the final round of those 1992 CityRock Nationals, Alison Osius beat Sport Climbing Championships mainstay Bobbi Bensman to claim victory in the women's division. In the men's division, Doug Englekirk defeated Jim Karn in a showdown that was separated at times by a single point. Such narrowness in the results proved that Florine's idea had merit, but paradoxically, it also illustrated the wildly diverse nature of American competitions at the time. The country's entire infrastructure was far from standardized in matters of production and calculation.

Six months later, CityRock hosted the United States' first "Redpoint Invitational," with each competitor allotted 25 minutes the day before the climbing competition's final round to assess and practice routes that had been created by expert routesetters Steve Schneider and Jim Redo. Englekirk again took first place in the men's division, and Anne Smith won the women's division.

Another event, more idiosyncratic in branding than any of the invitationals and championships, was the Horsetooth Hang On, sponsored by Budweiser as an outdoor contest on the boulders of Fort Collins, Colorado's Horsetooth Reservoir. It embraced unique formatting in its own right, making no delineation between local climbers and those from out of state—an area of reproach that had dogged some of the amateur outdoor competitions in the 1970s.

In an attempt to mitigate criticism from competitors of the combined format in 1992, the organizers of the Hang On designated low point values for the well-known boulders of the area and higher values for lesser-known ones.

In a way, the Hang On was a nostalgic nod to the earliest Southern California contests at Santee and Mount Rubidoux, unifying locals with a handful of outsiders in cordial climbing fellowship. Still, it demonstrated insouciance that had begun to precipitate the competition scene.

Without Lowe's revered tour to formalize the competition concept, many events fell back on climbing's recreational roots and integrated some levity. Budweiser infused the Hang On competition with adequate payouts of $1,000 for the winners of the men's and women's divisions, but opted to have a bouldering version of its mascot, Bud Man, take part in the festivities as well.[9] Another competition in Colorado featured cans of beer placed intermittently up the routes; competitors progressed toward the cans while blind-folded and wearing scuba diving fins. ("The object was to 'swim' to the top through as much beer as possible.")

The characteristics and quirks of other competitions ranged from uncommon to downright unusual, with witty names like Climbers Against Whiners, the Happy Climbers Competition, and the Manhattan Meltdown. Even events that attempted to maintain seriousness wrestled with periodic embarrassments and foibles. For example, when Christian Griffith claimed victory in a division of the Los Alamos Forearm Meltdown competition in 1991, his prize was a chalkbag from Verve—the very company he had founded. A later competition, the Sapphire Classic in Albuquerque, New Mexico, featured a grand prize of $3,000—in jewelry. The annual spectacle at Snowbird had regressed by the early 1990s, too. The climbing was still elite, but it was shoehorned into a larger Sports Expo that also included mountain bike races and volleyball games. An article by Alan Lester in *Rock and Ice* titled "The Endangered Snowbird" indicated that the famous Cliff Lodge wall, once the pinnacle of creative possibility and media acclaim for sport climbing, was on the decline too: "The panels creak, most of the T-nuts are unusable, and there are lots of small holds between the paneling on the vertical walls—but this is Snowbird, and that makes it all okay," wrote Lester. The climbing wall at Snowbird was a metaphor for how American climbing competitions had lost some of their novelty and prestige within just a few years.

---

9. An amusing recap of the event reads: "Bud Man stunned onlookers by nearly send-ing the difficult Pinch Problem on the Mental Block without changing out of his cape and tennis shoes."

Two well-publicized competitions that managed to provide some stability to the changing scene were the Phoenix Bouldering Contest in Arizona and the Pocatello Pump in Idaho. Both competitions had developed years' worth of respected history and lineage by the mid-1990s and had grown steadily in participatory numbers as well. The Phoenix Bouldering Contest, in particular, had persisted even while its founder, Jim Waugh, had aided in the organization of Lowe's 1990 Sport Climbing Championships.

But by 1992, Waugh's Phoenix Bouldering Contest (PBC) had grown to become arguably the most famous climbing competition in the United States, with some of the country's best climbers like Ron Kauk, Christian Griffith, Kurt Smith, Dale Goddard, and Bobbi Bensman having notched victories there at some point. It had also evolved to include a number of different categories and scoring divisions: Masters, Expert/Local, Expert/Out of Town, Intermediate/Local, Intermediate/Out of Town.

Beyond the competition aspect, Waugh's annual event had become among the most celebrated rendezvous for the greater climbing community. It featured dozens of vendors temporarily setting up booths to sell gear at discounted prices. Attendees were enticed to return with the budget-friendly retailing as much as the many climbing options.

Waugh would recall of the event's steady growth by the early 1990s, "It was the Seventh PBC where I pioneered a whole new area (Queen Creek) with 300+ new problems. That continued for another 3–4 years, with new problems almost every year. During that time, more sponsorship came on board that afforded the event more luxuries such as concert bands. Hard work and attention to details, along with a great staff of local, dedicated people, kept improving the event from local to state to national to international over the years."

Another highpoint in a period of decidedly muddled competition identity was For Women Only, the first major climbing competition to feature exclusively female competitors. Sponsored by Danskin, it was held on the 98-foot artificial wall of the Sporting Club in Chicago, Illinois, in July 1991. Alison Osius won the event, with Bobbi Bensman—the winner of Phoenix Bouldering Contests' Women/Out of Town division that same year—taking second place, and Diane Russell placing third.

In a way, the survival of American competitions in all their variations around the country allowed for the advancement of a grassroots ethos on a scale that the sport had never before experienced. Several small-scale publications emerged, including a magazine titled *The Connection* and later renamed *Sport Climbing,* headed by editor Elaine Chandler.[10] Although limited in distribution, Chandler's magazines contained in-depth sections devoted to competitions' results and broader news related to the growth of the United States' competition scene. For instance, a 1992 issue of *Sport Climbing* reported a commitment by ESPN to broadcast portions of the following year's World Cup season: "After the ill-fated Lowe Sport Climbing Championships, there has been some question as to whether sport climbing competitions would get the second chance that they deserve," noted the magazine. "The answer seems to be YES."

The same issue detailed new climbing gyms that had opened in Salt Lake City, Utah, and Redmond, Washington, as well as a list of reasons why readers should become members of the ASCF. Chief

---

10. This magazine is also sometimes referenced as *Sport Climbing Connection.*

among the reasons was, "You will be supporting the growth of our exciting new sport," but the list also nebulously mentioned climbing's "possible future Olympic status." New gyms were creating a network around the United States, of sorts, and becoming catalysts for a competition climbing revival in their own right. The Boulder Rock Club, the Sport Climbing Center in Colorado Springs, and other state-of-the-art facilities were becoming spaces for congregation and socializing as much as competing. Construction of the climbing walls at the Boulder Rock Club eventually spawned an entire wall-design company, Eldorado Climbing Walls, started by John McGowan and Steve Holmes, an alumnus of Lowe's competition ventures. A competition at Clipper City Rock Gym in Baltimore, Maryland, was featured on the popular CBS television program *Sunday Morning* in a news piece profiling "the current 'boom' in rock climbing." And in a hint of things to come, climbing was featured on ESPN's television program *Max Out* alongside snowboarding and mountain biking in a segment highlighting "extreme sports."

With new facilities as backdrops, and the media as promotional tools, climbing competitions were perfectly equipped to unveil new stars for a new generation. The need for rejuvenation of the whole scene was emphasized when Lynn Hill, the American stalwart since the 1970s, retired from competing after winning the final World Cup event of the 1992 season, in Birmingham, England. That season's overall World Cup victory, as well as the three succeeding seasons, would go to Hill's compatriot, Robyn Erbesfield. Hill would continue to make climbing history—particularly as the first person to complete a free ascent of the Nose of El Capitan in Yosemite. But never again would she reign in the realm of major organized competitions. She would cite a preference for "the freedom and creative expression of climbing outside with my friends" over competition, and expound: "Competition climbing by its nature is about climbing inside, and I didn't want to feel like I was climbing inside of a box any longer."

If new American icons could somehow emerge in the mid-1990s like they had in the late 1980s with the rise of Hill, Erbesfield, Kauk, Griffith, and others, perhaps a new roster could revive United States competition climbing's prestige—even carry it to unforeseen heights via popular media—before it faded in the country's collective sporting consciousness completely.

CHAPTER 10

A GUIDING LIGHT

A YEAR AFTER *CLIFFHANGER'S* BOX OFFICE SUCCESS, American competition climbing suddenly found itself with an unlikely new protagonist. Mia Axon, a 35-year-old environmentalist and employee of Colorado's Outward Bound School, made waves by unexpectedly placing fourth—narrowly missing a spot on the awards podium—at a UIAA World Cup event in Villach, Austria, on April 16, 1994.

Axon's high standing on the international stage was part of a progression of success that had included a sixth-place finish at a World Cup event in Nürnburg, Germany, the year before, a second-place finish at that same year's Snowbird competition, and the overall victory of the ASCF's Tour de Pump series for three years in a row beginning in 1992.

Despite her gradual rise, Axon felt like an epiphany to competition fans, partly because she did not fit the typical American climbing mold that was in vogue at the time. For better or worse, *Cliffhanger* had offered audiences the typical "Stallone-style action-adventure." It had thus presented climbing as a pastime for gritty, overly muscled heroes. And prior to the film, the dirtbag ethos of earlier decades had shaped climbers to be wholly devoted vagabonds, many of whom were scraggly males.

Axon, in contrast, was slight—barely taller than five feet and weighing 100 pounds. She worked a full-time, non-climbing job and volunteered with recycling campaigns around her home in Denver. Most fascinating was that by the time she started to gain recognition for her competition performances, Axon had lived a previous professional life as a harpist, having played the instrument since childhood. As a young adult, she had attended the prestigious New England Conservatory of Music in Boston, Massachusetts, performed for the Denver Symphony Orchestra, and become the lead harpist for the Colorado Ballet Orchestra.

Although fairly unusual among climbers, Axon was not the sole American competitor who found success abroad while the competitions in the United States continued to try out different formatting and branding styles; Shelley Presson, Georgia Phipps, and Bobbi Bensman participated in UIAA-sanctioned events overseas. Additionally, Robyn Erbesfield placed second in the 1993 World Championships in Innsbruck, Austria, ahead of France's Isabelle Patissier and behind that year's overall World Cup winner, Switzerland's Susi Good. Erbesfield consistently placed high in World Cup events overseas, often the sole American at the top among consistently adept Europeans like France's Nanette Raybaud and Liv Sansoz, Italy's Luisa Iovane, Germany's Marietta Uhden, and Russia's Elena Ovchinnikova. Erbesfield's greatest accomplishments were the securing of overall World Cup season championships in multiple, consecutive years.

Erbesfield also began dating Didier Raboutou, winner of the 1989 Snowbird competition, and moved to Europe. The international romance of Erbesfield and Raboutou provided climbing media with a temporary softening of the standard America versus Europe framework that had characterized competitions and reportage in the United States since the earliest iterations. One magazine even ran a dual interview with the couple titled "Love & Rockstars." Responding to a question in the interview about why there was a dearth of elite American competition climbers in the era, Erbesfield stated, "I think it's because sport climbing is a new sport in America. I believe that is the only thing that is keeping Americans from being as strong as the Europeans. If you look at Jim Karn or Lynn [Hill] or myself, you realize there is no difference between the top American climbers who have been exposed to sport climbing and their European counterparts."

Getting new people, particularly women, interested in the sport was something that Axon felt strongly about as well. At the time of her competition ascendancy, she began teaching courses specifically geared to women at American gyms and encouraged the women in her practicums to enroll in competitions.

In a profile from 1994, Axon said, "There has been a notable absence of elite women at competitions. Less than half the really strong women climbers in this country compete. Is it because they're not competitive, and therefore not interested? Or is it because they're so competitive they can't stand the thought of losing? I don't know."

Axon's observation about a gender gap was accurate. At one of the Tour de Pump events at the Boulder Rock Club in February 1994, the gym's co-owner, John McGowan, explicitly noted a particularly low turnout of women. At that competition, only six women participated at the elite level, skewing the winners' purses. McGowan would tell

Climbing, "We need more women to compete, otherwise we can't split the cash evenly. It's not fair that 44 men were competing for the same prizes as six women." At another event in Colorado, the Ute City Crank at the Aspen Athletic Club, Alison Osius was the only woman who had registered for an elite division—so she just entered the men's field instead.

The same month of Mia Axon's significant fourth-place finish at the World Cup in Austria, the ASCF held a national event called the Summit Hut Desert Draw at Tucson, Arizona's new gym, Rocks & Ropes— 33 men enrolled in the competition, compared with only 18 women.

Despite the disproportionate roster, the Desert Draw was marked by stirring climbing from the women who did participate, including flashes—initial attempts that result in competitors successfully reaching the top—of the semifinals route by climbers Bobbi Bensman, Mindy Shulak, and Kadi Johnston. Bensman flashed the finals' route too, with Johnston ultimately taking second place and Shulak placing third.

As Bensman and other women stole the show, the Desert Draw also signified the commencement of fresh opportunity for television coverage. ESPN had been in existence since the late 1970s and broadcast hockey, basketball, football, and other widely popular team sports in the 1980s. The network previously covered the Nameless Tower climbing endeavor of Jeff Lowe and Catherine Destivelle as well, but by the mid-1990s, ESPN was making an even greater move into niche sports markets. The embrace of contests that resided beneath the mainstream had been epitomized by the 1993 launch of another channel, ESPN2, for a younger viewing audience. Competition climbing, along with activities like poker, lacrosse, and even Spain's Running of the Bulls was selected as part of ESPN's program expansion and content diversification in the 1990s. Consequently, the

Desert Draw became one of ESPN's earliest test-runs for nationally broadcasting a climbing contest.

Although the adoption of climbing competitions by ESPN would quickly swell, the network's initial foray into the landscape was bumpy. Practically since the first Snowbird competition, the custom for large-scale climbing events had been to blare music— to get the crowd excited—while the climbers attempted the routes and progressed through the rounds. However, to avoid any songs being inadvertently overheard on a nation-wide television broadcast and thus spurring music proprietorship entanglements, ESPN had more recently decided to eliminate music from the background of its broadcast competitions. In the case of the Desert Draw, the result was an eerie silence for the competitors as well as the audience.

There remained presentation and production amendments that ESPN would need to make if it was to broadcast future competition climbing events. Nonetheless, the Desert Draw proved just how exciting organized climbing could be—and how there was potential for the sport to reside in the pop-culture consciousness of the average niche sport fan.

As mainstream media, led by ESPN, developed a resurging interest in climbing competitions, the ASCF deepened its operations. Within a few short years, the organization's administrative structure solidified: Hans Florine served as the ASCF's Executive Director and Shelley Presson served as the secretary. Mike Pont, who had been laboring over the construction of the Twin Towers for the World Cup at Berkeley just a few years prior, was selected as an active ASCF board member. Michelle Hurni was chosen to be the President, with Chris Bloch acting as Vice President.

Underpinning the staff was comprehensive dogma that made competition climbing under the ASCF's auspices the most systematized and validated it had ever been. The dogma ranged from itemized tenets clarifying the ASCF's overarching objectives (such as maintaining a national ranking system of competitive climbers, registering American competitors for World Cup events overseas, and sanctioning events domestically) to detailed breakdowns of the ASCF's competition prize purses.[11] The ASCF also distributed a quarterly newsletter with regularly updated competitor rankings.

One of the most important steps taken by the ASCF was to bolster the national ranking system in accordance with the growing number of national competitors. "We said, 'Let's rank people—not just the top 10, but let's rank everybody who ever competed,'" Florine would later reflect. "I think at one time we had, like, 270 men ranked and, like, 110 women. And I would get phone calls from people saying, 'Hey, you got my local [competition result] wrong—I actually should be in 160th place, not 175th!' And I'd get right on it and change it. People cared about a black and white printing of their names. People were psyched to see their names move up, and they'd go out of their way to go to local or regional events to get points."

As a result of the extensive points system that continued throughout a given year, the ASCF's annual victors were decided much in the World Cup style—not by a single concluding championship, but

---

11. Although prize purses fluctuated over the years, one ASCF document lists the total prize purse at local competitions of the mid-1990s to be $350, the total prize purse at regional competitions in the same period to be $2,000, and the total prize purse at a national championship to be $6,000. Competition organizers at the national level were given leeway to raise and distribute more than $6,000, but ASCF rules stipulated that any purse—in any amount—must be distributed equally to men and women competitors, at least down to third place.

by accrued points. In fact, a given year entailed multiple "national championship" competitions at several gyms.

In addition to such developments, the ASCF fashioned its true keystone with a comprehensive packet of rules. The packet delved into greater detail with each passing month and held the entire American competition configuration together. Consider the specificity in Article G, Section 13, of the ASCF rules at the time that Axon accidentally skipped a quickdraw clip at the finals of the ASCF's National Championship in 1994—an event organized by Florine at CityRock in Emeryville, California:

> The competitor shall be stopped immediately on the route and the highest hold touched or held from a legitimate position shall be measured in the event of the following: a) fall; b) exceeding the permitted climbing time; c) crossing over the boundaries of the route; d) using prohibited parts of the walls for climbing (in violation of art. G1); e) failing to clip all belay points in order; f) returning to the ground (as defined in art. G7); g) use of artificial aid.

In the instance that a competitor objected to particular article or section of the rules or wished to protest an event's decision, the ASCF accepted written appeals from competitors at a cost of $10. The appeals were to be lodged immediately following a given incident, and the fee was refundable if the appeal was eventually upheld. The enforcers of all such adjudicating matters were the ASCF's certified judges—personnel who had completed the organization's thorough Judges Training Course in conjunction with a regional-level or national-level competition.

Part of any would-be judge's extensive certification process involved an examination with random, itemized "discussion questions" of hypothetical competition mishaps, such as:

> *A competitor reports at the entrance to the isolation zone 30 minutes after the time limit. How is this dealt with?*
>
> *A sponsoring company provides non-UIAA ropes and requests that these be used. Are they accepted?*
>
> *A competitor begins climbing with socks over her/his shoes. What do you do?*
>
> *A power failure occurs as a climber is near the top, putting the wall in darkness. What is done?*
>
> *A competitor grasps a clearly visible hold which is out of bounds. What do you do?*

When added together, the judging criteria, the doctrine of rules and requirements, and the ongoing member correspondence raised the profile of the ASCF in the larger climbing world. One key component of competition climbing that was largely absent from ASCF's initial doctrines and documentation was routesetting. Nearly all competition routesetting matters were purposefully conceded to a separate organization called the American League of Forerunners (ALF). The ALF was born out of a formal routesetting training course given to Mike Pont, Steve Schneider, Tony Yaniro, and Christian Griffith at Paradise Rock Gym in Colorado by Hans Peter Seigrist, a Swiss representative of the UIAA. Yaniro and Pont were further credentialed when they traveled overseas to complete a UIAA routesetting practicum at a World Cup in St. Pölten, Austria.

The creative flame that became the ALF was kindled by ongoing formalization of routesetting that was taking place in Europe by

Antoine Le Ménestrel and others under the UIAA's command. As the chief American authority and a conduit to those routesetting methods in Europe, the ALF sharply monitored the routes of the ASCF-sanctioned competitions around the United States and worked in concurrence with the ASCF's personnel.

Much like the ASCF, the ALF had an administrative and clerical staff; Schneider acted as the ALF's President, with Chris Bloch eventually coming on board as the Secretary. Other contributors such as Nic Cocciolone acted as regional directors. An ALF newsletter was released on a quarterly basis to those routesetters around the country who paid a $25 annual membership to the ALF.

By 1995, the ALF had 38 active members. Of those members, most were certified to routeset at local and regional-level competitions. Under the organization's certification hierarchy, the next level of accreditation, beyond local and regional authority, was national accreditation. American routesetters with such esteemed national-level certification in the summer of 1995 were Florine, the organizer for most of the nation's highest-level competitions that year, as well as Tim Steele, Mike Call, Hank Caylor, Ty Foose, Jim Redo, Jacob Slaney, Kathy Yaniro, Rebecca Noyes, Jordi Salas, Doug Cosby, Jason Campbell, Doug Ayers, and Rob Butch. Only Pont, Schneider, Yaniro, and Griffith were certified to set at the international level.

A big part of the ALF's success was the extensiveness of its certification process. For instance, the requirement for a routesetter to obtain national-level status entailed a grueling three-day course. The course began with a routesetting and route-critiquing session on the first day, followed by a climbing ability test on the second day, during which the applicant had to onsight a 5.12b route and redpoint a 5.12d route. A written examination was also included as part of this day's ongoing evaluations. The final day entailed further routesetting and critiquing duties. Applicants were often kept awake late into the night to routeset, in order to simulate the probable routesetting schedule at a national championship.

The increased formality of the ASCF and ALF operations and each organization's constant solicitation for new members elevated the significance of the ASCF National Championships in 1995. One such competition, held at Mission Cliffs Gym in San Francisco, California, over the weekend of August 19 and 20, came on the heels of a Junior National Championship, which had been held the week prior at SolidRock Gym in San Diego. There, a 1995 Junior Nationals had included eight different age categories and amounted to a veritable showcase of climbing's booming popularity among American youth: A lanky climber from Colorado named Tommy Caldwell won the Male 16–17 division by flashing the finals' route. A shy 14-year-old from Kentucky, Katie Brown, flashed her respective final route too and won the Female 14–15 division.

Other standouts from that Junior Nationals were Chris Lindner, Chelsea Raymond, Shena Sturman, Jay Weber, Nancy McCullough, and a scrawny 14-year-old from Santa Cruz named Chris Sharma, a relative newcomer to the competition scene.

Although some of the competitors from that Junior Nationals at SolidRock also chose to compete at the Nationals at Mission Cliffs, the primary focus at Mission Cliffs was not on the sport's popularity and prominence among kids and adolescents. Instead, the narrative of the 1995 Nationals revolved around the adult women who were taking part, aided by the efforts of Erbesfield and Axon to advance and promote the role of women in climbing's competitive realm.

Fittingly, the well-publicized allure of the 1995 Nationals was Erbesfield's return to American competition after participating solely overseas for three years. But the 1995 Nationals also included France's newest star, Natalie Richer, and Russia's Elena Ovchinnikova, whose presence allowed for a continuation of the patriotic spin that had epitomized so many of Jeff Lowe's competitions years earlier; yet again, it seemed there would be an America versus the World theme.

Axon, the previous year's luminary, was also included in the 1995 Nationals' women's field, which was officially the largest in history, as were Bensman, Alison Osius, Shelley Presson, Diane Russell, and young Katie Brown—fresh off her dominant victory at the Junior Nationals the week before.

Such a sizable assemblage not only spanned generations (Brown being a teenager, other women being in their thirties), but it also crossed climbing lifestyles and ancillary interests. Erbesfield, though an Atlanta native, had taken up permanent residence in France. And Bensman and Osius had begun to parlay their climbing success into media opportunities, particularly as contributing writers to climbing magazines. Osius was on her way to becoming an editor at *Rock and Ice*.

The variety in the women competitors' backgrounds added narrative depth to a much-anticipated showdown: the 1995 Nationals would systematically determine which woman was the best competition climber in the world, and practically every participant had a compelling story to supplement her potential victory.

The men's division had intriguing storylines as well. The 1994 and 1995 Phoenix Bouldering Contest competitions had been won by an Albuquerque, New Mexico, native named Timy Fairfield, who thus entered the 1995 Nationals with two solid years of competition momentum behind him. In its official summer rankings for 1995, the ASCF ranked Fairfield second only to Doug Englekirk. Engle-kirk was also competing in those 1995 Nationals, having previously taken part in numerous World Cup events since bursting onto the international scene in 1990. In fact, at a number of ASCF Nation-als in the early 1990s, the men's podium order was a variation of the same trio—Englekirk, Jim Karn, and Scott Franklin—receiving the gold, silver, and bronze medals.

Also part of the spirited men's field in 1995 was a Colorado der-matologist, Steve Hong, and a Kentucky wunderkind, David Hume. Tommy Caldwell and Chris Sharma were entered as well, although few spectators suspected that either climber would be able to contend with the best adults beyond a nominal level.

ESPN was busy with its own climbing competition concept on the other side of the United States and chose not to broadcast any 1995 Nationals. However, despite the lack of a major broadcaster, sponsorship from French equipment company Petzl boosted the publicity of the Mission Cliffs Nationals. And routes designed by Christian Griffith, Jake Slaney, Kathy Yaniro, and Di Bailey, among the most established names in the rapidly growing gym industry at the time, gave the event some requisite technical prestige.

Griffith's staff presence, in particular, linked the 1995 Nation-als to Lowe's defunct Sport Climbing Championships, if only at a token level. Yet, even though less than half a decade had passed since Lowe's two-tiered business plan had dissolved, the competition climbing landscape was already markedly different. For example, Mission Cliffs possessed a permanent interior encirclement of arti-ficial climbing walls—fully functional and ready to be ascended in the standard gym style. Such permanence negated the need for the substantial cross-country transportation or wall construction crews, the likes of which had caused many labor woes for Lowe.

The existence of the frequently updated competitors' ranking system by the ASCF, as well as the depth of a national climbing team, also legitimized competition in ways that had been nascent just a few years before. Yet figurative headaches still arose.

"The ASCF would schedule comps and then not hold them—because the gym managers would realize that they were going to lose money," recalls Rene Keyzer-Andre, who sat on the ASCF's board of directors and also competed in events. Keyzer-Andre was adamant that a gym he helped open in 1995, RockQuest, in Ohio, did not cancel when opportunities for hosting big competitions emerged. But he understood well any gym's financial crux. "It was not financially feasible for a gym to shut down for a minimum of three days, if not five or six days, so the routesetters could come in beforehand. One year there were six national championships scheduled—but only a fraction of those competitions were held."

While there were such ongoing financial conflicts at the gym level, the appearance of the climbing competitions themselves revealed no such strife. Some competitors taking part in competitions in 1995 had traveled previously on the Sport Climbing Championships' circuit years prior, but the fact was American competition climbing was seeing perhaps for the first time a degree of major turnover. With that came spirited, youthful zeal and new personalities.

As a result, the 1995 Nationals at Mission Cliffs, in particular, would either be the proving ground for a new generation, or mere verification that competition's greatest stars belonged to a previous era that was unlikely to be surpassed.

The competition kicked off with a number of flashes in both the men's and women's divisions, including coasting tops by Erbesfield, Ovchinnikova, Richer, and Bensman. The cruising continued in the following round, which saw Sharma and Hume—among the youngest men in the competition—flash more routes and continue their surprising underdog runs. Erbesfield, Richer, Axon, Presson, and Brown flashed the ensuing women's routes. The women's final round was then christened by Erbesfield, the only woman to flash the respective finals route. The ascent marked her victory, affirmed her storied return to American competition climbing, and stamped her claim as the United States' greatest competition climber of the year. She would continue her success overseas shortly thereafter, winning World Cup events in Birmingham, England, and Aix-les-Bains, France, in the fall.

But as much as the summer's 1995 Nationals had been centered initially around the strong women's field, it became clear during the men's finals that another storyline had emerged: the unprecedented competition dominance of Chris Sharma, the wiry teenager from the Bay Area. He surpassed 33-year-old Englekirk on the scorecards, as well as his teenage generational contemporaries, Hume and Caldwell, to claim victory. And it was more than Sharma's climbing skill that heralded the dawning of a new competition era; it was his entire youthful aura—having "campused" through sections of the routes (using only his arms) at Nationals where other competitors had meticulously placed their feet, having bouldered in Mission Cliffs' isolation section while other competitors had rested idly, and having beamed the whole time with the enthusiastic exuberance of a participant simply having fun.

As a national champion, Sharma theoretically allowed climbing to be explicitly promoted as a teenage pursuit—a first for the sport. In an article, "Young Guns," from a 1995 issue of *Climbing*, well-known competitor Todd Berlier wrote, "For the past few years, the top five finishers have generally been a predictable cadre of adults. But in San Francisco a welcome shake-up began, with three 14-year-olds stealing the show: Chris Sharma in first place, and David Hume and Katie Brown, competing in their first nationals, in second and third (for women)."

Sharma had only been climbing for two years at the time of his dominant performance at these 1995 Nationals, although he had already chalked up successful ascents of famous, difficult outdoor climbs around his home of California. Hume and Brown had also cut their teeth outdoors, particularly as fixtures at Red River Gorge for several seasons before participating in major competitions.

The sudden youth influx paralleled the nation-wide climbing gym expansion. In fact, Sharma and Brown, in particular, had learned to climb primarily indoors—Sharma at the Pacific Edge Climbing Gym in Santa Cruz, California, and Brown at Climb Time in Lexington, Kentucky.

Following August's Nationals, both Sharma and Axon traveled to Laval, France, to participate in October's Youth World Championships, and each won in their respective age categories. For all intents and purposes, competition climbing had been recharged by teenage stars, and now it had to once again somehow breach the American mainstream and connect with the masses.

CHAPTER 11

COMPETITION GETS EXTREME

THE SAME SUMMER THAT THE NATIONALS AT MISSION CLIFFS heralded a new cadre of young elites, ESPN decided the time was right to stage its own assortment of competitions specifically targeting a youthful generation. For several years, the Generation X demographic had been carving a unique pop-culture identity, illustrated by the rise of popular musical acts like Nirvana and Pearl Jam, as well as innovation with a novel computer-based entity, the Internet. Yet, for all the targeted associations that had already been made with Generation X in the realms of music, technology, and movies, athletics remained largely an untapped arena—and ESPN aimed to change that. The previous generation, the Baby Boomers born in the aftermath of World War II, had largely embraced team sports such as football, baseball, and basketball. In dissimilarity, those within Generation X, while sharing some interest in team sports, noticeably lauded individual pursuits like skateboarding and rollerblading that fit the insouciant and alternative ethos of the 1990s. Skateboarding had even seen the creation of its own international organizational body, the World Cup of Skateboarding, in 1994 to oversee its competitions.

With such cultural fuel, ESPN fashioned an idea of holding an alternative sports festival, packaging assorted "extreme" recreational activities—like skateboarding—and drawing huge crowds of spectators and television viewers in the process. Eventually branded fittingly as the Extreme Games, the concept was the brainchild of ESPN executive Ron Semiao but had swelled to encompass multiple facets of the network. The large-scale production was to be like the Olympics for Generation Xers, packaged and showcased exclusively by ESPN, and as such, it would be a balance of competition stringency and artistic television showcase.

The activities chosen to be included in this Extreme Games extravaganza in 1995 spanned a wide gamut of physicality, with some such as skateboarding and mountain biking already possessing deep competition heritage, and others such as bungee jumping being fairly new to mainstream competition publicity in the United States. Other activities culled into the inaugural production package would include rollerblading, a distinctive discipline of skydiving known as skysurfing, a branded adventure race known as the Eco-Challenge, water skiing, windsurfing, and street luging.

But executives at ESPN had also taken notice of climbing's renewed popularity, particularly after the network covered massive events such as the National Championships in 1994 and smaller events such as the Summit Hut Desert Draw. Climbing, never far from the cultural periphery since the impecunious Stonemasters of the 1970s, now had a fairly solidified competition methodology that interlocked perfectly with the makeshift Olympics stylings of these proposed Extreme Games. It was also clear that competition climbing was becoming more prevalent in gyms across the country as the new decade progressed. Climbing was an obvious candidate for being looped into any major commercialization and collectivization of extreme sports.

Hired by ESPN to organize and ultimately produce a climbing portion for the 1995 Extreme Games was Ralph Erenzo, who had started a climbing-centric company, ExtraVertical Inc., since jump-starting the ASCF with Peter Darmi years before. Although Erenzo was involved in meetings with ESPN administrators practically from the onset of climbing's inclusion in the proposed Extreme Games, he was given significant autonomy by ESPN officials who knew little of competition climbing's nuance.

In fact, ESPN remained largely hands-off of Erenzo's resultant managerial undertakings, with the network's only major request being that the climbers and the procedures of the Extreme Games uphold World Cup levels of proficiency and presentation. Such official formatting, in accordance with the time-honored prestige of the World Cup circuit, would serve to augment the Extreme Games' climbing portion by unofficially connecting the climbs to all major competitions—mostly in Europe and Asia—that had come before them. Erenzo's Extreme Games would mark the first time since Jeff Lowe's World Cup at Berkeley in 1990 that an international competition had been formally held in the United States.

Allowed to create the climbing offerings for the television broadcast in manners he thought suitable, Erenzo formulated multiple climbing disciplines that adhered to those norms established in previous competitions sanctioned by the UIAA. The Extreme Games would feature roped climbing, most markedly with a Difficulty discipline, that would be divided into men's and women's fields. There would also be speed climbing disciplines separated by gender.

Unlike many American climbing competitions of an earlier era, the Extreme Games would steadily land sponsors that resided not in the respective recreational niches, but in the barefaced mainstream. Mountain Dew, Taco Bell, Chevrolet, Nike, and other major companies agreed to contribute funding and support for ESPN's groundbreaking blend of lifestyle and athletics, corporate branding, and unabashed nonconformity in festival-style presentation.

Despite the independence, Erenzo, along with a close colleague in matters of preparation, Jordan Mills, quickly found the planning and production for the Extreme Games' climbing events challenging. The competition was scheduled to be held in Rhode Island at the end of June 1995, but the state—and specifically Newport harbor—lacked artificial climbing walls that could be utilized for such a large-scale operation. As a result, and out of necessity, ESPN opted to have Erenzo's company, ExtraVertical Inc., erect new walls in an expansive open space beside the harbor that had formerly been a landfill. However, the soil foundation of the grassy area, suitable for gathered spectators and ground-based sports, proved to be inadequate for supporting the scaffolding of tall vertical climbing structures as the summer approached.

At one point while inspecting the site for the climbing walls, Erenzo and Mills were able to pull some scaffolding anchors from the soil with their bare hands. In shock, Erenzo contacted the site's construction engineers, and then sent all the walls' installation specifications and construction blueprints to manufacturer Entre-Prises for independent analysis.

Erenzo's concerns were validated; Entre-Prises determined that the foundation and the original calculations were unsafe for climbing wall scaffolding and support. The company recommended that Erenzo instead utilize immense concrete Jersey barriers to anchor the climbing walls. The heavy Jersey barriers, normally used to divide traffic on highways, ended up working as improvised solutions to the Newport site's foundational complications. But the whole process not only strained Erenzo's relationship with some ESPN executives, it in turn jeopardized the contract that he had signed for overseeing additional years' events.

Once the Newport site was declared safe and ready, and in order to give the climbing disciplines of the Extreme Games the formal World Cup spirit that ESPN wanted, Erenzo arranged for an esteemed panel of international judges to be the mediators for the ensuing competition. One of the judges, Sasha Akalski, was from Bulgaria, and had previously presided over a historic open international competition in Grenoble, France, in November 1987—the first use of the UIAA's official rules for competitive climbing. Akalski had also judged World Cup events and served as Jury President for both the Canadian Open National Championships and the American National Championships in the years preceding the Extreme Games. Having worked in a number of countries and dealt with an assortment of climbing organizational bodies, Akalski gave some international credibility to offset the Extreme Games' recreational rudiments.

Adding esteem to the event was Ivor Delafield, acting president of a technical commission that the UIAA had created to oversee international competitions. He would be present to observe the separate disciplines. Veteran judges Rick Orr and Doug Carson were also brought in to arbitrate the Extreme Games' climbing. Lynn Hill, who had won numerous large-scale competitions in years prior and had since become an American climbing icon, was even hired to be a color commentator; Hill also provided suggestions about camera angles and positioning to the ESPN crew that was tasked with filming all the dramatic climbing. And in order to create an extraordinarily strong roster of contemporary competitors, invitations to participate in the games were sent to the top six individuals in the ASCF's rankings, along with two "wild card" invitations.

The scrupulous preparations that Erenzo, the construction crew, and the judges put toward making the climbing portion of the Extreme Games a success was mirrored by substantial funding that ESPN executives pumped into the gathering itself. By the time the Extreme Games officially kicked off in a haze of summer heat on June 24, 1995, production costs for the massive gathering had reached nearly $10 million. All efforts and investments paid off: over the event's multiday period, the crowd of onlookers in Newport, primarily those of Generation X and younger, was estimated at 200,000.

Though certain sports were not affected by Rhode Island's extreme summer humidity, the moisture off the ocean quickly proved problematic for climbers trying at all costs to keep their hands dry and their grip firm on the walls' holds. Routesetters Tony Yaniro and Mike Pont even employed a hairdryer in between competitors' heats at one point—a desperate stab at trying to dry any moisture that had collected on the handholds. Years later, Pont would recall ascending the climbing wall in a mechanical lift with Yaniro and "pulling out whatever tricks we could come up with." Pont would explain, "We were up there poofing holds with chalk balls and grinding chalk into the holds—and then brushing them off and retapping them with chalk. We were probably 100 [or] 200 feet from the Atlantic Ocean, so there was also mist in the morning from being so close to the ocean. It was bad."

Despite the persistent heat and uncomfortable mugginess, the Difficulty and Speed portions progressed as intriguing continuations of the rivalries that had been established in other competitions the previous year. Robyn Erbesfield continued her competition supremacy by winning the women's Difficulty discipline, with Russia's Elena Ovchinnikova taking second place and Mia Axon placing third. The men's Difficulty event, on the other hand, was steered solely by international competitors, with Ian Vickers of Great Britain taking first place by a slim point margin of 0.6, and French brothers Arnaud and Francois Petit placing second and third, respectively.

In a way, the dominance of men from Europe echoed the inaugural Snowbird competition that Jeff Lowe had formulated with Dick Bass in 1988—at which France had claimed the whole podium. In another sense, continuing the status quo from competitions of years earlier bolstered the importance of Chris Sharma, Tommy Caldwell, and other young American men who were suddenly rising through the competition ranks by the mid-1990s. In fact, the same year as the Extreme Games, Caldwell, as something of a dark-horse wunderkind, wowed the crowd at the annual Snowbird competition by topping all the routes.

The steady resurgence of competition climbing's popularity in the United States, both for spectators and climbers, was contingent on a resurgence of homegrown stars—young as they were—to provide iconography and personality to the sport, too.

Still, the men's Difficulty podium at the Extreme Games lacked the American cachet and verve that the women's Difficulty possessed. An addendum to this, however, was the Speed podium. Although Ovchinnikova won the women's event, the men's event was won by an American—Hans Florine, who had ruled speed climbing competitions in the United States almost without exception since the days of Lowe's Sport Climbing Championships circuit. At the Extreme Games, Florine impressed the crowd with his "signature double dyno move," lunging upward on the wall, through several movements with seeming fluidity and a perfect degree of showmanship.

By all measures, ESPN's first big festival-style gamble into the realm of niche adventure sports paid off and continued to be marketable in the pop-culture mainstream for the remainder of 1995. Although the Extreme Games didn't anoint a young, fresh-faced American man as competition climbing's new king in the manner of that summer's Nationals at Mission Cliffs, the games received full coverage on ESPN's various channels, recaps in niche magazines continuing into the fall, and a soundtrack CD featuring "music from the Extreme Games," titled *You Ready for This?* A PlayStation video game, *ESPN Extreme Games*, was even released in September 1995. In a *New York Times* article titled "Most Exciting Part of Extreme Games Is Extreme Coverage," Richard Sandomir specifically commended the events' unconventional camerawork.[12]

Beyond the technical innovation and ancillary commodification, the Extreme Games were also praised for successfully blending various recreational subcultures—climbing's unique breed among them—that were otherwise proudly free from being pigeonholed or corporatized. Sasha Akalski would recall of the Extreme Games' sociality and impact on climbing:

> It was great exposure for the sport. It was fun to mingle
> with the other athletes from different sports. It was a

---

12. The article lightheartedly notes, "But in virtually every technical way, ESPN and ESPN2 were excellent, using every camera possible—on helmets, courses, walls, toes, eyelashes, nostrils, and toenails—to enliven the events."

success, for sure. It was apparent that competition climbing was safer than the other extreme sports presented. I
saw other athletes from different sports getting hurt on
a daily basis. Every morning at breakfast, I saw a new
athlete with a cast.

ESPN's Extreme Games was not initially guaranteed to be an
annual endeavor, but its success in 1995 resulted in speedy plans
within the network offices to hold a similar gathering in 1996, as well.
Erenzo was the logical choice for managing the climbing portion
of the impending 1996 competition too, having originally signed a
four-year contract with the network. However, several months into
preparations for the next Extreme Games, Erenzo received word that
ESPN was canceling his contract. To Erenzo's surprise, the disagree-
ment over the scaffolding site in preparation for the 1995 games
had ballooned into a lawsuit. Erenzo eventually countersued and
won, but the legal tangle would not be resolved in time for him to
organize the climbing portion of the 1996 gathering.

As a replacement, and at the recommendation of Alison Osius,
ESPN turned to Jim Waugh to organize and manage the Extreme
Games for 1996, which was eventually rebranded as the X Games.
Waugh was still enmeshed in the duties of recurrently organiz-
ing the Phoenix Bouldering Contest (PBC) at the time of his hir-
ing, but his attachment to ESPN—and the network's targeting of
Generation X—was appropriate given the steadily increasing num-
ber of younger competitors participating in his annual competi-
tions in Arizona. For instance, taking second place behind winner
Timy Fairfield at Waugh's PBC in 1995 had been youngster Tommy
Caldwell. And nearly 50 of the competitors at that year's contest
had been under the age of 20. Chris Sharma would participate in

the PBC the following year and claim the first-place prize. Caldwell would again place second.

As a suitable creative force and technical director for 1996's X Games II, as ESPN's gathering was now labeled, Waugh somewhat followed the methodology that Erenzo had formulated and established in the organizer role the year before. This included the balancing act of taking directives from ESPN's non-climber executives and also devising the competition in his own style. But Waugh also believed strongly in experimentation, particularly when repackaging climbing for the purpose of a television broadcast. "The whole format wasn't thought out for TV," he would say about climbing's earliest iteration in the X Games. "If you look, every sport that has had any modicum of success on TV has had to alter their sport in some way. And that's just the nature of it: if you want corporate sponsorship, you've got to be on TV."

To that end, Waugh pitched a number of ways to evolve competition climbing as entertainment in the X Games' flashy style. His ideas included adding speed climbing relays, and varying the length and routes of the speed climbing wall. Such ideas, inventive as they were, proved to be difficult sells for ESPN executives reluctant to stray too far from the previous year's format.

Another addition that Waugh considered was a bouldering discipline. He knew that the television executives considered the climbing wall to be the flagship; the wall could be framed grandly in the backdrop of camera shots, and it could also be plastered with sponsors' logos. In contrast to the quick speed climbing heats that were over in mere seconds, bouldering—at times slow and methodical as it was—would allow for longer camera shots on the impressive wall faces. Bouldering could also be made visually exciting in a unique way with the competitors falling into big foam pits. But again, the executives had no interest in adding a new discipline, particularly one that would deviate from the roped events' staging. "Bouldering was, in a lot of ways, even more complicated to explain on TV than the Difficulty [portion]," Waugh would say. "At least with Difficulty, it's whoever gets the highest wins. With bouldering, it required a leaderboard: Who's in the lead after route one? Who's in the lead after route two? Who's in the lead after route three?"[13]

Like the preceding event, X Games II was scheduled to be held in Rhode Island, at the Newport Yachting Center, at the end of June. On the international palette, this meant the event would be perfectly situated in between other prestigious climbing events—preceded by the European Championships in the winter, and followed by the UIAA Masters in Serre Chevalier, France, in the summer and a World Cup competition in Slovenia in the fall.

Mike Pont and Tony Yaniro were again hired as the routesetters for X Games II. Robyn Erbesfield was chosen to set routes, as well, instead of participating as a competitor. It was a significant change for Erbesfield, who was by this time the most decorated American in the history of the World Cup circuit. Now married to Didier Raboutou, Erbesfield had undergone multiple carpal tunnel surgeries and had expressed a desire to travel the world leisurely and pursue climbing projects outdoors, free from the competition grind. She and Raboutou had also recently constructed a large training and dormitory-like section of their home for coaching students. While

---

13. Waugh was given the chance to organize a bouldering portion years later at a subsequent X Games. The extravaganza had since moved to San Francisco, and ESPN executives had all but given up on trying to package climbing in the X Games mold by that time. Waugh would recall: "In the end, [the executives] said they were going to drop [climbing]. I said, 'Please, give me one more go—let's try bouldering.' And they did, they gave me one go with bouldering. But the truth of it was, [climbing] was in a revolving door on its way out."

her commentary at X Games II would not mark the formal end of her competition career, it was evident by the mid-1990s that Erbesfield and Raboutou had their sights set on roles beyond competing. In an interview at the time, Erbesfield stated prophetically, "Today, I don't have a lot of time for teaching, but when I stop competing myself, I will certainly invest in the others."

Although backed by such an experienced crew, Waugh encountered his own share of headaches in matters of event preparation. One of the main areas of contention with ESPN executives involved legitimizing the event on the international circuit while also presenting it compactly on television. Waugh would later explain: "If you're having a sanction-like World Cup event, you're required to have an Open [category]—a qualifier. But to hold a whole other day and facilitate that is a massive amount of money, and ESPN was thinking, quite frankly, 'Why do we need to pay this?' So the theory was: we'll just put more of that money into the prize purse and encourage people to come for that reason. What we did is we had to start listing it on the [IFSC's event] calendar with the help of Marco Scolaris and other people who were the leadership of IFSC at that time, with the idea of trying not to get other events close to it—because [international competitors] were always going to go to World Cups before they would come to the X Games."

The disagreements about whether or not to sanction the climbing portion illustrated the breadth of understanding and expertise that Waugh brought to ESPN's alternative sports marvel. And the climbing portion that Waugh eventually brought to fruition for X Games II proved to be successful—as Erenzo's had been the previous year. The men's Difficulty discipline for 1996's X Games II was won by France's Arnaud Petit, who had finished in second place in 1995.

Hans Florine won the men's speed climbing event again, and France's Cécile Le Flem won the women's speed climbing segment.

The most significant news by the climbing's end was about American teenager Katie Brown, who won the women's Difficulty portion by besting two of France's top stars of 1996, Laurence Guyon and Liv Sansoz, on a finals route rated 5.13a. Guyon had been a silver medalist at the World Championships in Geneva, Switzerland, the year before; Sansoz had earned the bronze medal at those same World Championships and was the 1996 European Champion. Those important anecdotes raised the profile of Brown's victory at X Games II even more; Brown had not simply won, she had won by beating two French climbers who were unequivocally among the best in the world.

Without necessarily intending to, X Games II played a role in pushing American climbers back into the European fray, particularly by inviting so many European climbers to come to the United States to take part. The victories by Brown and Florine reasserted the notion that Americans could compete and win on the biggest stage. Yet, behind the competitors from all the countries was a jumble of bureaucracy, national affiliations, and governing bodies exercising varying levels of authority. A later recap in *Rock and Ice* would proclaim that ESPN created "the most important climbing competition in North America," while "major competitions elsewhere in the world are floundering."

CHAPTER 12

AROUND THE WORLD

———

ESPN'S EFFORTS TO CAPITALIZE ON THE POPULARITY of "extreme" sport and recreation niches resulted in the undeniable highlighting of a new, younger generation in competition climbing. The remainder of 1996 proved that Katie Brown's stirring victory at X Games II and Chris Sharma's meteoric rise to the top of the competition climbing ranks were not flukes.

In fact, Brown's performance for ESPN viewers in June 1996 earned her a last-minute invitation to the World Masters at Arco, Italy, that September. The European competition had direct ties to the SportRoccia competition from 1986 and, like the Extreme Games and X Games II, drew some of the best international competitors, such as Liv Sansoz, Stephanie Bodet, and Cecile Le Flem of France, as well as two of the best female Italian climbers of the 1990s, Luisa Iovane and Rafaelle Valsecchi. Elena Ovchinnikova was also present for the World Masters, although she had relocated to the United States by this point and was thus competing as an American on the European competition circuit.

At Arco, in front of a vociferous crowd of European onlookers, Brown cruised through an early onsight round and found herself neck-and-neck with her X Games II rival, Sansoz, in the scores by the event's last day. Energized by the narrow margin, Brown rallied and bested Sansoz's highpoint by several feet in a rousing superfinal round. Brown fell only two moves from the wall's top in a performance that observers at the time labeled a "tour de force." The resultant buzz around Brown, the teenage American phenom who had now beaten Europe's top professionals at multiple competitions, became so expansive in climbing media throughout the fall that *Climbing* even ran an interview with her father at one point.

Not only did Brown's composure and resolve at the World Masters—one of most famous and time-honored competitions—mark her first victory abroad, it also underscored a shifting paradigm for the American contingent back in her home country; Brown was only 15 years old at the time of her win at Arco and not allowed to take part in World Cup events given the UIAA's 16-year-old age minimum. As a result, the climbing community, particularly in the United States, adjusted to a new reality: many of the best American climbers were now kids rather than experienced veterans who had cut their teeth as vagabonding dirtbags, acquired wisdom after years of trial and error, and then migrated to the competition scene. If the results of those recent high-profile events in the United States had not affirmed such evolution, Brown's masterful performance overseas at the World Masters certainly did. Not surprisingly, climbing classes at facilities around the United States started offering lessons aimed specifically at kids and teenagers. Several gyms started advertising "Great Youth Programs."

Sharma, too, continued a publicity blaze in an unwavering continuation of the hype that had first manifested following his victories at SolidRock's Junior Nationals and Mission Cliff's Nationals the year before.

In August 1996, Sharma again won in his age group at a Junior National Championship in Seattle, Washington. Held at Vertical World, the historic gym formerly known as Vertical Club, and sponsored by Clif Bar, these Junior Nationals featured a collection of difficult qualifying, semifinal, and final round sequences from routesetters Mike Pont and Marc Bourdon. The routes ranged from long traverses to extensive ascents that culminated in overhanging roof sections. Sharma was the only competitor in his age category to flash the boys' finals route, but the event also showcased a compelling close contest between youngsters Beth Rodden and Kathryn Embacher, both just a year older than Sharma, in the girls' division.

Just five days after the end of those Junior Nationals, Sharma, Rodden, and Embacher traveled to Canada to compete in the Continental Sport Climbing Championships as part of a family-fun festival that lasted for more than two weeks. Unlike the climbing events of X Games II, which had been observed by UIAA representatives but ultimately hosted by ESPN, the Continental Sport Climbing Championships in Canada were officially sanctioned by the UIAA. Pont and Bourdon, also fresh from Seattle's Junior Nationals, set the routes for the competition, which saw a surprising abundance of flashes in the qualifying and semifinal rounds. The final round, held on a wall at Vancouver's expansive Pacific National Exhibition grounds on September 1, drew nearly 1,000 spectators and became another showcase of Sharma's raw talent. He was the only competitor to flash the men's route. American Mia Axon, who had also made the trip north to participate in the competition, won in the women's division with the sole flash, while Embacher placed fourth and Rodden fifth.

It was not just the undeniable talent of Rodden, Sharma, and others in the new group of youngsters that was leaving an impression on the competition community. The juniors brought with them noticeable optimism—perhaps through youthful naiveté—to a degree that was unprecedented in the United States at the competitive level. Comparing his own generation with the younger newcomers, Pont would say: "The kids of that generation—Beth Rodden and Tommy Caldwell and Chris Sharma—were all very supportive of each other. They had a positive outlook on the way the sport was developing. We hadn't had that. In our generation, nobody had really ever believed [climbing] was going to be a successful sport because we witnessed firsthand a rise and fall. We based how we perceived the future on what we had seen happen: eventually we were all going to be living in a tent at a climbing area in a campground, and cowering under the overhang of a cliff to go try to climb something for our own reasons—so we ought to just live it up while we can. That had been our outlook."

The changing faces and evolving outlooks of the sport in the mid-1990s were representative of changes that were happening behind the scenes as well. Many governing forces that had influenced competitions on a national and international level began to advance with the changing athlete culture. For example, a year after the UIAA sanctioned the Continental Sport Climbing Championships in Canada, the organization officially formed the International Council for Competition Climbing (ICCC). Although less formalized commissions for handling competition matters around the world had existed for years, the formal establishment of the ICCC signified the global popularity of climbing competitions at the time.

The existence of the new ICCC ensured that there would be continued efforts to evolve and expand the competition climbing concept into new markets. In an immediate sense, one such evolution was a rise in bouldering-only competitions internationally. "Bouldering competitions have become as popular as baguettes and brie in France," *Climbing* declared in 1996, recapping an event in Val d'Isère, France, that was won by Liv Sansoz and Francois Petit. But the creation of the ICCC also reignited notions about climbing's potential for inclusion in an Olympics.

In the United States, as well, structural changes were afoot. For many years, Ralph Erenzo had served as the Executive Director of the United States' domestic governing body, the ASCF. As the head of the ASCF, Erenzo's duties had largely entailed the logistics of organizing competitions—like those at SolidRock and Mission Cliffs—at the numerous gyms around the country. In fact, the ASCF, which had first incubated as a passion project for Erenzo and Peter Darmi, owed its own formalization to work that Erenzo had done (with the help of American Alpine Club board member Bill Putnam) to petition and collect $35,000 in start-up funds from American Alpine Club board members in 1990. Those funds had stimulated the ASCF's creation and provided foundational capital for some of the major American competitions in the ensuing years.

By the mid-1990s, Erenzo was also acting as the American Alpine Club's delegate to the ICCC as American youngsters like Brown and Sharma were making headlines at competitions around the world. As such, Erenzo was the managerial bridge between the United States competition climbing scene and that of Europe. He was tasked with garnering funds for climbers from the United States who wanted to participate abroad—which could include everything from providing climbers' airfare and hotel accommodations to transportation and competition entry fees for those American competitors traveling around the European countries.

As necessary and well-intending as the objective was, it proved over time to be largely a futile effort—and beyond Erenzo's control. The American Alpine Club was more aligned with mountaineering than competition climbing; the club rarely approved or accepted financial requests for competitors' funding, even with such a new crop of talented and promising adolescent Americans emerging as dominant competitors. The result was that competitors from the United States, often young and not wealthy, were responsible for paying their own way to Europe if they wished to participate in international competitions. This individual-centric model stood in glaring contrast to Europe's, which saw countries' climbing federations sponsoring entire teams of competitors. The United States technically had a national climbing team, but the team was never able to acquire ample funding on a collective scale. European federations had far greater membership numbers than any of the climbing organizations in the United States—including the ASCF—and thus the European federations had far greater monetary resources.

The complex financial issues increasingly created rifts between the American competitors and the American executives. The competitors, knowing the European model and also akin to unions in other American professional sports, hoped that the ASCF would provide substantial subsidy for the whole lifestyle of being a competitive climber: insurance and benefits, as well as possible retirement assistance, in addition to international travel fare. When the reality hit that neither the ASCF nor the American Alpine Club was able to provide such amenities in full, questions arose about whether entire structural changes were necessary.

The tension also resulted in significant moves. Some American climbers like Robyn Erbesfield and Timy Fairfield had opted not only to train in Europe but to live there as well. And often these relocations meant training with European—and particularly French—teams, hiring French coaches, boarding with French climbing clubs, and benefiting from France's substantial athletic infrastructure.

For those Americans willing to live abroad, the global strategy resulted in positive competition placement. In addition to Erbesfield's consistent success on the World Cup circuit, Fairfield, as an expat, took part in more than 100 international competitions; at the aforementioned bouldering contest in Val d'Isère, he placed ninth, and the year before that, he won a speed climbing event at a World Cup stop in Birmingham, England. Two years later, he won a bouldering World Cup competition in Clamecy, France.

In fact, Fairfield's rise to prominence on the international scene occurred at a time when competition climbing benefited greatly from his charismatic persona and undeniable physical gifts. He was an all-around athlete, having first found success as an adolescent in soccer, gymnastics, and ski racing before climbing. And, in many ways, he was a product of a previous era's mentorship, coached by famed climber and routesetter Tony Yaniro as well as competitive gymnast Rob Candelaria. Candelaria had opened the first commercial climbing gym in Boulder, Colorado, called the Colorado Athletic Training School (and colloquially known as CATS), in 1988. This further connected Fairfield to the American competition lineage.

But Fairfield was refreshingly far from the status quo—and the previous era. Raised by a liberal-thinking father from California and a no-nonsense New Yorker mother from the South Bronx, he had traveled the world at a young age, experienced different cultures and countercultures by the time he was a teenager, learned foreign languages and diverse customs, and embraced a nonconformist mind-set that he found in punk rock and avant-garde art around the world. When he applied the same freethinking principles to his competition climbing, there was a realization that the best competitors and the best sponsorship opportunities still existed overseas, despite all of the United States' competition progress. Fairfield's determination to train abroad for the long term was also influenced by his background in soccer, a sport where American players frequently moved to Europe to get better and gain exposure to the world's elite.

The decision to live in Europe—mostly in France—for five years made Fairfield an outsider and an anti-hero to his American fan base, particularly as he captained the ASCF's national team. Furthermore, to Fairfield, competition climbing was the most rebellious form of climbing because it was still derided by some climbers of an older generation, those who considered traditional climbing on real rock to be the righteous discipline.

It all added to Fairfield's anti-hero aura. Furthermore, he was never afraid to speak his mind and express a preference for globalism over nationalism; he would later explain that he never considered nationality to be relevant to athletic performance—particularly in an individual international sport like competition climbing. At times, this unique ethos meant removing the American flag from his jersey at events; at other times—such as a World Championships in Geneva, Switzerland—it meant refusing to be the American flag bearer at the competition's opening ceremony. These choices inevitably forced Fairfield to endure accusations of being un-American, but he never saw it that way. "I suppose that for an aspiring archetypal angst-driven Gen-X, punk-rock, action-sports athlete like myself, such actions symbolized a method of transcendence typified by an informed counter-cultural abandonment of our inherently nationalistic myopia and dogma," he would later reflect. "I viewed such relinquishment as a mandatory rite of passage enabling the invigoration of the type of convicted self-reliance conducive to abandoning imposed constraints, cultivating the right mentality, embracing the unknown, exercising free will, adopting a more sophisticated training ethos and developing an expressively personalized style necessary to thrive at the world level. But from the existential standpoint, I was probably just going for effect."

Any nonconformity on Fairfield's part became a feature that the European media increasingly picked up on as a captivating statement of American culture at its finest: America was rebellious; America was punk rock. And Fairfield, as a competitor, epitomized that. "I wasn't competing with a telos of manifest destiny or pro-American ideologic proliferation at the forefront of my motives," he would expound. "I participated in the sport internationally as a means of becoming a more well traveled, cultured, informed and compassionate human being—global citizen, a member of the bigger family. Nothing against the Old Empire, but you can't achieve those types of personal growth staying at home celebrating freedom—you have to go exercise it by seeing the world."

As Fairfield continued to move up the national and international rankings while living abroad, he also tried out new training programs. He fashioned intense workouts that were a result of his drills with the best French athletes, as well as his own background in multiple sports that possessed more robust training programs than climbing did at the time. His climbing became so refined, and the movement in competitions so fluid, that Fairfield earned compliments from Patrick Edlinger and other competitors in France's venerated professional climbing scene. In fact, the legacy of Fairfield's generation of American competitors gradually became one of embracing more intense training programs than those exercise regimens of previous American generations. Fairfield and others took climbing fitness to greater systematic and physically demanding levels than ever before, largely aided by their immersion in European climbing circles.

But moving overseas and training with foreign teams was not the chosen course for most American competitors, nor was it reflective of the fact that public interest in competition climbing was healthy in the United States in the mid-1990s—even if funding for the best American competitors was minimal. For example, events that catered to specific markets were more prevalent than ever, including a women-only competition, the Rock Goddess Master Plastic Pull, held in Beaverton, Oregon. The Gay Games in New York City, an annual multisport spectacle supporting sexual diversity, also featured a climbing competition. The University of Montana held a fundraising competition, Climb for Cancer, and Stone Gardens Climbing Gym in Seattle, Washington, held a Northern Exposure Climbing Festival.

Tangential to the modest competitions, Bobbi Bensman embarked on a slideshow tour around the American Southeast in 1996 discussing her climbing career. Sponsored by *Climbing*, Pearl Izumi, and La Sportiva, Bensman's mini-circuit included a speaking presentation and Q&A session at equipment shops and gyms in Nashville, Tennessee; Birmingham, Alabama; Charlotte, North Carolina; and elsewhere.

At the same time, the gym industry continued to thrive around the country, aided by the mild celebrity of climbers such as Bensman, Christian Griffith, and others who involved themselves with gyms in speaking capacities, as wall designers or as facility employees.

CityRock, in Emeryville, California, was one of the gyms using specific names in its advertising at this time. One classified read: "Become a better climber with our expert staff including Dave Altman, Zoe Bundros, Jeff Follett, Scott Frye, Peter Mayfield, Mike Papciak, Christian Santelices, Steve Schneider & Abby Watkins."

Indoor climbing was permeating new city markets as well, a progression that traced back to early Berkeley and Oakland roots and the methodology of providing climbing to a clientele that did not have easy access to the outdoors. The ASCF had held a massive National Championship in the Hunter Mountain ski resort, north of New York City, in 1993, and within a few years, New York had its own vibrant gym scene. Ralph Erenzo repurposed the walls from 1995's Extreme Games and opened his own gym, ExtraVertical Climbing Center, at the intersection of 62nd Street and Broadway in Manhattan, in May of 1997. There also existed a 20-foot-tall wall at the Manhattan Plaza Health Club on 43rd Street, just west of the tourism hub of Times Square. Nearby, East Brunswick, New Jersey, also featured a gym, Up the Wall, with climbing walls that were even taller than those in New York City.

Other states that had never before had gyms also saw the opening of new facilities—Climb Time in Indiana, GAR Indoor Climbing Center in Illinois, Vertical Endeavors in Minnesota, Rocks and Ropes in Nevada, Cleveland Rock Gym in Ohio, Vertical Edge in North Carolina, and Dyno-Rock in Texas, to name a few. Costco's immense Sportsnation in Portland, Oregon, featured an array of climbable arches and caves within a large fitness facility that even boasted a restaurant. Urban Krag in Dayton, Ohio, was created out of the remnants of a 100-year-old church.

A significant addendum to the many city gyms being developed was the destruction of a particularly popular facility. In September,

1995, Clipper City Rocky Gym in Baltimore, Maryland, burned to the ground during an industrial park fire that killed one firefighter and injured more than a dozen others. The gym's owner, Jim Ellis, vowed to rebuild following the blaze, and a local high school held a Climb-A-Thon fundraiser in the ensuing weeks. The huge fire and the loss of a life, as well as the unexpected ruin of the gym's extravagant climbing walls, were among the first widely known tragedies related to the competition scene and specifically the facilities that accommodated climbers. They would not be the last.

With more gyms came increased specification in the realm of artificial handholds and footholds. New companies arose that manufactured the sculpted, ergonomic resin holds, which were quickly becoming preferred over real rocks that could be bolted onto indoor walls. Handholds made of carved wood and fired clay also became less common as the polyester resin handholds with flat edges and smooth globule forms grew in popularity. The newer resin handholds, often shaped from foam molds, were not as sharp or jagged as handholds of the past, and their surfaces were less harsh on climbers' skin.

Brands like Groperz, Nicros, and Franklin Climbing Equipment (started by longtime competitor Scott Franklin) started offering handholds in a wide variety of bright colors. Several Franklin Climbing Equipment holds in unique shapes, such as bulbous honeycombs and thick bowls—nicknamed "urinals" by competitors—became instantly identifiable on climbing walls because of their large size and swirling color designs. Training tools known as hangboards, large sculpted plates that featured multiple grooves and holds for finger-strength training, were more prevalent than ever on gym walls too.

Advertisements appeared in climbing magazines from one company, Exposed Heights, for an instructional video, *How To Make Your Own Climbing Holds*. Stone Holds, a manufacturer based in Denver, Colorado, launched a "monthly hold club" for gyms and also released a popular gargoyle-shaped line of holds. Boulder-based Straight Up was remarkably prolific as well and advertised the release of "ten new designs every month."

Expert hold shapers became more common, as did signature series of handholds branded with the names of elite routesetters and climbers. Bozeman, Montana–based Radholds featured a collection of holds by Steve Schneider. Radwall released a set of holds called the Radicals Crux series, designed by John Yablonski. Vertical Concepts released a Mike Beck Collection. Entre-Prises released its own symmetrical set, the Lynn Hill Holds. A Canadian company, Silhouette Climbing Systems, released Yaniro Powerholds that were designed by Tony Yaniro.

Some of the handholds that would prove most influential were offered by Climb It. The company released a set of pockets, jugs, and spherical slopers collectively called Jim Karn Monster Holds. But Climb It also released a set of small and medium-sized red handholds called the Mike Pont Bloodlines, with a goal of making the Bloodlines dissimilar to Karn's set and the standard shapes of the period. "Where [Karn's] holds were very simple and sleek, and perfected in a very Jim Karn kind of way—very correct shapes—mine were much different than that," remembers Pont. "They were flowy and sort of the way a routesetter now makes holds, [for example], 'This hold is designed to be a left hand thumb catch side pull.'"

The ergonomics and situational design of Pont's Bloodlines indicated how gym climbing and its components were on the cusp of a sea change. The abundance of handhold collections and increasing

specificity in handhold shaping prompted evolutions in routesetting as well. The various handhold designs that were available by
1997 were vastly different from what had been on the market just
a few years prior, and this only furthered competition climbing as
a unique discipline that was utterly different from its physiological
cousin, outdoors climbing. In an interview with *Climbing* from the
period about routesetting for competitions, Pont said, "You have
to find the gym's strongest lines and most visually appealing features, and work with them. Also, you have to be in tune with the
strengths and abilities of the climbers who compete. That's harder
than it sounds. It comes from the experience of working and climbing with the stronger competitors. Another thing I concentrate on
is the continuity of individual routes. I like to make them very
constant, either slowly increasing in difficulty or maintaining difficulty throughout the entire route."

Increasing technicality in routesetting also encouraged the development of a necessary skillset among competition climbers: being
able to quickly—properly—read a route given in the brief amount
of time that was typically allotted for route "previewing" at an event.
It was a subject so relevant that Yaniro was even invited to write
detailed pieces on route-reading for publications at the time. In one
such instructional article, he advised:

> Read the route as you will encounter it during the climb:
> one piece at a time. Later you can develop a more refined
> strategy. Imagine yourself grabbing the starting hold and
> taking a deep relaxed breath. Then smoothly proceed
> upward hold by hold, move by move, really feeling and
> visualizing the moves—even twisting your body and climb-
> ing 'in the air' with your hands and feet.

According to Yaniro, one of the biggest theoretical differences in competition-style sequences of the era compared with routes outdoors was the preferred absence of a particularly difficult section, commonly known as the crux. While routes on real rock in the outdoors typically featured a distinct crux at some point in the climber's ascent, having such an isolated difficult section in a competition route could lead to stalemates in the scoring. "In general, the routesetter tries to make a route without cruxes because the goal of the route is to separate the falling points of the climbers; he doesn't want bottlenecks," Yaniro wrote at the time.

The evolution of routesetting and the continued profusion of gyms created the perfect environment for new competition formats to gestate. Although not totally evident at the time, the ever-expanding youth movement was creating a mass of new competition fans and competitors who were eager to rally around a concept that they felt was their own. All the while, ESPN was continuing to showcase a new generation of competitors. Erenzo returned for 1997's X Games III, which were held in San Diego, California, and marked by a repeat victory for Katie Brown in the women's Difficulty discipline and a third-place finish for Chris Sharma in the men's Difficulty division.[14]

For all its success with the extreme niche, however, ESPN executives had all but forsaken bouldering as a discipline, opting instead to feature roped climbing that allowed for bigger, more exciting falls on television. Conversely, the network's preference of roped climbing was adopted right at the time when bouldering was becoming a particularly popular discipline for young climbers around the United

---

14. The men's Difficulty discipline at X Games III was won by France's Francois LeGrand. Hans Florine won a separate men's speed climbing discipline; Elena Ovchinnikova won a separate women's speed climbing discipline.

States. This created an opening for a homegrown American climbing competition that focused solely on bouldering—and youth. In the process, it also set the stage for a complete restructuring of the United States' competition system, with all the various organizational components about to combust.

CHAPTER 13

THE KIDS ARE ALRIGHT

A MID CLIMBING'S YOUTH MOVEMENT, which had been most visible from a marketing perspective by the Extreme Games and fueled most consistently by annual ASCF Junior National Championships, came increased interest and influence by the parents of the many young competitors. At first a rather unconnected group, these parents of the climbers steadily became more familiar with one another given the frequency of youth competitions and the consistency with which the same kids seemed to be taking part in many of them. Soon a camaraderie developed, and with that arose a collective parental interest in just how the ASCF's youth competitions were being run—and whether any improvements could be made.

This shared curiosity materialized first as a nondescript meeting in one of Portland, Oregon's most popular pubs, the Blue Moon. There, among the swirl of subdued rock music and strong drinks from the bar one afternoon, a group of parents gathered around a well-worn table to analyze in earnest the ASCF's methodology as it regarded the kids' competitions being held in the mid-1990s.

Among this group at the pub was Jeanne Niemer, whose six-year-old daughter, Kate, had recently expressed an interest in competition climbing. Niemer already had significant organizational experience and was able to evaluate the pros and cons of any organization's processes with laser precision. In fact, she had previously founded her own climbing-centric organization, Sheclimbs, with a goal of connecting and supporting women around the country who were interested in getting involved in the sport. One of her goals with this meeting at the Blue Moon had similar objectives to those of starting Sheclimbs, but with a slant toward kids rather than adult women; essentially, Niemer wanted to figure out a way that parents could better connect and support each other as competition climbing evolved and gained prominence.

Also seated at the table was Matt Stevens, the climbing coach of Niemer's daughter and an important keystone between the young competitors and their concerned parents. Stevens knew Hans Florine. Florine had cemented himself as a competition climbing legend by winning the speed climbing discipline at the UIAA's first World Championships in Frankfurt, Germany, in 1991. He was also still in a leadership role at the ASCF. In fact, it was Florine who had helped an organizer from Pennsylvania, Randy Hart, put together the ASCF's first Junior National Championships nearly five years prior. Florine had consistently given funding to the ASCF's juniors' tier over the years and helped with ASCF's junior competition logistics. The thinking now was that perhaps Stevens could relay pertinent details of any discussion—and any decisions made—at the Blue Moon to Florine, who could then use the ideas to improve the ASCF's youth ventures.

Scott Rider, an employee at Vertical World in Seattle, Washington, was also present at the meeting at the Blue Moon. Broadly, Rider's presence represented the important role that climbing gyms were playing in the youth boom. Gyms such as Vertical World were not only the hosts of many youth competitions, they were also becoming the main source for introducing kids to the sport. On a practical level, Rider also possessed valuable experience related to the practicalities of hosting youth competitions. He had previously managed a facility in Eugene, Oregon, the Crux Rock Gym. There, he developed a youth climbing program from scratch. Such development included implementing youth training curricula, recruiting volunteer coaches, and advertising various youth-centric events. He had also come up with the idea of having several gyms around the Pacific Northwest host youth climbing competitions, as a way of giving the gyms—many of which were quite new—opportunities to showcase their unique construction.

And at the table of the Blue Moon was Robb Rodden, whose daughter Beth was quickly rising through the competitors' rankings and was already being heralded as one of the best young climbers that the United States had ever seen.

Although the pub provided a relaxed, lighthearted atmosphere, it quickly became evident in the discussion that everyone seemed to share a similar, impassioned concern about the ASCF: for all the good the organization had done to keep competition climbing alive for years after Jeff Lowe's circuit folded, the ASCF's focus had undeniably become the adult climbers who were part of the federation and participating in the various events at gyms around the United States. And those adult competitors of the ASCF, likely influenced by the success of the European climbing organizations, seemingly wanted to be *professional* climbers—or at least obtain some sort of career sustainability as climbers—in a mode comparable to that in Europe. As a result, in the minds of Niemer, Rodden, and the other parents, the ASCF's junior division had become something of an afterthought while the organization's adult division garnered large cash prizes, featured substantial gear raffles, and experienced significant prestige.

Most of the parents were not wholly against the idea of the adult competitors aiming for professional status through the ASCF, but they did not want an organization's support of kids—and the development of climbing at a youth level—to be lost as collateral damage in the sport's professional aspirations.

As the afternoon progressed at the pub, Niemer and the others realized that the best solution to the disconnect between the adult competitors and the youth competitors was to create a whole new organization that was focused on kids. This new organization would, in effect, replace the ASCF's junior program. Competitions could be run similarly to how the ASCF had run its Junior National Championships, but with regional coordinators around the country tasked with promoting and running local youth events.

It was a landmark idea, prescient because these regional coordinators would naturally be far more familiar with local youth competitions' rosters than any single national director—or federation—could be. And given the sport's growing popularity, it just made sense for any new organization to station personnel in various locales; the coordinators could act partly as community organizers when need be, but also as unofficial talent scouts of the local climbing scenes throughout the year. They would play a primary role in developing and fostering youth climbing wherever there were gyms willing to participate in the venture.

Also, this new youth organization could focus on the longstanding aspirations of having climbing someday included in the Olympics. While the Olympics might not have been an overt goal at first for Niemer and the others, its sportsmanship certainly was. The ASCF's pushes to professionalize the sport in the 1990s somewhat philosophically clashed with the amateur ethos. So, a fresh organization that was solely focused on kids would, by default, embrace amateurism—friendly and fair competition for the sake of competition.

By the time the motivated group emerged from the Blue Moon into the mauve Portland dusk, they had formulated a rough set of competition rules and a mental list of possible competition host gyms. They also possessed an optimism that their new organization could manage youth climbing, on the whole, better than it ever had been managed in the United States.

When Florine was notified within the next few days of the parents' intention to separate from the ASCF, he did not object or urge them to reconsider. It was an act of altruism on Florine's part that nodded back to climbing's communal roots, as he ultimately wanted the sport to be promoted as well as possible to all demographics. "Ultimately, I just was happy to let the juniors run free on their own since they had the energy, the people, and the participants to run with it," Florine would say of the ASCF's relinquishment of its youth tier. "The junior organizing people were kicking ass, and [the ASCF] could never pull such a thing together with adults because we didn't have the participation. Parents spend money on their kids, and we learned that quickly."

Florine gave his blessing to Niemer, Rodden, and the others, and with that, the Junior Competition Climbing Association (JCCA), as the parents' organization was deemed, was born.

Almost immediately, the ideas conjured up around the pub table were put into practice. Stevens, who had been the acting Director of the ASCF's Junior Division, stepped down from the role and the ASCF's Junior Division promptly dissolved. Rider then became the official director of the JCCA. A spare bedroom in Niemer's house in Tigard, a half hour outside of Portland, became the JCCA's official headquarters. A post office box was rented for official JCCA correspondence. A toll free number went directly to Rider's home. An irreverent advertising campaign that proclaimed "Old Farts Need Not Apply" was rolled out in publications. It heralded the JCCA's advent and solidified an ideology for American competition climbing that was now youthful and distinctive.

The first issue of *Junior News*, a quarterly newsletter of the JCCA, was mailed out in January 1997, announcing the organizational shift: "With the blessings of the Adult ASCF, we have created a more autonomous organization strictly for youth climbers, operating under the non-profit umbrella of the ASCF. As the 'official' junior arm of the ASCF, we will provide all sanctioning of Junior events to determine national ranking and selection of the Junior National Team to attend the Youth Worlds."

A JCCA database was developed to keep track of the competition scoring and the fluid rankings. A board of JCCA directors was established, composed of Niemer, Rodden, Stevens, and Rider, along with Jeff Burton, Dain Smoland, Lynn Bleiweiss-Sande, Chip Schlegel, and Rich Johnston. Johnston was the founder of Seattle's Vertical World, but more relevantly, he was involved in a tangential organization, the Climbing Gym Association (CGA). The connection to the nation-wide CGA provided the JCCA and its board of directors with instant credibility across the United States.

In time, the JCCA board expanded to include additional members, including Dorelle Peters, whose daughter was also a young competitor. Other subsequent board members hailed from as far away as Texas (Bob Broun) and Illinois (Dave Hudson). Hudson, in fact, served as the organization's first Midwest Regional Coordinator largely due to friendships he had already established with climbing gym owners in Michigan, Wisconsin, and his home of Chicago.

To cultivate the JCCA's growing network of other regional coordinators, Niemer made a point to reach out to parents and organizers all over the country. Some regions, particularly New England, had a significant number of climbing gyms, but the JCCA board knew that equally important for furthering the vibrant youth scene on a holistic level was to connect with regions that lacked facilities and resources. One of the organizers who took on a role as a regional coordinator, Debbie Gawrych, became the JCCA's National Volunteer Coordinator and was tasked with managing the regional volunteers for all events.

Still, the JCCA was not immediately accepted by the entire climbing community. Particularly skeptical of any deviation from the long-standing ASCF norms were some parents of youth competitors on the East Coast—far from the JCCA's Tigard base—who preferred that kids compete strictly for cash and gear prizes. In contrast to that model, the JCCA's main aim of simply "developing the sport" was just nebulous enough to be criticized.

Almost from the start, Niemer also found herself unexpectedly receiving angry and threatening letters from East Coast parents who hated the idea of the main youth organization now being based in a distant geographic corner of the country. The angry parents also disliked the JCCA's $25 annual membership, and feared that the JCCA, with its Portland roots, would eventually develop into an organization with Pacific Northwest favoritism and bias. It became Niemer's job to assuage any apprehension, while also listening to everyone's anxieties and piecing together a unique competition circuit with the board of directors.

Another matter, equally as important but drawing less contention from those outside of the greater Portland area, was to establish an aesthetic for this new youth organization. This included the creation of JCCA promotional materials, posters, brochures, and advertising copy that could be sent to climbing gyms around the country. An artist named Brenna White, contributing her skills as a volunteer like most of the people in the JCCA's inner circle, designed a logo that quickly became the universal symbol of American youth climbing: an orangutan-like figure, anthropomorphized with a tank top and chalkbag, scaling the interior of an emblematic triangle.

The JCCA's abundant visual presence helped ease the concerns of the East Coast parents over time. Niemer's constant communication was effective as well. Years later, she would remember, "It took about a year for [the skeptical parents] to come around—they just needed to see that we weren't trying to ruin their climbing lives, I think. I even got e-mails apologizing for their behavior once they saw that we were doing a pretty good job."

Adhering to the promise to hold events in disparate regions and promote youth climbing everywhere, the early JCCA circuits crisscrossed the country in a twisty path from one gym to another. Scott Rider even authored a handbook that was given to gyms, containing all the intricacies of hosting a competition. It answered basic questions ("What is Isolation?") and provided in-depth information such as guidelines for JCCA eligibility. Rider recalls, "Basically the goal was to create a document where, if you can read, you can host a youth competition. This had never been done before. No one had attempted to create a road map for gyms, to eliminate the barriers to entry and make it as turnkey as possible to get involved and host an event."

On June 6, 1997, AK Rock in Silverthorne, Colorado, hosted a JCCA local competition; the following weekend, a similar event was held at Jugheads in Birmingham, Alabama; the next weekend—on June 21—the host gym was Rok Haus in Lafayette, Louisiana, followed quickly by events in New Orleans and Houston, Texas. The JCCA's Regional Championship that year was held at Houston's Texas Rock Gym, with the National Championship being at Planet Rock in Pontiac, Michigan.

Amid the initial success, Scott Rider also wrote a comprehensive handbook for gyms about how to start youth teams. The handbook included important curricula and example team training drills. Coupled with the other handbook on hosting competitions, American competition climbing had raw materials for its systematic reconstruction as a result of the JCCA. "Some gyms were ahead of the curve, the right staff and expertise to build their own program, and some had already hosted events," Rider would recall. "But there were lots and lots of brand new gyms with no experience at all in setting this stuff up. By drawing on our experience coaching in the gym and running events, we tried to make it as easy as possible for any gym to start a youth team and host a local/regional event."

The following year saw similar variety in the JCCA's itinerary—local and regional competitions at gyms such as Roc Ltd., ClimbMax, and Vertical Edge in North Carolina, as well as Vertical Extremes in Pennsylvania and Stronghold Athletic Club in South Carolina, and a National Championship at Rock'n & Jam'n in Colorado.

The next year, even more gyms joined the JCCA's network, particularly Pyramid's Climbing Gym in Greensboro, North Carolina, and Get A Grip in Selinsgrove, Pennsylvania.

With each passing season, new climbing gyms emerged—and expressed an interest in joining the JCCA's regional whirl. At times a gym's desire to take part outweighed its ability to adequately host events. The day before one competition, Niemer showed up to find that the facility's climbing walls had not been finished. So, she and her daughter worked through the night putting handholds and footholds on the wall and setting up an adequate warmup area for the competitors.

Even when well-equipped for competition, gyms would sometimes not have enough routes set to accommodate all the competitors. Since most JCCA events were done in a redpoint format, meaning that the routes could be practiced and climbed repeatedly within a certain competition period, gyms would often have long lines of kids waiting anxiously to try certain routes when options were limited.

There were also issues with the spectators. Many of the host gyms were not used to accommodating the substantial crowds that the JCCA events began to draw. On one such occurrence of a gym exceeding its legal occupancy, the local fire department arrived to usher away a portion of the spectating crowd. But soon the firemen, themselves, became transfixed by the excitement of the competition that was taking place on the walls and amusingly stayed to watch a significant portion of the event.

From modest beginnings and such variation in host capabilities, the JCCA grew into its role as the chief custodian of youth climbing. Aiding this was the high quality of climbing that was being featured on a regular basis at the regional level and every summer at the National Championships. Among the most dominant JCCA competitors were Lisa Lage, who won nearly a dozen regional competitions in one season, and Beth Rodden, who went undefeated in her age group at national championships for three years in a row. Emily Harrington and Angie Payne also began their careers with impressive JCCA showings.

The foundation of all the climbing at the various events was the routesetting. However, like the gyms, the routes had their share of growing pains. In the beginning, it was not uncommon for some JCCA routesetters to overlook the important detail that they were setting for youths. Competitions' categories were separated into ages 11 & Under, 12–13, 14–15, 16–17, and 18–19, but capability miscalculations were frequently made given the varying growth rates of children. The results in competitions were handholds that were far too reachy and footholds that required uncomfortable leg extensions from the kids. On occasion, the young competitors would impress the crowd with their physical improvisation—doing the splits, planting a foot onto a hold that was high up at ear level, or dynamically jumping through multiple moves in a single route. Former JCCA competitor Kate McShane Urban (*née* Johnson) recalls not even being able to reach the starting holds of a route at one of her first JCCA National Championships. The organizers conferred and eventually allowed her to stand on a box to reach the holds.

As the routesetters became more aware of the differences in kids' body mechanics and more experienced routesetters from the ASCF also got involved in the JCCA, the sequencing of the holds on the wall and the rouesetting methodology improved. Tony Yaniro was brought in as the routesetter for most of the larger competitions. Mike Pont also contributed in the setting, as did Derek Waggoner, Kevin Branford, and Molly Beard. "We often had little time to set," recalls Beard, particularly of the JCCA's formative events. "We often worked stupid long hours for little or no pay. There were no lifts, no crews of more than five people, no color-coded routes, and not a lot of creative hold choices. There were also not nearly as many competitors, so grades were not as hard and the National was initially only two days versus the current four. Given these constraints, we recycled routes like crazy."

However, with more events came a further understanding of routesetting nuance. "Over time, many gyms had youth teams, which meant most gyms had at least a bare understanding of how to set for youth," Beard says of the way routesetting evolved with additional JCCA events. "This meant not only an improvement in the setting at locals but a rapid ability level increase across all categories. Events went from clear favorite-to-win situations to who-is-having-a-good-day. At the [national competitions], crew sizes increased to a consistent 6–8, and interns, while not official, were expected. Setting became much less dependent on recycling routes. We often would set finals, hide the routes behind tarps or banners, or disguise them but not use them, while qualis and semis were still recycled. We also had a much greater understanding of how the kids were sized and how they climbed. We could predict better about moves they would or would not do or skip, and technical abilities. Far from perfect, but the knowledge base was increasing and the events were more fair."

As the JCCA grew, so too did the community of young climbers that it was nurturing. In most regions, the competitors were a close-knit group. "My school friends were completely separate from the climbing scene, so it was a completely separate circle of people," recalls former JCCA competitor Zoe Mark (*née* Raab), who placed high at a number of events—including third place at a JCCA national championship. "It made competitions even more special because I would see friends and people who had become like family."

Families often traveled together and carpooled to practices and competitions. Naturally, this closeness—and the sheer abundance of kids—invited a wide array of shenanigans prompted by everything from boredom along long stretches of highway to childish rabble-rousing at the gyms.

Most of the time, the mischief was harmless. JCCA regional coordinators and event volunteers were constantly having to gently admonish kids who were caught swinging on unused ropes or climbing over the bouldering walls in climbing gyms' warmup sections. Gym vending machines had to be closely monitored, as the kids often hunted for candy and soda to break up any lulls in competition. It became a post-competition tradition for JCCA kids in one region to fill their mouths with as many M&Ms of a particular color that they could fit. And gyms' padded floor mats had to be constantly supervised so unsupervised competitors did not attempt overly ambitious acrobatic feats while waiting for their turns to climb.

But on more than one occasion, the tomfoolery got a little out of hand—particularly when kids traveled to events and stayed in hotels. Sometimes hotel staff would be alerted that the JCCA kids had playfully tossed the poolside furniture into the water. Prior to one particular competition, a group of young boys secretly poured laundry detergent into a hotel's courtyard fountain. The prank resulted in a fountain of overflowing bubbles, an angry hotel staff, and a substantial fine for the parents the next day.

Emily Varisco was a JCCA competitor who was on the Boulder Rock Club's climbing team in Colorado, taught by distinguished coaches Justen Sjong, Chris Wall, and Jim Redo. Varisco also had a private trainer—Michelle Hurni. Additionally, Varisco took part in a series of local competitions organized by Bryan Mallin at Paradise Rock Gym called the Denver Climbing League. The DCL, as this series was colloquially known, catered to middle school and high school students in the greater Denver area. The various events helped fashion a youth scene that was competitive but also friendly. "One thing that I really liked about it then was the fact that not many parents went to the World Cups, and if they did, they didn't travel with us," Varisco would recall. "The kids all had rooms together and the coaches ran things. I think this made for greater team unity and took some of the stress out of it."

Even with the occasional lively pranks from the kids and occasional overzealous parents, the early years of the JCCA were marked mostly by friendly competition atmospheres and tireless efforts by Niemer, Rodden, Rider, and Peters to successfully grow the sport of climbing. Each season ended with an in-depth assessment by the board of any official rules that needed to be modified or adjustments that needed to be made to the malleable organizational model.

On the competitors' side, kids started to train in more systematic and regimented ways than ever before. Kate McShane Urban recalls of her time as a JCCA competitor: "I had coaches from a pretty young age, initially as part of a local team and later a couple of folks who worked with me individually. I remember doing some periodization training, a lot of endurance in the fall and more strength training and harder routes closer to the summer competition season. We played a lot of games—add-on, elimination, and this diabolical thing my team coach came up with that was basically the climbing equivalent of running lines, picking an easy route and doing one move up, one move down, two moves up, two moves down, et cetera, until you'd climbed the entire route."

Despite the JCCA's modest origin—over drinks at a pub—its success increasingly positioned it as the chief body to preside over virtually all child and teenage climbers in the United States. Kids' competitions became systematized and well-regulated affairs. Gone at all levels and ages was that freewheeling ethos that had long epitomized the United States climbing competitions. But such formalization, particularly as the JCCA grew to include other board members and more competitors, left room for creative planners to emerge at the end of the 1990s that were not necessarily under to the ASCF or the JCCA umbrella.

With the competition network so aptly streamlined and buttoned up by the end of the twentieth century, the atmosphere was just right for organizational outliers to arrive on the scene, tout some alternatives, and really shake things up.

CHAPTER 14

BOULDERING BOOMS

I N MARCH OF 1997, just as the ASCF and JCCA were beginning to forge their own competition trajectories separate from one another, a Midwestern climber named Scott Rennak purchased a box of carpentry tools and started a handhold company, Crater Holds. Rennak's decision was spurred by the many other brands in place by the mid-1990s that had created a veritable market for artificial climbing holds. His founding of the company was a logical extension of the craftsmanship he was already deeply immersed in as a wood carver and resin shaper of pieces for his own attic climbing wall.

Crater Holds' success came slowly, but its founding set in motion a series of events that ultimately changed the aesthetic and direction of competition climbing in the United States.

Three months after he got his modest handhold company off the ground, Rennak scrounged up some money and acquired a bank loan to purchase Climb Time, a Cincinnati, Ohio–based climbing gym that was pugnaciously trying to find an identity in a region that lacked any mountain heritage and had only a very fringe climbing population. But what the Midwestern city, snuggled between Kentucky and Indiana, lacked in steep topography and alpinism, it made up for in metropolitan potential.

From the onset, Rennak, as the new owner, was able to use Climb Time's walls as a test space for innovative handhold concepts and grip ideas. The patrons who had long frequented the facility were removed enough from all preconceptions to be completely open-minded to Rennak's new shapes, styles, and materials. Handholds from other brands were utilized on the Climb Time walls over time as well, and so Rennak's gym quickly established itself as a stage for both the status quo and innovative ideas that were still percolating and not yet completely refined in the burgeoning industry of artificial-handhold creation.

In October 1997, just a few months after buying Climb Time, Rennak constructed a new bouldering wall in the gym. He smattered it with his new handholds, as well as holds from other shapers. To christen the new wall's completion and stage a grand opening–type ceremony to celebrate Climb Time's new identity, Rennak decided to host a bouldering competition for Cincinnati locals. Unlike the highly structured nature of the federation and association competitions that were popping up around the country as 1998 approached, Rennak's first bouldering competition at Climb Time was intentionally low-fi, a no-frills contest that was structurally unstructured. It ended up being so well-received by the Ohio climbing community that another bouldering competition was held a few months later in the same insouciant vein.

In many ways, Rennak's earliest bouldering events were analogous to the initial Phoenix Bouldering Contests that Jim Waugh had hosted in Arizona in the 1980s. As Rennak's ambition grew and his endeavors became more noticeable beyond just the Ohio niche, he would increasingly look at Waugh as a mentor—and the earliest Phoenix Bouldering Contests as models for his own—to steadily adopt a similar unperturbed operational philosophy for climbing competitions; the most important aspect was always that everyone should have a good time.

To that point, Rennak handled the earliest Climb Time bouldering contests more like parties than rigorous competitions, with resultant beer kegs and reverie as principal as the official results. The foundation of the events for patrons was not competing, but simply enjoying new boulders and seeing which competitors could complete the most routes. At times Rennak would set as many as 150 new boulders for his Climb Time clientele in a single push.

The public continued to respond positively. So, in the fall of 1998, Rennak, still only in his early twenties, expanded the competitions beyond his own gym. He reached out to other gyms within a reasonable radius of Cincinnati to see if they would want to be included in the venture. What resulted was a circuit of 12 bouldering competitions at 11 gyms, all contained within a single season that would stretch from November 1998 to May 1999. The gyms would include Hoosier Heights in Bloomington, Indiana; The Rock in Florence, Kentucky; Rocksport in Louisville, Kentucky; Vertical Adventures in Columbus, Ohio; Urban Krag in Dayton, Ohio; as well as Rennak's Climb Time in Cincinnati and other Climb Time gyms in Indianapolis and Lexington. Select other multiuse facilities, such as the indoor climbing wall at Miami University in Oxford, Ohio, would also be included. Competitors at the various gyms' events would hail from nearby cities as well as smaller towns within the chosen Midwestern expanse. "Climbers of all ages, genders and abilities will compete for prizes on boulder problems—short climbs (under 15 ft. in length), characterized by overhangs that do not necessitate ropes," wrote Rennak in an announcement that he mailed out to gyms. Scores for the many competitions would be tabulated at the end of the circuit in order to crown seasonal winners in different skill-level categories.

Rennak called his circuit the Midwest Bouldering Tour. While each competition was not exactly groundbreaking in format or presentation as the inaugural season progressed, the competitions' joining together to form a series that was separate from the national lineage of the ASCF or the JCCA was bold. Rather than focusing on immediate expansion or eventual unification with national governing entities, Rennak chose to stay regional in his focus. The Midwest Bouldering Tour earned $1,700 and Rennak promptly parceled it out in the form of donations to the Ohio Climbing Association, Red River Gorge's Climbers' Coalition, and other local causes.

The next year, Rennak significantly expanded the concept and proposed 60 events—a 400 percent increase from the prior season—and rebranded the circuit the Eastern Bouldering Series to account for participatory gyms that resided outside of the Midwestern perimeter. Although national recognition had not been a goal for Rennak's string of competitions, news quickly spread of the tour's grassroots nature and its popularity among climbers in Middle America. Participants in the Eastern Bouldering Series included several young competitors who would quickly rise to national prominence. Among them were Angie Payne, Tori Allen, and a young, shaggy-haired climber in the kids' division named Paul Robinson.

Aiding the recognition of Rennak's circuit was an eight-hour routesetting workshop called the Course Setting Clinic. Rennak created and led classes for it at gyms around the country. An instructional tour of clinics kicked off in late October 1999 at

Climb Time in Lexington, Kentucky. Rennak then traveled north to gyms in Rhode Island and New York before circling back to the Midwest and concluding with workshops at Vertical Reality in Whitewater, Wisconsin, and Climb Time in Cincinnati in mid-December.

Paralleling Rennak's success with organizing routesetting clinics and bouldering competitions was his increasing frustration with the ASCF. This crystalized when Rennak learned that the ASCF had looped in his bouldering competitions—to be part of the federation's calendar of annual sanctioned events—without his knowledge. Rennak responded with a letter of objection to the ASCF, and although the animosity would swell and lessen over time, it established an early, formal rift between Rennak and climbing's national governing body that would exist for seasons to come.

With his own competition series proving to be successful without the resources of a major governing entity, Rennak's future as a unique event organizer seemed all but certain. Then, in April 1999, a huge storm rolled through southwestern Ohio with devastating consequences. It would prove to change the course of Rennak's life and, subsequently, change the course of American competition climbing.

In the storm's fury, tornados touched down and destroyed dozens of homes in Rennak's community. Numerous local businesses were destroyed as well. All totaled, the massive weather event killed several people in greater Cincinnati and caused millions of dollars in damages. Although Rennak's Climb Time facility survived the disaster, the main thoroughfare to the gym was made inaccessible by debris and destruction. As a result, the gym's attendance numbers dipped drastically—by as much as 40 percent in the tornado's aftermath. Adding to access woes was the fact that authorities of

Rennak's municipality instituted an evening curfew. The intention of such restrictiveness was to keep the neighborhoods safe as crews worked to repair a devastated infrastructure. But for Rennak, the curfew cut deeply into his climbing gym's potential evening profits.

Uninterested with the idea of staying in Ohio to endure what would assuredly be an agonizing year of rebuilding and recovering, Rennak decided to pack up his belongings and move on. He sold Climb Time and headed west to Colorado, a state that already had deep roots in American competition climbing history. Bankrupt but undeterred in the fresh western environment, Rennak became determined to continue his annual bouldering series from a new home base in Boulder. He eventually met with Matt O'Connor, the manager of the Boulder Rock Club, one of the most well-known climbing gyms in Colorado, and shared ideas for an expanded bouldering circuit. O'Connor was intrigued and wanted the Boulder Rock Club to be involved in the vision.

Rennak's new circuit would be called the American Bouldering Series (ABS), and it would be bigger and better than his first touring ventures in the Midwest.

Amid this evolution, Rennak also drafted a letter for gym owners around the country. It was primarily an invitation for facilities to host competitions in the ABS' forthcoming season. However, it also served as a call to organize and included maxims that signified the ABS' collectivist philosophy: "We need to feed off each other's strengths and learn from our weaknesses," the letter stated. "We need to be willing to give and take a little. But most importantly we need to work toward what should be our common goal—to improve the quality of indoor climbing."

Further in the letter, Rennak expressed his intentions to advance routesetting by holding more training clinics and offering certification for individuals who wished to become ABS routesetters. Underpinning all of this was Rennak's idea that a competition climbing circuit is best commenced when there is a large degree of autonomy given to the participatory gyms. The end of the letter formalized this sentiment by stating explicitly: "Perhaps you've heard of the American Sport Climbing Federation. They're the sanctioning body that represents U.S. competition climbing at the international level. Their sole position, which is largely misunderstood, is to provide U.S. competitors a means of entering World Cup events, not to 'organize or otherwise run competitions.' They are our voice to the international community, but we've got to self-regulate."

Complementing the rebranding of his bouldering series, Rennak set his sights on authoring an organizer's handbook that could serve as a how-to manual for any gym manager who opted to host an ABS competition. Since Rennak allowed gyms taking part in the ABS to choose from a variety of different competition formats such as Redpoint, Onsight, and Worked, the book would prove to be a valuable tool—an encyclopedia, of sorts, that managers could reference for every aspect of any such event.

Once published, the book would continue to be revised by Rennak for each subsequent ABS season. From its inception it contained information on event planning and competition structuring. In a later edition, a section would even lay out the format for a dyno competition, modeled after a similar competition that Rennak's mentor, Jim Waugh, was employing for the Phoenix Bouldering Contest.

Rennak's handbook, in subsequent iterations, also contained detailed tips for routesetters (For example, "Set some easy problems with bad holds"). Explanations were given for routesetters on how to properly grade boulders on the V-scale, the American grading standard, and how to convert those grades to the unique ABS point system.[15]

Perhaps more than any other widely available American text that had come before it, Rennak's handbook openly expressed concepts such as "flow" and "variety" in regard to routes. Such intangible—but important—aspects had long been embraced by the routesetting community but rarely given thorough treatment in a written form distributed to the masses. Consider the thorough explanation that followed the tip "Watch the flow of difficulty throughout a problem" in Rennak's handbook:

> Indoor problems are normally internally consistent—cruxes tend to be within a few grades of the rest of the moves. Early cruxes, while possibly realistic, leave us deflated for the finish—it's best to spread the difficulty out. Problems that continually get harder, or have several successive cruxes, are perfect for weeding out competitors. Avoid good rests in boulder problems for comps—competitors will hang and shake versus trying, falling and letting the next person go.

The result of Rennak's writings and such extensive competition preparations was a circuit of events for the ABS that was greater than that of the preceding Midwest Bouldering Tour and the Eastern Bouldering Series. Beginning in October 2000 and spanning into the following year, ABS 1, as Rennak's new season's circuit was known, eventually incorporated 90 events from gyms all around the country.

---

15. Under the ABS' scoring, completion of a boulder rated V1 equaled 30 ABS points, V2 equaled 40 points, V3 equaled 60 points, and so forth.

The separate bouldering events culminated in a rousing championship at Rennak's old Climb Time headquarters in Cincinnati, which was won by John Stack in the men's Open division, and Tori Allen in the women's Open division. Other divisions were also featured in the ABS 1 championship, including Recreational, Intermediate, Advanced, and Youth categories.

Part of the allure for participating gyms throughout the first season of the ABS was a "Comp Box" that Rennak had provided to those facilities that opted to host events. The large boxes included products and accoutrements from various sponsors: chalk, energy bars, gift certificates, magazines, clothing, bags, handholds and footholds, and more. The packages absolved gyms from having to wrangle sponsors (and the sponsors' goods) on their own. "My [host gyms] loved me because if you signed up with me, I gave you all your raffle," Rennak would later explain. "I sent you a crash pad, a gift certificate for a pair of shoes. It took away the huge burden of host gyms having to corral and manage sponsors—and headaches that went all the way back to Jeff Lowe having to court North Face and Danskin and others."

Rennak worked tirelessly to deliver the boxes' contents to gyms around the country from his ABS post in Boulder. He never set up a formal office and never established a warehouse, nor did he opt to build a sizable staff to help him further develop the ABS brand. Amid his wide-ranging operations, his ethos remained entirely do-it-yourself. He subsisted by storing his ABS materials and sponsor supplies in a patch of free space at La Sportiva's North American headquarters in Boulder.

To make ends meet, Rennak got a job delivering pizzas. "Domino's Pizza fueled ABS for at least two years. Hucking pizzas until 3:00 AM, then I'd sleep in, go bouldering all afternoon, and then huck pizzas—I don't know how I got it all done," he would later recall.

He also continued to sell his handholds and footholds. To improve his acumen for running what was quickly becoming the most successful national bouldering competition series that the country had ever seen, he enrolled in business classes at the local college. It all contributed to the ABS being a one-man show, reliant solely on Rennak's determination to somehow make it work.

The following season, ABS 2 continued the trend of growth and expansion. Through a connection with Hans Florine, California's Touchstone Climbing, one of the largest gyms in the country, donated $2,000 to Rennak's competition endeavor—a significant and generous contribution since Rennak had managed to run previous years' circuits with a total annual budget of just $10,000. A graphic designer, Sasha Halenda, designed a new ABS logo that gave the organization an even greater professional sheen. And the number of events looped into the ABS circuit was further expanded, doubling to 120 over the course of the 2001–02 season. In the eventual ABS 2 championship at the Boulder Rock Club, Tori Allen again claimed victory in the women's division. The previous year's men's champion, John Stack, took second place to Obe Carrion.

Using a metric of participation, Rennak's ABS signified that competition climbing in the United States was more widespread than it ever had been. This was mirrored in other competitions that had taken place—and drawn substantial crowds—around the United States during the ABS' founding years. For example, ESPN's summer X Games extravaganza had moved from Newport, Rhode Island, to San Diego, California, and featured 24 American climbers, along with a cadre of international stars. Katie Brown had emerged victorious in the women's lead climbing division by the event's end, with Chris Sharma, perhaps the most famous young American climber at the time, placing third in the men's division.

The next summer, in 1998, X Games IV commenced in San Diego and featured Brown employing a fluid dropknee in the women's finals to reach a distant hold that had proved ungraspable by previous competitors Mi Sun Go of South Korea and Elena Choumilova of Russia. Brown's eventual victory at the competition—yet again—did not just invigorate the spectators; it gave the event a nationalistic flare. The highest-placing Americans in the men's division were Vadim Vinokur in third place and Steve Hong in eighth place. Sharma had been sidelined by a snowboarding accident and was unable to participate. An article in *Climbing* lamented his X Games IV absence: "Chris Sharma has an injured knee and is not competing, so the men's difficulty event is destined to be a disappointment. His absence is also a bummer for the TV people, who would dearly love an American victory for their viewers."

But in a way, Sharma's exclusion that summer had made Brown's victory even more of a patriotic statement, and thus aided in branding the year's X Games offering as anything but a disappointment by its awe-inspiring end. The same article, in its conclusion, conceded and called Brown's X Games IV victory the "perfect result."

Another competition with significant promotional push that same year had been the JCCA Junior Invitational in San Francisco. It had featured victories in various divisions by names that would be mainstays in the climbing industry for years to come: Ethan Pringle, Beth Rodden, Robert D'Anastasio, and others.

Smaller-scale competitions flourished in significant numbers too. Often more relaxed than their larger, invitational-style counterparts, these contests were ways for climbing gyms to earn quick profits and grow memberships—and often draw from the local community, much in the manner that Rennak was championing. The Gym Rat Jamboree at Peak Performers Gym in Jacksonville, Florida; the South Texas Heat at San Antonio Rock Gym in Texas; and the Top Gun Competition at Adventure Sports Rock Gym in Logan, Utah, were samples of this more concentrated event model at the time.

University recreation centers—featuring climbing walls in growing numbers—acted as event hosts too, illustrated by the Alamosa Crux Open at Adams State University in Alamosa, Colorado, and the Fall Rock Rodeo in Miami University in Oxford, Ohio—not too far from where Rennak had originally kicked off his bouldering series. Annual outdoor competitions with growing fame, such as the Hound Ears Bouldering Competition in Boone, North Carolina, and the Rock Rodeo in Hueco Tanks, Texas, also grew outward in popularity from local clientele bases.

In fact, competitions became so common that nearly every week featured a competitive climbing event taking place *somewhere* in the country. Consider one representative string of fall weekends, during which the Pump-Kin Pull-Down at Thornton, Colorado's Rock'n & Jam'n gym (October 31) was followed by the Hold On or Go Home competition at Vertical Endeavors in Columbus, Ohio (November 7), which was succeeded by the larger-scale Touchstone Invitational at Mission Cliffs in San Francisco (November 14), which was followed by the Cranksgiving at Vertical Relief Rock Gym in Flagstaff, Arizona (November 22).

The rise of bouldering competitions around the United States contributed to a more general interest in the bouldering discipline. This resulted in more climbers bouldering outdoors as well. "At first, bouldering wasn't really seen as that legitimate," recalls Tim

Steele, a climber out of Miami University who was immersed in the scene first as a national-level routesetter by the American League of Forerunners, and then as a developer of outdoor bouldering areas such as Bishop, California. "Certainly sponsors didn't care as much about what you had bouldered—they wanted to know what you had climbed, as far as routes go. And it seems like the comp scene was still more or less focused on routes, at least until Scott [Rennak] came out with the ABS. And then everyone all of a sudden was carrying around a crash pad."

Crash pads, portable cushions for bouldering, had been part of the discipline's minimalistic paraphernalia for years—and available to purchase on the retail market primarily through a company run by climber Bruce Pottenger. Pottenger's company, Kinnaloa, called its chief bouldering mat the Sketch Pad. However, early iterations of crash pads, although well made, were expensive. Prohibitive pricing resulted in boulderers like Steele periodically resorting to grassroots approaches when it came to acquiring cushions for bouldering outings. Steele remembers: "When I first went to [Hueco Tanks, Texas], I didn't have a pad. Nobody was toting around pads at all—you hit the ground every time, and it hurt. I met John Sherman and he had a pad. Being in college, I couldn't afford a commercial pad, but I thought, 'Damn, how do you make that thing?' I went back to college after the trip and lucked out and found a bunch of wrestling mats being thrown away in a dumpster one day behind one of the gymnasiums. My friends and I scavenged the foam—took all the foam out of the mats and basically sewed our own fabric around the outside to make our own crash pads. And then we took them back to Hueco and we were psyched because now we didn't have to hit the ground as hard."

The ABS began to thrive and so too did equipment on the commercial bouldering market. An Oregon-based climber, Clark

Shelk, started a company, Cordless, that made budget-friendly crash pads. Shelk recalls a feeling that bouldering's imminent boom was "obvious," especially because of its ease of entry—"just the natural movement of climbing without the use or knowledge of gear, rope techniques, belayer, etc." Shelk would explain. "Learning how all the gear works is a time-consuming process, whereas bouldering allows you to just climb on your first day out."

Shelk soon had a feeling that his Cordless pads would find a niche: "The first 12 or so pads I made really had no long-term business plan behind them; I just wanted a means to make some money while spending a winter in Hueco," he would recall. "After that first winter, I started getting calls from across the country. The crew that would spend winter in Hueco went back to their local areas in the spring, and that's how the word spread. It just went viral from there, eventually Cordless had enough money to place print ads, attend trade shows, and sponsor a few climbers."

Such unique growth of the Cordless brand was indicative of bouldering's uniqueness. According to Shelk, bouldering was an "underground movement" that radically grew throughout the climbing world, "not because of support or recognition in the climbing industry, but in spite of it." He would later say, "Unlike sport climbing and competitions, which were developed by and focused on the 'elite' climbers, the bouldering community was a bunch of nobodies and average Joes who changed it all from the ground up."

Another company out of Oregon, Metolius, began marketing more affordable crash pads too. And crash pad manufacturer Revolution launched a highly publicized recycling program called R.A.P.P., wherein preowned crash pads could be returned to the company for a 15 percent discount on the purchase of a new pad.

Along with utilitarian equipment like crash pads, chalk buckets, and scrub brushes, bouldering media became more common. Print advertisements featuring boulderers were more prevalent than they had been in years past. A book on American bouldering that John Sherman had published nearly a decade earlier called *Stone Crusade* became the discipline's preeminent doctrine, more relevant than ever as a historical record and a comprehensive guide book. And with filmmaking partner Steve Montesanto, Tim Steele released a landmark film on VHS, *West Coast Pimp*, that focused entirely on bouldering in California. The video featured a soundtrack of thumping electronic music and exuberant voiceovers accompanying an array of climbing highlights. Its packaging reiterated that the sudden bouldering craze encapsulated more than just the climbing discipline—it comprised a whole fast-paced, youthful aura: "*West Coast Pimp* captures the camaraderie, the energy, the synergy of lifestyle, attitude, fashion and sheer joy of climbing unroped." One particular segment in *West Coast Pimp* followed a young climber traversing not secluded stone but the Doe Library on the Berkeley campus of the University of California. In a sense, the scene connected the widespread bouldering culture of the time to the Cal Crank competitions that had taken place on the same campus years prior. Another segment featured Scott Frye, by then a bouldering veteran, completing a famous boulder, Nat's Traverse, in Berkeley.

With more affordable gear on the market, more videos, and a host of young climbers exclusively interested in bouldering, the longstanding stigma of bouldering being the "runt" discipline or merely skill practice for longer sport climbing routes quickly faded.

Over time, the surge in bouldering's general popularity and the success of big entities like the X Games (which expanded to include the Winter X Games with an ice climbing competition and an X Games Asia in cities such as Kuala Lumpur, Malaysia; Seoul, South Korea; and Shanghai, China) as well as the ABS and the JCCA, helped attract considerable non-endemic sponsorships to competitions.

One example of such substantial backing was from Japanese car manufacturer Subaru, which sponsored a bouldering competition in Hood River, Oregon, as part of the Gorge Games in July 2000. The grand prize for the competitors at that year's Gorge Games was $1,500. Chris Sharma was fully healed from his debilitating knee injury and dominated the event. He only missed winning due to a technicality—failing to match with both hands at the top of a handhold in the finals. Yet, his "inadvertent blunder" with his hands seemed to fuel his motivation for another bouldering competition called Bring the Ruckus the following month in Salt Lake City, Utah. While other competitors in the field struggled to make progress beyond the boulders' halfway points at the event, Sharma ascended effortlessly. When he became troubled by complex sequences, he campused through the cruxes of the boulders without bothering to secure his feet on the awkward footholds.

Sharma's dominant performance at Bring the Ruckus earned him a victory in the men's division, while Liv Sansoz won the women's division following a superfinal round with Claire Murphy of England. Highlights of all the performances were immortalized in the first volume of Big UP Productions' *Dosage*, a series started by filmmakers Brett and Josh Lowell. Released on DVD, it marked one of the first instances of a bouldering competition's replay being made available on the American retail market.

In addition to the electrifying events taking place, competition climbing's popularity could be gauged increasingly by elaborate projects being proposed—but not necessarily brought to fruition—in the era. One such venture that Rennak was eventually involved in was a bouldering contest to be held on the high-up observation deck of Rockefeller Center in Manhattan, one of the most popular tourist destinations in New York City. Early conceptions entailed constructing a deepwater soloing pool below a 40-foot arch at Manhattan's famed skating rink at Fifth Avenue. "Climb to the Top of the Rock," as the completed project was to be labeled and promoted, would also include a marquee five-day celebration with climbing-themed films and presentations in a plaza demonstration area between 50th and 51st Streets. Invitations were sent to 300 competitors to take part in ongoing competitions among the city festivities, with the number of total participants for the entertainment activities estimated to be 10,000 people. All totaled, the extravagant expanse would reside on the streets of New York City for an entire month.

As grandiose as the Rockefeller Center project was, plans fizzled when requisite costs were tabulated to be in the multi-million-dollar range. But a substantial aspect of the proposal was always ease of access for spectators; the project's "free and open to the public" foundation signified a belief that the masses were once again ready and willing to respond ardently to competition climbing, particularly in the mainstream capital of the nation.

Elsewhere, Jim Waugh, having successfully overseen the climbing portion of multiple X Games events and the Gorge Games, was contacted by Disney and informed of an idea to construct a climbing wall inside one of the company's theme parks. The wall would have been a primary feature of a mountaineering exhibit that never materialized; climbing performers would have been trained to ascend the wall and greet theme park visitors.

The abundance of climbing-themed imaginings, as well as the wealth of competitions in the new millennium, masked and belied that there were problems steeping at the unseen, organizational level. If the competitive scene was to continue with the positive momentum generated by Rennak and the ABS, Jeanne Niemer and the JCCA, Ralph Erenzo and Waugh and the X Games, many underlying issues would have to be resolved, and that meant that the competition scene's disparate parts would likely have to shift from working separately and independently to working uniformly at all costs.

The climbing wall at the first X Games (known as the Extreme Games at the time) rises high above the harbor grounds at Newport, Rhode Island. Spectators congregate to watch the climbing, while cranes and lifts are used to film the action for ESPN. (Sasha Akalski)

A group of young climbers stand atop the podium of a Junior Competition Climbing Association (JCCA) competition. Highest among them—in first place (center)—is Daniel Woods, at the onset of a competition career that would quickly become legendary. (Steve Woods)

Scott Rennak deep in organizational duties for his creation, the American Bouldering Series. The headset and the multiple laptops hint at the substantial logistical load of running the series. The cardboard box in the background is filled with programs, books, magazines, and gifts—a collection of prizes that Rennak deemed the "Comp Box." These boxes became a calling card for the American Bouldering Series, enticing gyms to take part in the competition series that was quickly becoming a national phenomenon. (Photo courtesy of Scott Rennak/The Spot Bouldering Gym

In the early 2000s, Chris Sharma was one of the biggest names in the sport of climbing, and his participation at competitions such as the American Bouldering Series (pictured here) and the Professional Climbers Association attracted a wide fan base. (Steve Woods)

Chris Sharma (wearing bib No. 5) shares a celebratory moment with Daniel Woods during 2006's SendFest at The Front in Salt Lake City, Utah. In many ways, Sharma was a representative of one generation of competition climber at the time, and Woods was a representative of the subsequent generation—a new breed of talent that would usher competition climbing into an even greater level of fandom and renown. (Steve Woods)

Daniel Woods, nearly a decade after his early JCCA days, gets horizontal as he eyes a hold at the World Cup in Vail, Colorado, in 2008. (Steve Woods)

American Alex Johnson stands highest atop the podium on the evening of June 7, 2008, at the end of the World Cup in Vail, Colorado. Johnson's gold medal victory was one of the most thrilling narratives in the history of the sport. In second place is Austria's Katharina Saurwein, and in third place is Austrian Anna Stöhr. (Steve Woods)

Daniel Woods claims victory at the American Bouldering Series National Championship (commonly known as "ABS 10") in 2009. Woods had previously won the prestigious national championship in 2005, 2006, and 2007. He would win again in 2010, 2012, 2013, 2014, and 2015. (Steve Woods)

Competitors race each other to the top of the climbing wall during the 2016 Psicobloc Masters at the Utah Olympic Park in Salt Lake City. Due largely to exciting performances by Delaney Miller, Sasha DiGiulian, Claire Buhrfeind, and other participants over the years, the event became one of the United States' most famous annual climbing competitions. It showcased not only blazing climbing speeds, but also spectacular falls into a pool of water far below. (Colton Marsala)

Sean Bailey goes airborne, dynoing for holds on his way up a boulder at the 2019 Bouldering Open National Championship in Redmond, Oregon. Bailey earned a spot on the United States' Overall National Team of Americans, members of which aimed to qualify for the Olympics. (Daniel Gajda)

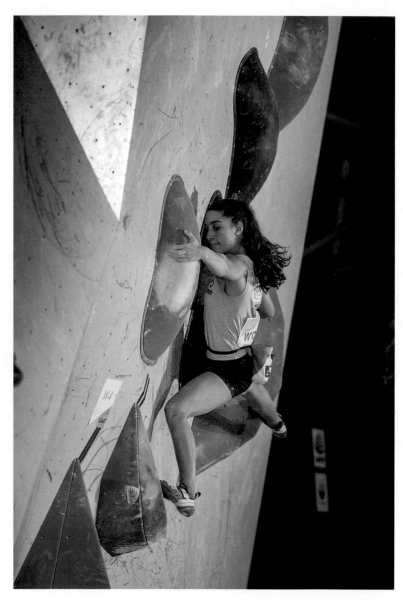

Brooke Raboutou positions herself midway up a boulder at the 2019 World Championships in Hachioji, Japan. The championships served as a qualification event for the Tokyo 2020 Olympics. Raboutou's place in the standings at the conclusion of the World Championship's combined discipline was enough to earn her an Olympic berth—the first-ever for an American climber. (Daniel Gajda)

CHAPTER 15

MOVING PARTS

IN A SPIRITED SPEECH given at the Boulder Rock Club in 2002 during ABS 2's end-of-the-season championship, Scott Rennak asked the crowd rhetorically and sarcastically, "Is comp climbing dead, or what?" He continued, "That seems to be all I've heard lately—especially from you older-school competitors: 'Yeah, yeah...we already tried that, it didn't take.'"

Rennak continued to espouse in detail how the United States was in the midst of a new, active epoch of competition climbing. If the early formulations of competitive events—highlighted by Werner Landry and his Southern California bouldering contests, and then Jeff Lowe and Bob Carmichael's visions for Snowbird—had prompted a Golden Age of American competition climbing by the late 1980s and early 1990s, then the 2000s marked a Silver Age that borrowed certain older organizational concepts while also fashioning new trends.

Rennak continued to push routesetting as a skill that could be taught to gyms around the country—a philosophy the JCCA was also actively promoting by enlisting its own routesetter certification process. Also, the Climbing Wall Industry Group, a segment of the Outdoor Industry Association, released a 25-page manual, *Route Setting Guide*. It included a glossary of climbing techniques and handhold types, along with instructions on subjects ranging from route aesthetics to hold selection.

Rennak was also in the midst of putting together an ABS scholarship fund. Under the fund, 10 percent of all ABS membership fees would be allocated to youths in various ABS regions for scholastic use. In a fitting blend of competition climbing's heritage with its present, Rennak even met up with Roy McClenahan at one point. McClenahan had acted as Lowe's de facto Deputy Director of Operations in 1990, making him one of the United States' foremost experts on the grind of competition organizing. At a pub called Conor O'Neill's in Boulder, Colorado, Rennak perused the budgetary minutiae of the 1990 Berkeley World Cup that were contained in McClenahan's famed "janal" notebook. The thinking was perhaps an opportune time was approaching for the United States to once again host a World Cup.

Separate from those initiatives, the JCCA was inspiring gyms around the country to foster youth climbing teams and even selecting association members to participate in the World Championships overseas.

All these new formulations and operational designs were elevating competition climbing to levels of prominence and nuance. So quick was the progression that it went largely underreported at first. Climbing videos and publications, beholden to substantial viewerships and readerships with outdoor predilections, often only featured brief snippets about competitors or blurbs with the ABS and JCCA results—despite the fact that those organizations' respective competitions were drawing great crowds and playing a primary role in the sport's growth. And when climbers like Chris Sharma, Tommy Caldwell, or Tori Allen were profiled by media outlets, the coverage was usually devoted to those climbers' outdoor projects—like Allen's send of Paranoia in Red River Gorge, Kentucky, or Sharma's projecting an extension of Biographie, a world-famous outdoor route in Céüse, France, in 2001.

Rennak noted this disparity in his 2002 speech at the Boulder Rock Club: "I wonder how we can all—the climbing media included—be so jaded in the face of what's actually happening. The facts point to the exact opposite of stagnation. We have two huge, thriving comp climbing programs and dozens of large-scale cash comps every year. There is more activity surrounding U.S. comp climbing than ever before."

In fact, Rennak's mention of the profusion of activity hinted that there were, perhaps, too many moving parts to the competition sphere. In addition to the ABS, another bouldering series had emerged and carved out a space in a tableau that was already becoming crowded. The Professional Climbers Association (PCA), as the bouldering series was known, had been born out of The Front Climbing Club, a bouldering-only gym founded in Salt Lake City, Utah, by Mike Uchitel in the summer of 2001. The first bouldering competition of the PCA tour, which was spearheaded by Uchitel and an accomplished routesetter from Pennsylvania named Scott Mechler, was the Pusher Open. It was sponsored by the Salt Lake City–based climbing hold company of the same name and held on August 18 and 19 that summer. It attracted 200 competitors (and 300 spectators) and featured a number of memorable moments, including first-round boulder flashes by Tori Allen and Liv Sansoz in the women's division, and some dyno-campusing by Chris

Sharma in the men's division that earned him a standing ovation. "Can anyone stop Sharma?" one magazine posed in a review of that first PCA competition.[16]

The Cordless Cup, another event in the inaugural PCA tour, would be held in Salt Lake City and sponsored by the eponymous crash pad manufacturer. Plans changed suddenly after the terrorist attacks of September 11, 2001, however, and the event was rebranded as the Cordless Benefit. Upon its commencement, a decree was made that half of the winners' purses would be donated to charity. Several competitors taking part, including Obe Carrion and Jason Kehl, decided to give away all of their winnings to aid in post–September 11 relief efforts.

The standouts of the Cordless Benefit, which featured a DJ blaring electronic music within a decidedly somber context, were Lisa Rands and one of France's best boulderers, Jérôme Meyer. Also noteworthy were the specially made red, white, and blue handholds that befit the competition's patriotic theme. The centerpiece on the climbing walls, however, was a large red, white, and blue Molecule sloper hold from Pusher that Kehl had personally designed. Rather than being painted in the various colors, Kehl's Molecule was given its American aesthetic via different colored pigments in the plastic during the hold's manufacturing process—a significant achievement in handhold design at the time.

Although the PCA did not have the quantity of events that Rennak's extensive ABS circuit did, it immediately had a high profile. Those initial PCA competitions featured $20,000 purses—substantial

---

16. In practice, if not in attitude, the PCA tour had some of its roots in a four-stop competition tour that Scott Mechler and another routesetter, Mark Eller, had organized a few years earlier on the East Coast. Cryptically titled the Size Matters Tour, the small circuit featured events at climbing gyms in Connecticut, New Jersey, and Pennsylvania.

payouts that were practically unheard of for any climbing competitions, let alone events of a new association. In fact, the total prize purses for the Pusher Open and the Cordless Benefit were larger than what was being offered at World Cups at the time. Also, with the PCA's organizers having close ties to companies such as Pusher and Cordless—or owning the brands outright—the competition series was always associated closely with some of the newest and most noteworthy gear on the climbing market. PCA events were frequently filmed by Mike Call, which added to the prestige and fanfare.

The combination of the various factors, as well as ostentatious prizes like PCA-branded belt buckles and flashy rings, and the introduction of popular handholds from an upstart company called Teknik (started by competitors Zoe Kozub and Seth Johnston) made the PCA among the most highly touted entities to ever materialize so suddenly on the American climbing scene. "In the ebb and flow of American competition climbing, the Professional Climbers Association (PCA) brings the flow," read one glowing recap of a PCA competition known as the Boulder Brawl.

Chris Danielson, who took part in the PCA tour as a competitor at a time when he was also honing his skills as a world-class routesetter, would later reflect on the PCA's panorama, lofty and ultimately fragile as it was: "I don't know how to describe it. I've been in every type of bouldering competition there can be, and there's high energy at all types of competitions. But that energy was tightened into a small space. And the people who were competing had a higher level of energy, passion. All the names from those days—whether Chris [Sharma] and Nels [Rosaasen] and their competitiveness, or John Stack, or Obe Carrion, or Seth Johnston and Zoe Kozub, and many others—they all gave it a unique quality.

"They were stars. They were characters. Scott Mechler driving all of it with the setting and then being on the mic.... And the audience got heightened by all that. And when you put together so many people who were psyched about that stuff—bouldering, climbing hard on plastic—put 300 of them together in one small, tight space. It was just different."

In a way, the ABS and the PCA coexisted for a while as the perfect complements to each other. Both circuits were led by charismatic visionaries who worked tirelessly outside of climbing's main governing body at the time, and both featured bouldering in lieu of lead or speed disciplines. But Rennak and Uchitel had different methodologies. Where the ABS' tour had amateur appeal, the PCA's circuit had professional cachet, and where the ABS embraced localism, the PCA benefited greatly from superstars like Sharma, Kehl, and Lisa Rands, as well as some of Europe's top competitors—like Meyer—taking part. Also, geographically, the ABS circuit reached outward from its Boulder grounding, while the PCA's anchor throughout its expansion was always Salt Lake City, Utah, despite a few competitions held in Colorado to coincide with festivals.

But as the ABS and PCA had launched and boomed independently, and the JCCA had persisted as the organization leading the cultivation of kids' climbing in regional pockets all across the nation, the main governing body for competitors—the ASCF—had struggled to maintain the relevance it had basked in during the mid-1990s. For example, an ASCF lead competition at Planet Rock in Ann Arbor, Michigan, in June 2000 had attracted only 21 competitors—a small fraction of the great participatory rosters of events put on by the federation just a few years prior.

"Why the ASCF has foundered is readily apparent," said author Matt Stanley in an article from 2002 in *Climbing* titled "Alphabet Soup: Whither the Fragmented Comp Scene?" "Adult competitors at all levels are into bouldering comps, events that provide a party atmosphere and greater group interaction, and the ASCF has left that arena to other organizations."

There was still a vibrant UIAA-sanctioned World Cup scene in the early 2000s, with competitions taking place in a plethora of foreign cities like Kranj, Slovenia; Chamonix, France; and Munich, Germany. In fact, in December 2001, Lisa Rands traveled to Birmingham, England, and competed in a bouldering World Cup for the first time; she placed second behind France's Sandrine Levet. The event drew a massive crowd of 6,000 spectators throughout the weekend, and Rands' performance was dubbed "extraordinary." The Rockmaster competition in Arco, Italy, continued each year with a festival-style atmosphere too, held in largely the same manner since the mid-1980s.

Despite the existence of many international competition opportunities, particularly by 2002, the ASCF did not have enough money to finance any overseas circuit travel for a whole American team. Athletes were thus left to finance any far-flung trips mostly on their own, which very few chose to do—especially with such new life being breathed into the scene at home in America.

The ASCF, in conjunction with the American Alpine Club, was still acting as the main American representative to the UIAA and its technical commission overseeing international competitions at this time, but it was increasingly clear that newer organizations like the ABS, the PCA, and the JCCA were inadvertently challenging the status quo.

In an attempt to bring some uniformity to the clutter of groups and associations, Hans Florine started a system called the Competitive

Climbing Rank (CCR) to catalogue American climbers' performances across the entire national spectrum. The motivation behind the CCR was a constant feeling by Florine and a prominent California gym, Touchstone, that the 40th to 1000th best competitors were not being fully recognized by the ASCF.

Florine's CCR was a big success. By early 2002, it had amassed 3,000 competitors in a database that culled results from each separate organization's events. It was a step toward clarity and homogeneity on at a countrywide level.

As widely appreciated as it was by competitors, the CCR was mainly a ranking system and not a formal unification of the scene's disparate parts. In the aforementioned 2002 article, Stanley wrote: "Even with several healthy competition organizations and a nascent ranking body, little else holds together the U.S. comp scene. Everyone involved agrees that the country needs an effective national governing body that sanctions events, ranks competitors, and promotes U.S. competitive climbing on an international level."

The swirling alphabet soup of organizations and their respective acronyms finally started to calm with discussions that took place between representatives of the ASCF and the JCCA. Beginning with a meeting on January 5, 2002, in Berkeley, California, the organizations collectively deliberated on the idea of a possible merger. Eventually the ASCF agreed to grant the JCCA the authority to organize youth events that resided under the UIAA's auspices. This formalized the JCCA's role as the main governing body for the United States' junior competitors, although the JCCA had been assuming such a role in a de facto manner before the negotiations. In an interview at the time, the ASCF's spokesperson, Steve Allen, said of the ongoing deliberations, "Our goal is to create a national governing body that represents climbing at the adult level, the junior level, bouldering, difficulty, etc."

Complicating matters, however, was a decision by the JCCA to expand beyond the confines of youth climbing and start its own adult division. As a result, the "Junior" aspect of the JCCA's moniker became inaccurate, so, in a series of press releases, the JCCA was rebranded as the United States Competition Climbing Association (USCCA). An announcement in the March 2002 issue of *Climbing* read: "The name, and the mission, of the highly successful Junior Competition Climbing Association (JCCA) is about to change. In addition to promoting and organizing youth climbing, The United States Competition Climbing Association (USCCA) will sponsor adult competitions in 2002."

The result of these changes and deliberations when the dust cleared was the presence of two main American organizations—the ASCF and the USCCA—overseeing the United States' adult climbing competitions by early 2002. The impractical and likely unsustainable nature of the multiple administrations governing American competitions was magnified when an old-yet-familiar refrain reemerged in climbing circles: climbing could soon become an Olympic sport.

Previous efforts to get climbing into the purview of the International Olympic Committee (IOC) had been unsuccessful, but upcoming Games reinvigorated interest. Not long after the JCCA rebranded itself as the USCCA, the UIAA's technical commission for competition climbing filed a formal proposal with the IOC to consider adopting climbing as an Olympic sport.[17] While the forthcoming 2004 Olympics, to be held in Athens, Greece, would be too

---

17. The UIAA's technical commission for competition climbing was founded officially as the International Council for Competition Climbing (ICCC), although the moniker was also truncated as International Climbing Council (ICC). Both appear in historical accounts, adding even more acronyms to the alphabet soup of climbing groups in the late 1990s and early 2000s.

soon for anything to come to fruition, climbing's presence in the
2008 Olympics in Beijing, China; the 2012 Games in London, England; the Games 2016 in Rio de Janeiro, Brazil; or Games in later
quadrenniums seemed quite possible. Climbing's practical and promotional inclusion would take time—years, certainly—if it were to
be accepted by the IOC, but the likelihood was aided by the efforts
of the technical commission's head at the UIAA, Marco Scolaris.

Scolaris made Olympics inclusion one of his professional priori-
ties and enacted a worldwide approach for climbing competitions
that particularly highlighted the Asian continent. "As a sport, Olympics is the goal," he said in an interview at the time. "We are working on other events including the University Games and the Asian
Games. We would like to invest in developing countries, in Asia,
and in South America. We are working well with China. China's
interest demonstrates that this is a sport that can be very popular
at a very low cost."

Yet, if climbing was progressing slowly toward an Olympics realization after more than a decade of false starts, this meant that the
United States would possibly be tasked with sending representative
American climbers to take part. Thus, the presence of *two* American governing bodies not only prompted questions about which
organization, the ASCF or the USCCA, would be more qualified
to select and direct representative athletes to be Olympians, it also
risked dividing the climbing tribe and fan base for an event—the
Olympics—that, in an ideal sense, embodied unity and cooperation
above all else.

At the very least, it was obvious that American competition
climbing could be better managed domestically and endorsed internationally at the Olympics and elsewhere if there were not two
acting nuclei, but just one. In that spirit, after more deliberation

throughout 2002, the ASCF and USCCA agreed to officially merge. In what could have been a contentious fusion of philosophies and operational practices, both organizations embraced the logic and the Olympics ideal.

Amid the Olympic enthusiasm, Rennak continued to spearhead his ABS—even as the other major bouldering circuit, the PCA, lost a main sponsor and vital capital and ended just a few years after its highly celebrated launch. "The PCA was the best thing to happen to climbing at the time," recalls Zoe Johnston (*née* Kozub), who had been one of the PCA's foremost competitors while also operating the climbing hold company Teknik. "It was really motivating to us as competitors, and also motivating for [Teknik] as sponsors to create new holds for a new style of events. The PCA was great for making everyone feel like superstars. On the mic it was the personalities, nicknames, and storylines that they pushed, making everyone look good and feel like they were part of something exciting. It was unfortunate that it ended abruptly, but on the other hand, it's kind of good that it was awesome right through to the end and didn't just fizzle out or devolve into something boring."

Although the PCA faded into the tapestry of American sports' organizational history, competition climbing in the United States still flourished. A third season of Rennak's ABS combined with a summer-only fourth season to host nearly 200 total events. In the process, the ABS circuit signaled the ascendency of Alex Johnson from child phenom to credentialed competitor; she won the women's championship at ABS 3 in 2003, while Tom Durant won the men's division.

With a surplus of young competitors like Johnson, who was only 13 years old, as well as Durant, Ethan Pringle, and Emily Harrington now aiding in bouldering's preeminence and popularity,

Rennak was more content running the ABS without getting involved in any Olympics push. Not only did he have little personal interest in whether climbing was featured in an upcoming Games, but the entire concept of Olympics inclusion seemed to contradict the grassroots spirit upon which the ABS had been founded.

To Rennak, a highly structured and meticulously scheduled Olympics would be the polar opposite of climbing, or at least clash with climbing's recreational—and perhaps even transcendent—qualities. Beyond that, Rennak had his hands full figuring out exactly where ABS fit into the USCCA now that the "alphabet soup" of acronyms had been depleted. To gain some clarity from all involved, he penned an extensive statement recommending that the USCCA employ four key initiatives as the new governing body for competition climbing. The four points Rennak itemized were: the USCCA should re-establish a junior tour, should establish and empower a committee to deal with "serious adult competitors," should embrace the ABS as the USCCA's branch that coordinates bouldering competitions for all ages, and should establish a public relations committee with an objective of expanding the presence of both organizations—the USCCA and the ABS—in the media.

At its core, Rennak's detailed statement was an account of how the ABS and USCCA could work as a union, while also being a declaration that he was not willing to concede control of the ABS over to the USCCA simply because the USCCA was now the chief governing body. "The biggest question should be directed at me: 'Why give up the ABS?'" Rennak posed in the piece. "I've spent thousands of hours and dollars and lost 2 inches of hairline in the process of building the ABS. Plus, the USCCA has a history of strong-arm politics with hosts, quite un-ABS-like. Some people worry the USCCA will corrupt the good thing that is the ABS."

Despite strong language at points, the whole of Rennak's message was complimentary of the USCCA, as Rennak pointed out that both the ABS and the USCCA shared a common goal of developing and improving the sport of climbing.

And Rennak was right to vie for continued autonomy with the ABS, as he was in the midst of a profitable surge. In late 2003, for instance, he negotiated $20,000 in title sponsorship from Eastern Mountain Sports for the upcoming tour, ABS 5. The influx of money would make ABS 5 easily the most well-funded of all ABS seasons. A $20 membership initiative for participating gyms also contributed to ABS' financial support, and Rennak found his circuit suddenly well bankrolled.

The downside to all the ABS success was the hefty toll it was taking on Rennak physically and emotionally. The USCCA eventually accepted the contention that the ABS should manage the United States bouldering scene with a degree of sovereignty. In doing so, the USCCA also gave the ABS the authority to form a national bouldering team with eligibility for World Cup events. With such responsibilities, Rennak would continue to lead his ABS administratively as a one-man show. He was steadfastly dedicated to the series that he had created from scratch, but he was also getting burned out from the inherent nonstop logistics. As soon as one season wrapped up with a championship, host gyms needed to be contacted and committed for the following season. If gyms balked at the ABS membership fee, Rennak had to deal with the resentment himself. He also had to continue to court sponsors to contribute to each season's "Comp Box."

Although Rennak kept his exhaustion a secret from others involved in the ABS—which, by the fifth season, included popular brands like Krieg, Flashed, Metolius, Clif Bar, Petzl, and

Sterling—the reality was that he was too drained from more than half a decade of crafting bouldering competition circuits dating back to the Midwest Bouldering Tour. He had reached a threshold that had massive implications. By the start of ABS 5, bouldering was the most popular form of competition climbing in the country, and the ABS was its preeminent network. But if Rennak were to step aside at some point, the ABS might quickly dissolve and the American competition climbing scene would once again be left in disarray—perhaps irreparably.

CHAPTER 16

FRESH STARTS

———

O N OCTOBER 30, 2003, a letter went out to personnel in all areas of the climbing industry announcing that the United States Competition Climbing Association (USCCA) was changing its name to USA Climbing. "The name is easier to remember, better reflects our role as the national governing body, and presents us in a similar manner to Olympic sport organizations in the United States," said the letter, penned by Debbie Gawrych, who had ascended to a role of President in the organization since first becoming administratively involved in competition climbing as a regional coordinator for the JCCA.

Gawrych's mention of the Olympics in the letter was not understated. The letter also listed several goals that the organization had for the coming year; the third of which, behind increasing membership numbers and improving the organization's website, was to pursue the objective of making climbing an Olympic sport:

Our Olympic Committee includes executives of some of the top companies in the industry. This Committee will collaborate with the USOC, UIAA and ICC, among other organizations, to bring this goal to fruition. This will only happen if we increase membership (recreational, indoor gym facilities, coaches, teams, and elites), bring together the fragmented programs and events of competition climbing under a singular sanctioning body (USA Climbing) and support adult teams that compete regularly in World Cup events.

In fact, the designation of USA Climbing as the official governing body heralded the start of one of the single most important years in United States climbing history. USA Climbing, as a brand, would gradually become pervasive in climbing media and synonymous with virtually all major indoor competitions.

The year's significance accelerated when Scott Rennak made a decision to sell a portion of the ownership of the ABS to two colleagues from the Boulder, Colorado, gym community, Anne-Worley Bauknight and Mike Moelter, in February 2004. Moelter and Bauknight, both employees at the Boulder Rock Club, were close friends of Rennak's. They each paid $8,000 for a 20 percent stake in the ABS brand.

The bouldering tour was now too great to have just one season-culminating event, so that year's ABS championship was to be spread over three gyms—The Spot, in Boulder, on February 26–28, Touchstone's Sacramento Pipeworks in California on March 18–20, and Earth Treks in Timonium, Maryland, on March 31–April 2.

The geographic variety of facilities illustrated just how expansive the ABS had become—and why Rennak now needed other architects like Moelter and Bauknight to help him manage it. But while the addition of Moelter and Bauknight saved the ABS from potentially dissolving, the abundant operational duties were continuing to consume Rennak. ABS 5 featured more routesetting instruction and resources for host gyms than ever before—nearly all of which were authored by Rennak himself—and a massive promotional drive with posters and advertisements.

The arrangement and the challenges all came to a head a week after that trio of ABS 5 championships, when Rennak sent a letter of resignation to Moelter and Bauknight. With the notice, Rennak tendered all future ABS control to his two friends. "There was no one in the country that was better positioned to take over," Rennak would say of Moelter and Bauknight. "They were passionate about our mission and had proven their dedication as volunteers. Mike and [Anne-]Worley were the best thing that ever happened to ABS. After they joined as owners I realized I could now step away, my baby was in safe hands."

Although Rennak would remain an associate of the ABS in an ambassadorial way, his resignation marked the end of an era that had utilized grassroots, self-actualized competitions to spawn a country-wide bouldering craze. From his humble roots at Climb Time in Ohio, Rennak had managed to tie the nation's glut of gyms to a greater, cohesive purpose with his bouldering series, thus connecting disparate regions, towns, and cities through climbing competitions. By the time he stepped down and Moelter and Bauknight assumed full control, the United States had a successful bouldering competition circuit model, similar to the one that Europe had been employing for sport climbing since the 1980s. But the ABS had proved to be far more interconnected than any tour on the European continent and, with its season championships, more purposeful.

Throughout Rennak's tenure with the ABS, he had looked at Jim Waugh as a mentor and as the forefather of the United States' whole bouldering culture. Thus, it was fitting that 2004 marked a terminus for Waugh as well. His own grassroots creation, the Phoenix Bouldering Contest (PBC), had continued annually since 1983, with just one hiatal year in 1999, and was now reaching its end.

Like Rennak's ABS, Waugh's PBC had seen its share of locational moves, from Camelback Mountain and the Beardsley Rockpile to South Mountain to the Oak Flat Campground in Arizona. Format evolutions of the PBC over its 20-year span had included the addition of an invitational category in 1998 for the best American climbers—such as Chris Sharma, Tommy Caldwell, Mia Axon, and Elena Ovchinnikova—to coincide with the more layperson-focused local and non-local categories. But perhaps the greatest storyline of the PBC's long tenure had been the dominance of Bobbi Bensman, who won the competition more than a dozen times. In a significant addendum to her legendary PBC career, which dated back to the 1980s, Bensman had returned to the competition in 2002 after giving birth to a daughter—and won again in her age division.

In total, Waugh's contests had attracted thousands of competitors over the years and involved a steady surplus of faithful volunteers. Monetarily, some seasons' total prizes amounted to nearly $60,000. Entire vendor cities were created and then dismantled on the contest's April weekend every year, but this aspect of the PBC had increasingly rankled local retailers in the greater Phoenix area. Waugh would recall, "People went [to the PBC] because they got to see friends from all over the country, but also people went for the vending. Lots of people came in and got rid of their factory seconds and got rid of their old inventory. So, it had great deals on gear. As this went on, local retailers got more and more concerned and started giving complaints to their reps, and their reps took [the complaints] to the manufacturers. And basically a lot of the local retailers around Southern California, New Mexico, Arizona, Utah, Colorado—they all basically kind of got together and said [to the manufacturers], 'We're not going to buy your gear because we don't sell enough of it—everybody waits and saves their money and goes to the bouldering contest where they can buy things cheaper. When that started to happen, we started to lose sponsors."

In addition to the many vendors and the issues related to their finances, tangential PBC activities by the 2000s included everything from catered picnics and tug-of-war games to communal pancake breakfasts and awards ceremonies. Arizona-based bands like the Scones and the Nitpickers performed concerts on a main stage. The PBC had become an American climbing institution.

All the peripheral flourishes aside, Waugh had made certain that bouldering was always the PBC's driving force. In doing so, the PBC had contributed largely to bouldering's rise in popularity. Particularly by 2004, the festival-style design was the operational setup that most climbing gyms used for their own bouldering competitions, featuring product vendors, food trucks, and DJs (or occasionally live concerts) to augment the climbing. Such miscellany connected virtually all bouldering competitions, no matter the gym or region, to the PBC, in essence if not in fact. "Things have changed as [the PBC] has grown, but its spirit has remained the same: a group of like-minded people coming together to boulder and have fun," read one report of one year's festivities.

Waugh held his last PBC, rechristened as the Phoenix Boulder-Blast and promoted as "the world's largest outdoor climbing competition," on the weekend of April 23–25, 2004. It included everything from photography clinics to dyno contests. Fittingly, Chris Sharma won the men's (non-local) bouldering contest, and Lisa Rands won the women's. Sharma placed 10th in an exciting men's dyno contest that was won by Zak Farmer; Rachael Blievernicht won the dyno event in the women's division.

The narrative after the 2004 PBC was less about the competitors' victories, though, and more about the changing quintessence of the entire American competition climbing scene. It was fitting that Waugh had thought to conclude his bouldering institution just six months after the official establishment of USA Climbing, as the presence of an overseeing governing body significantly altered the sphere in which contests like Waugh's could operate.

Later that year, Waugh corresponded with USA Climbing about the possibility of continuing the PBC and developing a cooperative relationship with USA Climbing that would be mutually beneficial. Waugh was inquiring about a feasible way that his PBC could still exist in a collaborative manner with the governing body in ensuing years. In response, USA Climbing offered to recognize the PBC as a component of a "Pro Tour" or "Outdoor Series" that would include other climbing competitions like the Gorge Games and the Teva Mountain Games that resided slightly outside the confines of a slick circuit. And USA Climbing also offered to promote the PBC, in exchange for a percentage of the PBC's revenues. It was a tempting proposal.

Waugh's inquiry was comparable to discussions that Moelter and Bauknight were having with USA Climbing about the ABS at the time too. One demonstrative letter they addressed to the board of USA Climbing stated, "The entire climbing community will benefit greatly from a close association between the ABS and USA Climbing. It will improve communication to competitors, hosts and sponsors and will help to unite much of the competitive climbing energy in the U.S. A united effort allows USA Climbing the time and resources to pursue the myriad of other possibilities ahead, such as improving the adult difficulty and speed scene, continuing to develop the youth following, building university and club-level programs, providing for the US Climbing Teams, constructing a permanent venue, creating a setting curriculum and much more."

It was clear that under the skillful direction of Bauknight and Moelter, the ABS had a forward-focused vision. Although young, Bauknight had worked in the corporate world prior to getting involved with climbing, and she brought sharp instincts when it came to the organization's business strategy and the potential for unification. A dedicated climber herself, she knew that a singular national competition organization would play better to the public's perception and potential business partners than would disparate separate competition entities.

As 2004 came to a close, the PBC and the ABS, two of the most influential bouldering conceptions to ever exist on American soil, found themselves on divergent paths. While Moelter and Bauknight eventually negotiated the merger between the ABS and USA Climbing, Waugh chose not to continue the PBC; he had already ventured into an organizer role at other competitions, like the summer and winter X Games and the Gorge Games, and he was content with the multidecade run that the PBC had enjoyed and the history it had carved. "It was a very difficult decision," Waugh would say of PBC's conclusion after its multidecade run. "The bouldering contest was one of the very earliest events, and it grew and it grew. But as it became more successful, so did competition climbing start to grow and become more successful. So, the result was that there were a lot more people competing for sponsorship dollars. That made it difficult because the event became pretty expensive to put on. It was sort of like putting on a Burning Man—but of climbing. And the fact that it was a one-off event as opposed to a series where competitors were going to get exposure in several cities made it much more difficult." He would add, "I kind of felt like it had reached a pinnacle, and I felt like it was better to go out on top."

As Waugh took on new ventures, so too did Rennak. Although Rennak was no longer tied to the administrative rigors of running the ABS, he was still a dedicated boulderer—and he still liked throwing parties. This made him ideally suited for the climbing competition version of freelance work, able to create unique events that filled some of the spiritual and communal void left in the climbing world by the PBC's termination.

Such skills were put to good use when Rennak organized Send-Fest at The Front Climbing Club (a different facility from The Front's original gym, but still in Salt Lake City, Utah), to be held on August 12, 2005. Anchored by the Outdoor Retailer trade show taking place in the city at the same time and hosted by Cordless founder Clark Shelk, the weekend-long bouldering competition was meant to be a throwback to the insouciant competitions of just a few years prior. And SendFest was held in the same city where the Professional Climbers Association, at one time the counterpoint to Rennak's ABS, had been spawned.

Music by a Salt Lake City DJ, Underground Chuck, and climbing-themed movies flickered on a side screen to accompany various competitions. As the event continued into its later rounds, it adopted an increasingly dance-club-like feel, aided by standing-room-only for the spectators. Competitors were given five minutes to climb, with five minutes of rest in a format that adhered to that of the defunct Professional Climbers Association and the ABS championships.

"SendFest was exactly that—a festival for comp and plastic climbing," reported *Urban Climber*, a magazine that emerged at the time to focus on the freewheeling bouldering ethos. "Just having the pro comp, citizens comp, and dyno comp would have been adequate, but the lifestyle element of hanging out, cheering for your friends, slacklining, and checking out new videos added another dimension to the entire event."

While SendFest donned an outward clubhouse-like nonchalance, it also possessed a substantial level of routesetting seriousness behind the scenes. A week before the event, the gym's walls had been completely stripped of all handholds and footholds. Rennak had brought in Moelter, who had adopted the role of head routesetter for the entire ABS. Accompanying Moelter in creating the competition's boulders had been a team of Jamie Emerson, Chris Danielson, Kyle Musgrove, Sean Stitt, Tim Barnett, and Kevin Branford.

Branford, as a former competitor of ASCF and JCCA competitions and a five-time youth national champion, was particularly attuned to how routesetting had changed to accommodate the nation wide competition boom. He had also been mentored by several routesetting pioneers. "When I started competing, I wasn't looking at the competition routes as different than normal gym routes—they just happened to be on a beautifully blank wall and anything that was between me and the top of the route was fair game," Branford would later say. "I suppose it wasn't until later that I began to consider that competition routes were vastly different. That was one of the things that drew me to competition climbing and routesetting: how to create challenging routes that weren't only fun to climb, but also served a purpose. I remember thinking that if Tony Yaniro or Mike Pont were the head routesetters for an event, then it would be perfect—no bottlenecks, fair routes for short and tall competitors, and [Yaniro and Pont] were masterful at making sure only one person would be at the top at the end of finals."

The fact that such a sizable and experienced crew contributed to the engineering of sufficient boulders for SendFest was illustrative of routesetting's continued popularity and transformation to a pedagogical craft; its expertise could be cultivated, clarified, taught, and refined within a like-minded group. And the routesetting community was fostered by increased video content. "We made SendFest recap videos and they were just on compact discs," recalls Danielson. "But within a year or two, they were put up on YouTube, and the PCA videos and others were all being seen by the old generation that was there and a bunch of new young kids too. I created a little YouTube page myself of some climbing moves I'd set and used them in some clinics. Climb X Media, NoRope.com, then I think a bit later *Momentum Video Magazine*—those all gave attention not always just to outdoor climbing but more to bouldering than before and also to comps."

SendFest's roster of competitors proved to be prophetic as well. By the competition's end, buried in the results and standings were two names that would influence American bouldering—and the United States competition scene—more than any others in the coming years: Daniel Woods, who tied for seventh place in the men's division at SendFest, and Alex Puccio, who earned eighth place in the women's division.

Woods, in particular, was in the midst of a blockbuster year. His competition career had begun years prior, when he won the 11 & Under division at a JCCA National Championship in Richmond, Virginia, in 1999. But since then, he had won the USCCA's Youth National Championship for the 12–13 age division in 2002, placed second in his division at the World Youth Championships in Bulgaria in 2003, placed first at a UIAA North American Championship in Mexico in 2004, and won in his age division at a slew of other smaller-scale competitions. Less than six months prior to SendFest in 2005, he had affirmed his superiority by winning the ABS 6 Nationals in Boulder, Colorado. Alex Puccio's respective breakout would be largely in the following year, but both competitors would dominate the bulk of major American bouldering competitions for many seasons to come.

The spirit of Waugh's PBC was kept alive by another phenomenon that began to thrive as Woods and Puccio began their legendary careers: outdoor competitions that donated profits to local access advocacy groups. These charity-focused contests not only harkened back to the earliest competitions around Southern California, but bridged a stylistic gap between indoor events on gyms' walls and the grimy dirtbag heritage of crag climbing.

One of the most notable examples in 2005 was a trio of outdoor bouldering events collectively called the Triple Crown that spanned the fall. It began with an event at Hound Ears, North Carolina, caravanned south to the popular nature park Horse Pens 40 in Steele, Alabama, and concluded with a competition in Chattanooga, Tennessee. Although the contests featured world-class competitors like Woods, Ethan Pringle, Kate Reese, and Claire Bell, the series maintained an altruistic focus; even the difficulty of the boulders became secondary to the reverie and the cause. "Grades had lost their importance and people were actually describing problems by sequences or overall aesthetic characteristics, rather than spewing numbers," reported Robert Semple in a write-up for *Urban Climber*. The brainchild of co-organizers Jim Horton and Chad Wykle, the Triple Crown was mainly a vehicle for contributing funds to the Southeastern Climbers Coalition.

Another outdoor competition that fall, separate from the Triple Crown but similarly inclined, was the Vedauwoo Bouldering Competition in Wyoming, sponsored by two equipment brands, Organic Climbing and So iLL. It featured 70 problems that ranged in difficulty grades from V0 to V11. Although Woods put on a masterful performance and won the co-educational heat, the overarching theme of the event was to provide upstart funding for the newly formed Laramie Climbers' Coalition nonprofit organization.

Charity competitions would continue in subsequent seasons. One of these was the New River Rendezvous, which raised money for the New River Alliance of Climbers and routinely attracted more than 1,000 attendees. Yet these competitions, as helpful and popular as they were, were ancillary to the strides that USA Climbing was making to cultivate an American competitive presence on the international stage. With the ABS now absorbed into USA Climbing's stock and the Olympics continuing as a long-term prospect, American climbing was more systemized than ever. Competition climbing in the United States had successfully amassed a comeback and coalesced from an array of contrasting components. Fittingly, the country was on the cusp of having its largest showcase of competition climbing since the Berkeley World Cup more than 15 years before.

CHAPTER 17

TAKING HOLD

———————

I N 2006, *THE NEW YORK TIMES* ran an article titled "Kids Scale the Walls, and the Principal Approves." It profiled the competition climbing team at Adams City High School in Commerce City, Colorado, and noted an increasing trend of high schools around the country establishing comparable co-ed teams for the nation's ever-expanding competition circuit. A short-lived organization, the High School Climbers' Federation, even emerged to nurture such teams, and climbing gyms in respective districts served as the schools' facility proxies for training.

The development of school climbing teams on a widespread scale was buttressed by advancements continuing to take place in tangential areas of handhold design and routesetting. With the ABS having a foothold in the public consciousness of a young demographic, boulder routesetting was more than just a loosely codified system with a zealous group of artistic practitioners—it was an increasingly enticing career track for gym employees. Although the craft of setting diverse routes in a gym or at a competition inherently relied on elements of unpredictability to give competitors the optimal physical and problem-solving challenges, most routesetters saw the logic and promise of adhering to certain best practices and procedures with the craft. The organization that had been the standard-bearer of routesetting standards throughout the 1990s, the American League of Forerunners, had since disbanded. But most routesetters around the country still felt that there was continued benefit in advancing the craft beyond a methodological free-for-all, especially as more vocational opportunities arose.

By 2006, the most prevalent routesetting strategies and tactics had been borrowed from approaches and processes developed by a group of routesetters at Miami University in Oxford, Ohio, in previous years. Miami University had been among a select group of colleges and universities to implement regularly occurring climbing competitions on artificial walls beginning in the late 1980s. In doing so, Miami University helped resuscitate competition climbing after Jeff Lowe's Sport Climbing Championships dissolved—but with a focus on mostly college-aged students. The artificial climbing wall at Miami University proved wildly popular; at times, there were more than 20 people waiting in a line to attempt the routes at the competitions.

A college-centric competition swell was fostered when many universities built elaborate recreation facilities that featured indoor climbing walls; for example, at a total cost of $25 million, Miami University constructed a multilevel Recreational Sports Center that featured a climbing wall by Radwall in 1994.

But the aspect that truly set Miami University apart for more than a decade and made it a consistent stronghold for competitions was that its wall attracted students and non-students alike. The university's original climbing wall, located in its Outdoor Pursuits Center on campus, was opened to the general public several times per week, and such openness allowed any social group or climbing sect to congregate indoors. "The Miami [University] wall was a magnet," recalls Tim Steele, who worked at the school's indoor climbing wall as a student. "It drew all the climbers from Indianapolis, Cincinnati, and Columbus—some people were doing two-hour drives to get there. And it was a lot of mostly trad climbers because the whole sport climbing thing was just taking off."

Steele and his roommate, Ted Welser, frequently helped organize events at the climbing wall at Miami University with upperclassmen. As the upperclassmen graduated, Steele and Welser rose to greater positions of organizational authority. "We were aware of the first comps that had been held at Snowbird," recalls Welser. "In the early 1990s I actually went out there, to Snowbird, and climbed on the famous wall on the side of the lodge. It had some holds that were left over from the first comp—it wasn't the whole route anymore, but it was still exciting to climb on it."

Welser and Steele were given significant leeway by those in charge of Miami University's outdoor recreation programs; their climbing competitions became more than just athletic contests; they became climbing's foothold in the Midwest. "The competitions were definitely viewed as community-building things, as forms of outreach," says Welser. "We would advertise them well in advance and spend a lot of time trying to line up some sponsors and set the routes. We would also bring in speakers like Bob Kamps—who was a key Yosemite guy, Mark Wilford—who was a famous Colorado climber, and Steve Ilg, and others. There was no climbing culture at the time, so we were just starved for community. The competitions were a way to get that."

Another Miami University student, Chris Danielson, soon joined Steele, Welser, and a small cadre of amateur routesetters and Ohio-based climbers. With a lack of mountain topography outdoors, the group conjured up a style of routesetting that was initiated and fine-tuned almost entirely on the indoor climbing wall. "We were working for student minimum wage, and we were having fun, and we were setting routes for fun—we weren't getting paid any extra to set," says Steele. "We were bumbling through it and learning from basically going to other competitions and emulating styles."

The styles of routesetting at Miami University ranged from flashy—such as using large jugs to force big, flailing dynos—to nuanced, such as screwing small jibs onto slopers to create subtle thumb catches. "The way I remember we'd sometimes set in the bouldering cave was just take all the holds off, put them back up in miscellaneous ways, and then make up problems on the existing holds," Danielson would recall. "I remember very little of any educational lessons on hold selection when routesetting. I remember there was a lot of sessioning. I think that's where most of the learning took place, through just climbing together, trial and error, everyone gradually expanding their movement vocabulary, but not with any plan."

Miami University also secured a place in routesetting history as one of the first facilities anywhere to incorporate large three-dimensional shapes known as volumes onto its climbing wall—long before such changeable features became standard in competitions. "I actually built a volume for the 1991 competition at Miami University," recalls Rene Keyzer-Andre, who routeset for competitions while holding a managerial role at RockQuest, an Ohio gym he helped build in the mid-1990s.[18] "Miami University's walls couldn't move—they weren't very changeable, and many competitors were returning year after year for the competitions. So to change things up, I built a big pyramid that was rotatable, and we threw it onto the wall for the finals. I had seen the rotating piece from the Berkeley [1990 World Cup], and triangles [features] from Snowbird comps. Those had given me the idea to make something that stood out and changed the wall's terrain but was not permanent."

Keyzer-Andre's routesetting protégés, Steele and Welser, were continually inventive and successful in their own right. The duo was asked at one point to travel to a conference at Cornell University in Ithaca, New York, where they gave a presentation to representatives of other universities' outdoor recreation programs on hosting climbing competitions. "Climbing events have become more widespread and complex in the last few years," Steele wrote in a handout for the crowd at Cornell. "More consistency exists between events now than ever before. It is important to have a well-organized, well-run, 'professional' event to add to the growth of this exciting sport."

Steele also specified what he dubbed the Golden Rule of competition organizing: "Allow yourself time. After the event, reflect on changes that could be made to make your next event even better."

Steele and Welser took their routesetting methodology to Rock-Quest after college, where they both worked as routesetters for Keyzer-Andre. Another young climber, Bill Kelly, soon joined them. For Steele, in particular, a serendipitous meeting with Jason Campbell

---

18. Keyzer-Andre and his wife, Margarita Martinez, were married in a ceremony that took place at Climb Time, in Cincinnati, Ohio, in 1993. Martinez was also very important to the development of the competition scene in the mid-1990s, earning a spot on the American national team for two consecutive years and participating in numerous competitions around the United States.

and Tiffany Levine-Campbell, two of the best American climbers at the time, allowed for rote progression of the new routesetting ideas that were incubating. "Jason Campbell and Tiffany Levine-Campbell had just come back from Europe and they decided to just hang out and train at our gym for a couple months," remembers Steele. "They wanted me to set some harder routes—with grades of 5.12c, 12d, 13a, 13b—so that they would have some routes to do laps on. Those couple of months were really the formative time. Even though I went to routesetting clinics, it was really the daily feedback of those two that was most helpful."

While working at RockQuest, Steele continued to write about competition organization and penned a philosophical manifesto that he titled the Routesetting Sermon. The document contained much of the technical nuance that he, Welser, Danielson, and others had spent years refining in college. "Routes can elicit emotion as much as any poem, from thrutchy, hate your way to the top, eulogies, to serene, Zen-like experiences," Steele asserted in the text. "The routesetter sets the tone that the climber must react to or with."

Steele's Routesetting Sermon was groundbreaking in the way it combined broad ruminations on the routesetting craft with practical approaches and processes taught by the American League of Forerunners (ALF), through which Steele had earned national-level certification. As an ALF member, Steele had been specifically mentored by Mike Pont and Steve Schneider, yet he was also among the first generation of routesetters to possess a climbing skillset honed exclusively on plastic holds rather than real rock. The pillars of his sermon were six "commandments," universal tenets annotated for aspiring and experienced routesetters alike, with asides on ways in which plastic holds merited separate, unique methodology:

1. Plastic does not climb like rock, and routesetters should thus not attempt to emulate nature. "Routes should make people dance, a connotation which to me, involves balance, flexibility, grace, precision, innovation, tenacity, power, subtlety, finesse, will (both physical and emotional), and techno."

2. The climber/competitor should *learn* from the climb. "This does not mean that every move has to be a learning experience," wrote Steele. "The climb is the sum of its parts."

3. There is no longer a significant difference between routes set in a gym for a general patron and routes set at a competition. "Difficulty [in competition] arises from the cumulative effect of all the moves (ie, power-endurance), not from the sheer difficulty of the moves (ie, power)," said Steele. "Most gym routes should act in a similar vein, as most people trying the routes are practicing (or training) to climb outdoors or to at least improve their skills."

4. Difficulty should not stem from reachiness: "In a gym or in a competition, a climb should be accessible to all," wrote Steele, thereby explaining a setting technique of using his elbow to measure distance when setting handholds, rather than his full arm—"If I can't make the reach in this manner, I begin to consider what shorter climbers would have to do to make the move; or if they could do it at all."

5. Routesetters should be cognizant of general size and body-type differences. "In general strive to set for people in the height range of 5 to 6 ft (the average adult)."

6. A good route has a perceivable flow and is fun. "Learn what people like and don't like," advised Steele. "It will vary from region to region."

Steele concluded his Routesetting Sermon by urging all partakers in the craft to learn from other routesetters, particularly those certified by the ALF.[19] The result of routesetting's increased sanctification—articulated by Steele, anchored by his college-aged peers, and soon expanding outward as the Midwestern crew took their expertise elsewhere—was an eventual rise of a larger group of well-trained, experienced routesetters. The routes that these young routesetters created on boulders soon became the backbone of United States competition climbing. The routes in the climbing gyms connected the competitors to the layperson climbers, as the routes remained on the gym walls—open for anyone to attempt—long after competitions had concluded.

As the influence of universities' routesetting spread outward, USA Climbing began to emphasize routesetting to a more formal degree. For example, after college, Danielson moved to Colorado and, along with Mike Moelter and a routesetter from Miami, Florida, named Kynan Waggoner, established USA Climbing's Routesetting Committee, mainly with the aim of systematizing the trade and certifying capable routesetters in the same way that the ALF had in the early 1990s.

Waggoner was an interesting addition to the USA Climbing milieu, having previously founded his own gym in Florida, X-treme Rock Climbing. He had also helped cruise ships around the world install artificial climbing walls for passengers' recreation and trained those ships' staff to inspect the walls and safely belay climbers. His

---

19. Steele's Routesetting Sermon was never made available to the general public in print form, but it is one of the most important documents in the history of American routesetting, along with print materials—such as the newsletters and certification courses—of the ALF, as well as the *ABS Organizer Handbook* published annually for a period by Scott Rennak.

diverse background made Waggoner adroit at seeing climbing's potential for significant growth and evolution, but he was also an enthusiastic advocate for competition; he had dabbled in all aspects of USA Climbing's competition-related operations, as well as the operations of its organizational precursor, the United States Competition Climbing Association (USCCA). He would recall, "Between the years of 1999 and 2005, I was working as an independent contractor for the USCCA as coach, team coach, national team head coach, or in a routesetting capacity. I was also volunteering as a regional coordinator; I was a member of the Coaches Committee; I was a member of the Adults Committee. Effectively, I was just trying to get myself involved in competitions in any way possible because I knew that I really liked something about competition. The routesetting, the coaching—whatever it was about that thing, I just enjoyed that environment."

Routesetting clinics around the United States became more common, too, and were most often attended by gym staffers seeking a degree of mentorship. This trainee model soon solidified into an official selection program for national competitions with assistant, apprentice, and intern titles.

One figure to emerge from the vibrant scene was Mike Helt. Helt hailed from the Pacific Northwest and was mentored by Molly Beard and other routesetters from the JCCA scene. As a competitor, Helt had been an ABS national finalist. He quickly parlayed his climbing talent into a full-fledged career as a routesetter, first at local events for the ABS and at competitions for the Sport Climbing Series (SCS), which was the label given to non-bouldering (roped) events under the USA Climbing umbrella. Helt eventually joined USA Climbing's Routesetting Committee and became the chief routesetter at regional, divisional, and national levels.

But Helt took his combination of competition experience and routesetting expertise in a unique direction in 2006 by founding a website, Routesetter.com. It was among the first websites of its kind, devoted exclusively to dispersing routesetting ideas and identifying industry trends. Helt's professional credentials gave the website an authority that surpassed all other routesetting and competition-themed resources online at the time. Also, Routesetter was a completely open forum for discourse. It included write-ups from Chris Danielson and other prominent figures of the time, as well as newcomers to the routsetting trade.

With a distinctly populist approach, Routesetter spurred the advancement of an eclectic community of setters; the website was not exclusive to people who were enrolled in USA Climbing's training program or enmeshed in routesetting at any sanctioned level. The website's maxim was, simply, "to bring ideas and psych to the routesetters that huddle in climbing gyms all over the world."

Underlying the routesetting advancements was new science for handhold and foothold creation. Innovative ideas permeated the climbing industry with regard to hold sizes, shapes, and uses. One of the handhold companies that had been born on the cusp of the bouldering boom was eGrips, started by climbers Ian Powell and Keith Fletcher in Boulder, Colorado. A childhood friend of Powell's, routesetter Ty Foose, soon joined the company and added to the creative interplay. Together, Powell and Foose devised textured surfaces for handholds that were more detailed and diverse than the climbing industry had ever seen.

A couple years after eGrips' founding, Powell had an epiphany while talking to an employee of a nearby factory producing inline skating wheels: the same polyurethane that gave skates' wheels their rubbery toughness might work for climbing holds.

Powell soon conjured up a mixture for climbing holds that was similarly polyurethane-based, and stronger than climbing's industry standard at the time. When molded, the new eGrips concoction coagulated to create handholds and footholds that were less breakable and more reusable in routesetting. Sometimes Powell would bounce the holds on concrete gym floors to illustrate the holds' durability to gym managers.

At first, the production of eGrips' polyurethane holds on a large scale moved from factory to factory. Early versions of the holds incorporated sand into the chemical mixture to create a sandstone-esque rubber. That mixture proved too damaging to the factory polyurethane pumps, but an opportune union occurred as inline skating's cultural popularity began to wane. The skating wheel company Kryptonics decided to work with eGrips on the development of new climbing holds. A Colorado company, Aragon Elastomers, guided by a plastics engineer named Chuck Demarest, became the epicenter for climbing's polyurethane revolution, and the entire handhold industry was rapidly transformed by the new chemical formula.

Powell would later comment on polyurethane being applied to a climbing context on an episode of the podcast *Plastic Weekly*: "We thought about patenting it and then we realized we were a couple of stoned 25-year-olds in a warehouse and we couldn't defend a patent—we didn't want to, we didn't want to spend our life like that, so we just gave up and we just told everybody, 'Yeah, can we all just start making [holds] out of urethane, please?'"

Although eGrips was doing groundbreaking work, it was subjected to a series of swift, significant business changes—first getting sold to one of the other leading handhold companies, Pusher, before evolving into a new brand, Choke Holds, under the direction of hold shaper Jessica Franco. But even with multiple transformations, eGrips' innovation was continual and analogous to developments taking place at other companies as well. Rob Mulligan, hold shaper for Voodoo Climbing, also conjured up a polyurethane-based mixture for handholds and footholds. He created holds with multiple surface textures, coarse in certain sections but smooth in others. Eventually this "dual-texture" design would be adopted by numerous other brands. And like eGrips, Voodoo Climbing saw several business changes, beginning as a grassroots endeavor of climber Frank Cornelius, then steered by Gina Richer and expanded with a modest staff.

In the process of its growth, Voodoo Climbing featured collaborations with a number of artistic climbers and routesetters such as Tony Reynaldo, Tyson Atwell, and Louie Anderson. Each hold shaper forged ahead, at times in accordance with other brands, maintaining an ongoing collective focus on the development of new hold shapes and styles. A creative vortex quickly emerged, with climbing hold shapers blending attributes of sculptors, chemists, geometrists, and artists-for-hire. Anderson, in particular, had previously worked for Radwall but now found himself as a highly sought-after "freelance hold shaper." In finding regular work, he would come up with approximately 500 different hold designs in a given year. He also published a book, *The Art of Coursesetting*, that compiled many of routesetting's fundamentals. The book included a section on competition organization and management penned by the ABS' mastermind, Scott Rennak. Anderson reflected on this time being a watershed period with its profusion of hold designs and ongoing routesetting specification. He labeled it as "the point at which the industry left its childhood and became adolescent, maturing and changing as it continued on its path toward the adulthood it enjoys currently."

Routesetting opportunities were expanded even more with the growing prevalence of extremely large holds on the American market. These holds, often uniformly textured and featuring asymmetrical curves, could be utilized in a variety of ways on a wall and force movement ranging from kneebars and rests to matched feet and slopey finishes. One of the first holds of this kind was Pusher's Boss, conceptualized by climbers Mike Call and Marc Russo, but other brands quickly released similar full-sized holds.

While the revolutions in handhold construction and design had mostly recreational implications, there was also a degree of solemnness behind certain changes taking place in the industry as well. The changes arched back to a tragedy that continued to reverberate: In 2003, a 22-year-old woman named Christine Ewing had been killed when she fell from a 20-foot-tall mobile artificial climbing wall in Missouri. Investigations found that the auto-belay cable to which Ewing was attached had been frayed and inadequate.

As a result of Ewing's fall and the media interest that followed it, the United States Consumer Products Safety Commission released a notice to climbing gym managers and "wall operators" around the country that focused on the hazards posed by well-worn gear—and particularly equipment related to Ewing's accident. The result of the notice in the years that followed was increased inspections of gym walls and equipment by their respective owners. Systematic efforts were made to preempt and prevent additional tragedies related to climbing indoors and on artificial structures. The widespread concern and alertness calcified into the formation of the Climbing Wall

Association (CWA), first as a tier of the broader Outdoor Recreation Coalition of America, and eventually as a separate entity.

Practically from its inception, the CWA's role was multifaceted: to merge common interests of climbing gym owners; to address safety matters (related to everything from wall construction to floor padding); and to work on industry-wide guidelines for gyms and other facilities.

The creation of the CWA indicated that the industry of gyms and their artificial climbing walls was expansive enough to merit a unified voice. Ewing's tragic death had represented the worst that could happen if such amalgamation did not exist.

The outcome of it all was an era of enlightenment for gym owners and managers, and a more cerebral attentiveness to "plastic" from all within the ever-expanding competition realm of the industry. The efforts devoted to "indoor climbing" now matched the thoughtfulness long given to real rock surfaces outdoors.

Another keystone for competition climbing in the new millennium was a generational shift that was taking place. Many of the most important names from the United States' competition past were assuming new roles and, in doing so, adding depth to the American competition infrastructure.

Robyn Erbesfield and Didier Raboutou, both of whom had been mainstays on event rosters throughout the 1990s, founded a youth-based training program in October 2004, called ABC Kids Climbing (an acronym that stood for Agility, Balance, and Coordination). In just a few years, the couple's ABC Kids Climbing platform and its eponymous facility in Boulder, Colorado, became one of the country's most famous institutions for training children to climb and compete. Among the pupils was a child gymnast named Margo Hayes; she would rocket through the competitive ranks and become one of the country's most promising young stars. The daughter of Robyn Erbesfield and Didier Raboutou, Brooke, would also train and find fast success as part of ABC Kids' youth team.

But ABC Kids Climbing was just one of several establishments that made Boulder the epicenter of competition climbing. The college city with 94,000 residents also featured the Boulder Rock Club and The Spot, a gym started by climber Dan Howley that was wholly devoted to bouldering. The Spot began holding its own series of competitions, The Spot Bouldering Series, in 2006. The series' eclectic themed events included a contest called Psychedelia that featured blacklights and a competition called the Gun Show, which entailed paintballing in between bouldering rounds. One competition in the series, advertised as the Night of the Rising Sun, included karate demonstrations beneath paper lantern decorations. Regional ABS competitions were also looped into The Spot Bouldering Series. The routesetters for these competitions were a particularly talented group, comprising many of the leading routesetters in the country at the time: Kynan Waggoner, Ty Foose, Ian Powell, and Jackie Hueftle, along with Neely Quinn, Seth Lytton, Chris Rogers, Joe Deshazo, Melinda Ryder, Greg Bruce, Jonny Hork, Ben Alexandra, Mike Auldridge, Wade David, Matt O'Connor, and others.

Boulder was not just the epicenter for competitions. It was also the location of USA Climbing's headquarters. Numerous gear companies also had their offices in the city and fed off the climbing craze by peddling everything from grip strengtheners to climbing-themed photography prints. Popular climbing films in the increasingly prevalent format of DVD, including titles like *Return 2 Sender*, *Big Game*, *Higher Ground*, *Inertia*, *Specimen*, and additional volumes of the *Dosage* series, were more popular than ever and could be found in all retail corners of the city.

In a fitting move, the generational shift and Boulder's flourishing also brought Roy McClenahan back into the forefront of the competition climbing fray. McClenahan had stayed on the periphery of the gym industry's expansion after the Berkeley World Cup of 1990, at first being connected with the growth of California's CityRock and later with the starting of the Boulder Rock Club. He had also devoted much of his time to establishing and overseeing a soft-goods sewing business, Persona, in Marshall, Colorado, just five miles south of Boulder.

Always a dyed-in-the-wool climber, McClenahan's recreational focuses were almost exclusively outdoor projects throughout the 1990s, with trips to nearby Eldorado Canyon; Vedauwoo, Wyoming; the Needles of South Dakota; and Yosemite, California.

However, in 2004, McClenahan took a job as a sales representative for a new shoe brand, Evolv. Over the next 15 months, he amassed 50,000 road miles traversing the country to demo Evolv's climbing shoes at gyms and competitions of all sizes and scales. Many of the events that McClenahan attended in the period were the contemporary iterations of competition heritage that traced back to the late 1980s. In fact, McClenahan was bearing witness firsthand to the unforeseen lineage of Jeff Lowe's sport climbing circuit, in which he had played a pivotal role.

It was undoubtedly a different scene, and McClenahan knew it. Most of the competitors in the 1980s—McClenahan's peers—had been birthed in an era of solely trad climbing. In contrast, the twenty-first century saw sport climbing and bouldering well-established and widely accepted. Techniques once scorned for training, like toproping and hangdogging, were now standard. Competition walls were no longer erected on the sides of buildings or lodges, or inside theaters, and competition organizers did not have to transport walls piece by piece to faraway host venues.

"This was nothing short of a sea change, but it was not a surprise because it was gradual and I'd had my hand in the industry all along," McClenahan would say of the scene's many transformations. Competitive climbing had now been fully reimagined and realized in gyms, nearly twenty years after the big-budget christenings at Snowbird in the 1980s.

"The endeavor of producing climbing competitions went from a requirement of massive overhead, involving significant investments in personnel and material, to extremely lean, grassroots operations, opportunistically leveraging the existence of all those climbing gyms which had proliferated across the country throughout the 1990s," McClenahan would later reflect. "Even more interesting were the changes to be seen in the composition of the pool of competitors. By 2004, the average age of competition climbers ranged from mid-teens to early twenties, while most of the competition climbers of the 1980s were a bit older than that—most being firmly planted in their twenties or even late twenties. Even more notable was the contrast in the vector of the climbing careers of the different generations: the later generation comprised kids and young adults whose apprenticeship unrolled in the opposite direction from what I had seen in the 1980s. In the 1980s, we went from climbing outside to competing indoors. Most of the generation of competitors from the 2000s got their start indoors, and many had little outdoor experience save for the older youths having been invested in bouldering, and sometimes, though rarely, sport climbing outside."

While competition climbing was gaining its new generational identity on a professional level, a subculture continued to thrive. One of the most popular competition series to develop outside

of the scope of USA Climbing was the Mammut-EMS Bouldering Championships, created by Jason Danforth, Pete Ward, and
Lu Yan.

Anchored by a consortium called the New England Climbing
Consultation, and recognized for its excellence in crowd-pleasing
routesetting, the Mammut-EMS series embraced a level of jubilance
that belied its formalization. As the culmination of a circuit that visited
Fairfield, New Jersey; Salt Lake City, Utah; and Boston, Massachusetts,
the 2007–08 championship concluded with overall victories by Alex
Puccio and Paul Robinson—the latter being an alumnus of Scott Rennak's Eastern Bouldering Series from nearly a decade prior. Other
competitors relished the spotlight at various moments throughout
the three-city tour as well. For instance, at the series' penultimate
competition, held on an artificial outdoor wall constructed under the
sweltering summer sun in Salt Lake City, a championship field of
25 top competitors was systematically whittled down on technical
routes set by Chris Danielson, Jackie Hueftle, Tim Kemple, Shannon
White, and Ryan Torcicollo. Chris Sharma topped three out of the
five boulders in the finals at Salt Lake City to win that specific city's
men's division, and Alex Johnson won the women's division by flashing all five respective boulders.

In between the routesetting of "crazy technical, body tension,
campus, dynamic problems," the Mammut-EMS Bouldering tour—
and particularly the annual championships—featured a revelry that
could not exist in a more professionalized organizational context.
"The energy reverberates off of the multifaced walls like light showing
through an impeccably well-cut diamond, and the MC of the event,
Jason Danforth, who's dressed in pornographic red leather pants,
screams his call of action so loud that his voice shudders violently

before going completely hoarse," recounted Tim Keenan in covering the championship for *Urban Climber.*

Keenan noted that New England Climbing Consultation "brought the soul of competition back to the people" with its Mammut-EMS series. In using personnel like Ward and Danforth and Danielson especially, the series was linked to an eventual group of competitions connected to USA Climbing under the moniker of the Unified Bouldering Championships (UBC). Mike Helt served as a chief routesetter. Alluring facets of most of the UBC events was that they were held outside—away from the gym model that was standard for competition hosting—and worked in conjunction with an unpredictable array of architectural miscellany. Although UBC only ran a handful of competitions, locations included the top of a Salt Lake City hotel parking garage and New York City's Central Park.

The fifth annual Red Rock Rendezvous, held in Red Rock Canyon National Conservation Area in Las Vegas, Nevada, over the weekend of March 28–30, 2008, touted a goal similar to that of the UBC: "to bring new people into climbing." The Red Rock Rendezvous featured a number of instructional clinics such as *Introduction to Climbing* taught by members of the American Alpine Club. Adding to the beginner-friendly offerings were 45 professional climbers, such as Tommy Caldwell, Beth Rodden, Joe Kinder, Chris Lindner, Dean Potter, and Alex Puccio, taking part by bouldering, speaking at the clinics, and motivating participants for a "graffiti clean-up and trail maintenance project."

The manifestation of such popular interest—bouldering as a sport of the people, by the people—and all the professional progress that had been made with American routesetting would come into full relief in the months that followed. Soon the rebirth of competition climbing would be fully realized in a renowned event that was equal parts new and old.

It was time for the young generation to take the crown and assume the throne, and Colorado would once again provide the backdrop.

CHAPTER 18

THE BEST IN THE WORLD

BY 2008, USA CLIMBING had progressed to become not only the chief governing body for American competitors, but also the vessel for a steady stream of well-organized and well-attended events that could span an entire given year. The raucous American Boulder Series (ABS) was positioned to be the fall and winter circuit, running from October through February. The Sport Climbing Series (SCS) was situated to commence promptly at the end of the ABS tour and run from February to July. Exhibition competitions—such as popular, festival-style events like the Teva Mountain Games in Colorado, Adventures NYC in New York, the Smith Rock Detour in Oregon, and SendFest in Utah—were intended to populate the remainder of any given summer and keep spectators and athletes satiated until another annual push could begin.

Supporting all competitions was a list of USA Climbing sponsors, including Sterling Rope, Clif Bar, eGrips, Prana, Vibram, Mountain Khakis, and others. Some major backers such as The North Face had associations with climbing competitions that traced back to the pioneering endeavors of Jeff Lowe.

Beyond corporate sponsorships, USA Climbing had monetary support from seasonal memberships of every competitor. These membership dollars funded the substantial annual offering of varied circuits. The cost was $20 for a competitor to participate in an ABS season and $45 to participate in an SCS season. Of that membership revenue, five percent went toward a USA Climbing scholarship, awarded to competitors who submitted essays extolling the virtues of climbing and community involvement.

Similar but separate, Clif Bar partnered with USA Climbing to establish a $1,000 scholarship called Respect the Rock. The scholarship was aimed at developing climbing in areas around the country otherwise lacking in finances and community support. There were also numerous companies willing to sponsor individual climbers, and the ABS and SCS events thus served as earnest platforms and makeshift auditions for ensuing professional relationships. La Sportiva even created a unique reward system based on a ranking algorithm of competitors' four best competitions, known as the Believe in Achievement award. The grand prize for the competitor who ranked highest and earned the award was a year-long La Sportiva sponsorship.

Much of these peripheral initiatives, which gave competitions and their organizational body a noteworthy presence beyond just the competitive events, were created or shaped by the leadership of USA Climbing at the time—Jim Concannon as president, Bob Broun as vice president, Anne-Worley Moelter (formerly Bauknight) as executive director, Mike Moelter as operations director and routesetter organizer, Kynan Waggoner as project manager, and a cast of dedicated personnel that included Kyle Clinkscales, Paul Gagner,

Debbie Gawrych, Emily Harrington, Scott Rennak, Chris Warner, and others.

Along with adept leadership and multiple sponsorships, one of the most remarkable aspects of USA Climbing by 2008 was the depth of young world-class competitors, many of whom had been incubated in the gym system that had begun to emerge in the mid-1990s.

To maintain a degree of order and schematization amid the abundance of competitor members, USA Climbing's competitions were divided into age and gender categories for any participants under the age of 19—methodology that had been retained from the Junior Competition Climbing Association (JCCA) of previous years. For USA Climbing's adult competitors, there were multiple divisions as well—known as the Difficulty categories—based on skill level: Recreational, Intermediate, Advanced, and Open divisions. Competitions sanctioned by USA Climbing also often featured a Masters category for competitors over the age of 40.

Of particular note was that competitors within the age range of 16 and 19 years old were given the choice to compete in a respective youth age category or compete in one of the Difficulty (adult) categories. The age-based configuration allowed for many of the top American young stars of the period—such as Alex Puccio, Alex Johnson, Daniel Woods, Ryan Olson, and Tyler Haack, who were all hovering around 18 years of age, as well as Tiffany Hensley, who was only 16 years old—to compete against and alongside compatriots who were older, such as Paul Robinson who was 20 years old, Angie Payne, who was 23 years old, Chris Sharma, who was 27 years old, and Lisa Rands, who was 32 years old.

Such fluidity encouraged a competitive ethos by permitting talented American youths to dabble in the upper echelon of competition before having to commit fully to it. Over time, this also meant that the youth phenoms were systematically competing at a world-class level—against world-class adults.

Along with progress in the competition arena on a domestic level, the international competition scene continued to evolve. In January, 2007, in Frankfurt, Germany, 57 climbing federations from countries around the world had endorsed the formal establishment of the International Federation of Sport Climbing (IFSC). Although new in name, this global governing body was a succession of the UIAA's technical commission for competition climbing (the International Climbing Council), which had been managing a worldwide network of events for years.

The freshly branded IFSC continued the UIAA's longstanding tradition of holding World Cup circuits—primarily in Europe and Asia—with bouldering, lead, and speed climbing disciplines. A para-climbing Cup was also soon established. The inaugural IFSC circuit featured events in Erlangen, Germany; Sofia, Bulgaria; Trento, Italy; Chamonix, France; Zürich, Switzerland; Kazo, Japan; Qinghai, China; and elsewhere.

American competitors occasionally traveled abroad to participate in these international competitions. For example, in September 2007, Emily Harrington competed in the IFSC's World Cup lead climbing discipline in Avilés, Spain, and finished in 14th place. At the same competition, in the bouldering discipline, Daniel Woods finished in 43rd place.

As USA Climbing continued to strengthen and support a strong American system of gyms and events, questions and curiosities arose about how the top American competitors would do against the world's top competitors under more advantageous conditions. To participate in an IFSC event generally required a long airplane flight overseas, not to mention the rigmarole of securing proper visa paperwork, booking lodging, making transportation arrangements in a foreign country, and training in an unfamiliar gym. Where would the elite Americans place in the final standings of an IFSC competition if extraneous detriments like jetlag, travel anxiety, and general cultural foreignness could be alleviated or eliminated altogether?

That question would be answered in a thrilling narrative that began with an announcement that one of the stops on the IFSC's 2008 bouldering World Cup circuit would be Vail, Colorado. There, the summer's Teva Mountain Games would provide an optimal backdrop for the prestigious climbing happening by featuring a festival atmosphere and a host of other competitive events like mountain biking, river rafting, kayaking, and a "mud run."

Economically, the Teva Mountain Games was the only feasible platform for holding any competition in the United States at the level of an IFSC World Cup. USA Climbing's gross annual operating budget was only a few hundred thousand dollars, which would not have been enough to cover the hefty World Cup expenses by itself. But by linking up with the Teva Mountain Games, among the largest outdoor recreation festivals in the country, USA Climbing was able to pass along some of the World Cup's promotional costs to other entities. And for years the Teva Mountain Games had been run by Anne-Worley Moelter and Mike Moelter, whose associations with USA Climbing made for fairly logical inroads. In fact, Anne-Worley Moelter had a seat on the IFSC's board at the time and proved to be instrumental in convincing the rest of the board members of the IFSC that the Teva Mountain Games possessed the necessary infrastructure to incorporate a World Cup climbing competition into its jam-packed schedule.

The Teva Mountain Games of 2008 were to be overseen by a local non-profit, the Vail Valley Foundation, and promoted by a local marketing company, Untraditional Marketing, owned by executives Joe Blair and Joel Heath. These companies would also significantly lighten the logistic load for USA Climbing. Blair and Heath were already fans of climbing competitions. They had witnessed climbing's popularity with previous annual competitions held at the Mountain Games that were not part of the World Cup circuit.[20]

But more important than bankable crowd interest at Vail was the reality that the United States was finally going to be given the chance to host another World Cup; the previous American World Cup competition had occurred 18 years prior with Jeff Lowe's event at the University of California's Greek Theater in Berkeley.

In matters of evolution and persistence, the summer of 2008 would thus mark the full renaissance of the United States competition scene—which had successfully wound through a maze of organizational deviations and acronyms, from the ASCF to the JCCA and the USCCA, to finally become its stable self. Flanking such large alterations since the 1990s as well had been innumerable grassroots movements in matters of competition formatting, gym design, sports

---

20. These initial climbing competitions at the Mountain Games in Vail had been held on a 360-degree freestanding artificial boulder created by Massachusetts-based Rockwerx and nicknamed the Mushroom Boulder. However, with the World Cup announcement came a stipulation that a new competition structure had to be built to meet IFSC standards. It would have to reside on a single plane—not 360 degrees—so spectators could watch the competition without having to move. Thus, a modular wall system with adjustable angles was designed by Kynan Waggoner and Mike Moelter and eventually built by a French company, Pyramide. The old Mushroom Boulder was discarded in a junkyard, where it remained for years before being moved to the exterior of Pure Bouldering Gym in Colorado Springs, Colorado. Like Lowe's Twin Towers from 1990, the Mushroom Boulder is another unique and venerable structure in the United States' competition history.

training, and gear construction. Underlying all of the evolutions and relentless creativity over the span of nearly two decades had been a steady roster of elite American competition climbers.

Indeed, for the rest of the world, the upcoming Vail World Cup was situated to be an important pit stop on the eight-city annual tour, slated in between other bouldering World Cup events that season in Grindelwald, Switzerland, and Fiera di Primiero, Italy. In keeping with tradition, a Rockmaster event, also part of the 2008 IFSC bouldering circuit, would represent competition climbing's early roots. But for the United States, in particular, the event in Vail would be a symbol of a long, multigenerational journey that spanned nearly all states and all gyms; it represented the United States' competition climbing saga as it pertained to the rest of the world. *Urban Climber* reported at the time, "The hosting of a truly global comp, one with an expected 30-nation attendance and sponsored by the International Federation of Sport Climbing (IFSC), marks a new day in top-flight plastic pulling for the US."

In order for the long chronicle of the United States' competition identity to culminate in 2008 at Vail, though, the abundance of top-level, primarily gym-trained climbers around the country first had to be whittled down to a select group of athletes who would represent the United States on the World Cup stage. It would be a monumental task. The World Cup was the pinnacle for adult competitors, but the United States did not even have an active adult national team anymore, not to mention any coaches for such a team.

But it did have a vibrant climbing culture, more keen and varied than ever before.

So, rather than create an entirely new system for narrowing the vast, country-wide field of climbers to a small, esteemed national team, USA Climbing opted to utilize the competition framework that was already entrenched in the consciousness of American climbers-at-large. Following that logic, 2008's ABS championship, held February 14–16, was chosen to be the official qualification platform for the World Cup event scheduled to take place in Vail six months later. The top six male competitors and the top six female competitors at the ABS championship would thus compose the United States' national bouldering team.

And if any tangible proof was needed that the American competition scene had been successfully revitalized to form a robust coupling of athletes and fans—of icons and icon admirers—it was evident in the crowd that turned up at that ABS championship, held at The Spot gym in Boulder, Colorado. Nearly 700 fans steadily crowded into the gym's cozy interior throughout the three-day period. At times, the line of people wanting to enter the building snaked around the outside parking lot—all fans eager and willing to endure the frigid mountain cold of a Colorado February to witness the christening of the United States' World Cup representatives.

Inside the warm venue, the atmosphere for the 2008 ABS championship continued in the party style established by previous years' events. Eclectic music was provided over The Spot's main speakers by DJ AJ, with running commentary of the competition provided by Scott Mechler and several other emcees. The energy and the excitement were building to a fever pitch.

Employees of The Spot such as Jackie Hueftle, who had become one of the most distinguished routesetters in the country, balanced the onus of tending to the massive crowd of hyped spectators with the charge of controlling more than 100 participatory competitors, 60 personal coaches, and myriad photographers from national media outlets that were also present. "The Spot was really futuristic in its design, as it had a great workout area, an upstairs conference room, yoga room, and cafe with a really nice professional espresso machine and lots of room to sit," Hueftle would reflect on the climbing gym's layout being well suited for crowded events, and particularly one as significant as the 2008 ABS championship. "There was a whole section of balcony in front of the yoga room just for viewing events. The upstairs—cafe and balconies—were always packed, the stairways were packed, and the entire rest of the gym that wasn't cordoned off was also packed. It was hard to get around during these things, and the energy was palpable."

As the ABS championship progressed through its early rounds and its initial competition boulders—and eventually tapered to a rousing final round—the party aura turned more serious with the crowd's collective realization that history was being made. The upcoming results would have hefty international implications.

The chief routesetter for the ABS' Open categories was Kynan Waggoner, and he had set a diverse smattering of boulders in varying styles to challenge the competition's finalists. Some of the competition boulders that Waggoner and his setting squad had created in The Spot were highly technical and required methodical movement on crimps, while others featured far reaches—or dynos—to bulbous slopers. Several boulders involved sequences of a dozen moves, which was longer than typical IFSC boulders that had only approximately five or six total moves. The combination of styles and the quantity of moves provided spectators with a mix of visual flash and finesse, ensuring that any victory would be had in a most decisive fashion.

The men's field of finalists was enlivened by strong, consistent climbing from Boulder resident Mark Hobson. Hobson's close connection to the host city endeared him to the immense crowd. But the eventual victory in the men's division came down to a struggle between two of the most established names in the sport: Chris

Sharma and Paul Robinson—both of whom flashed the first three of four total finals boulders to best Hobson in the scoring.

The fourth—and last—boulder in the men's division finals featured a pinch hang with a precision toe-hook. Although the boulder was a crowd favorite for the way it forced competitors to hang and peer through their legs at the mass of spectators in The Spot, neither Sharma nor Robinson found success in powering through the necessary physicality. When the points were tallied, however, Robinson won the 2008 ABS championship and qualified in first place for the men's World Cup team.

Robinson's victory offered its own brand of localism, as he was originally from New Jersey but in the midst of his sophomore year at the University of Colorado Boulder. He had lived in the city for more than a year and trained indoors at the nearby gym, CATS. But coupled with his gutsy victory was an awareness of the international battle that now loomed. "It was a dream of mine that I had had for a very long time," Robinson would remember of the ABS accomplishment. "It was epic to win at home in Boulder and in front of such a psyched and huge crowd at the Spot. Knowing that I had qualified for the World Cup, I was excited but also very nervous. I had no idea how strong those guys were and how well I would do on an international platform."

Sharma placed second in the ABS results behind Robinson. Third place went to Sean McColl, but his Canadian nationality negated him from United States national team contention. Hobson ultimately placed fourth. Daniel Woods, who had won the ABS championship the three previous years, did not take part. However, Woods was given a position on the United States' World Cup bouldering team because he had won the ABS championship and the climbing portion at the Teva Mountain Games the previous year.

The women's finals proved to be equally electrifying, supported by a storyline that traced back to previous championships. Beginning in 2006, Alex Puccio had begun transitioning out of the youth scene and into events with more adult competitors. With that, Puccio, as the decorated youngster often enmeshed in rosters of older stars, launched a surge of dominance on the ABS stage—winning the championship in both 2006 and 2007.

Constantly nipping at Puccio's heels had been Alex Johnson, who had earned second place at the championship in 2006. Adding to the plot was that the two American women were the same age, yet had vastly different climbing styles. Johnson was 5'9", and she used her extensive reach as the cornerstone of her consistently smooth movement on a given route. Puccio, in contrast, was a muscular 5'5"—not notoriously short for a competition climber, but nonetheless at a reach disadvantage when compared with taller competitors. Puccio had developed a climbing style that relied on strength, not range. A catchphrase had even developed—"Puccio Power"—to describe the way Puccio was able to pull through taxing physical movements with seeming ease on a consistent basis in competitions.

Fittingly, the 2008 ABS championship saw Puccio and Johnson, friendly and polite rivals, once again going head-to-head in the finals. Each competitor appeared to match the gauntlet thrown down by the other in the inaugural boulders. The duo's parity started to dissolve by the third boulder, a sloper sequence that suited neither Johnson's lauded reachy methods nor Puccio's ferociously strong style. Puccio reached the highest point of the boulder's sequence and was ultimately awarded a higher score. Johnson, ever tenacious, responded by reaching the top of the fourth boulder—a feat that Puccio could not duplicate.

The close battle between Johnson and Puccio in the finals equated to rousing sports theater, appropriate for such a historic event. When the competition finally concluded and all the narrow scores were tabulated, it was Puccio who arose victorious. Johnson earned a close second place, and Paige Claassen earned third place. Tiffany Hensley and Lisa Rands were also awarded places on the American World Cup roster. The nail-biting excitement in the women's division had suddenly added another layer to the United States' competition saga. Johnson, Hensley, Rands, and Claassen would have another chance to best Puccio in a few months. The Vail World Cup loomed, and everyone knew it would be the biggest competition stage of all.

CHAPTER 19

THE STUFF OF LEGEND

F OLLOWING THE EXCITEMENT OF THE ABS CHAMPIONSHIP, and with a roster of national bouldering team members officially set, USA Climbing began to expedite the preparations necessary to ensure that the upcoming World Cup in Vail would be a success.

Among the most pressing matters was to connect the American competitors with an established team of coaches. Those coaches selected to lead the team could also oversee national team rosters for years to come, which would most certainly vary with future competitions, championships, and the respective careers of the team members.

One of the most logical choices for the head coaching position of the American team was Kyle Clinkscales, who had acted as USA Climbing's national team coach since the organization's inception.[21]

---

21. Clinkscales is generally recognized as the first USA Climbing national team head coach. The distinction traces back to an international event in Italy in 1999 that featured American climbers Sarah Brown and Alice Braginsky competing under Clinkscales' tutelage. It's worth noting that USA Climbing—as a moniker—did not yet exist at the time, but the technicality should not diminish the accuracy of the designation or Clinkscales' coaching longevity at the national level.

A vast majority of USA Climbing's professionalism as it related to coaching at the time was directly linked to Clinkscales' ideas and efforts. He had created an inaugural national team training camp in 2005, started a coaches' committee, and penned USA Climbing's official code of conduct for coaches. On the occasion that other American climbing instructors had needed funding to travel to competitions in various parts of the world in USA Climbing's nascent days, Clinkscales had most often been the one lobbying the organization for the necessary capital.

But by early 2008, Clinkscales had also become deeply involved in other initiatives related to American climbing's larger presence. He and an assistant, Stan Borodyansky, had grown a modest gym team at Exposure Rock Climbing near Dallas, Texas, into the prestigious Team Texas, one of the largest and most successful competition climbing teams in the nation's history. Maintaining consistent success with individual competitors and Team Texas lineups of all ages kept Clinkscales busy. As a result, he was given a much deserved coaching role for the 2008 bouldering national team, but the head coaching position was given to a former competitor named Claudiu Vidulescu.

Vidulescu hailed from Romania but had been living in the United States since 2001. His initial base of operations had been Sportrock Climbing Center in Washington, D.C., where he had worked as a routesetter and a coach of the gym's junior team. But he had broken from tradition by creating the Evolution Climbing team. Rather than being associated with a single gym, the Evolution team was an assemblage of operationally independent climbing squads. It was collectively more professional than the average regional youth team. Vidulescu would visit and coach the different groups on a regular basis. All combined, the Evolution team included young athletes from Washington, D.C., Philadelphia, New York City, and Boston, and quickly expanded beyond its metropolitan East Coast roots.

"Step by step, month by month, more people would be on board with what I was trying to do, and that was put together the best climbers in each [geographic] area, go to that area—maybe bring some from other areas—and have everyone training together with high-intensity and high-performance type of climbing," Vidulescu explains of Evolution's methodology. "I'd write down what the climbers should do until our next meeting. Then we'd email or call back and forth and talk about what was working or what was not working."

In the first year of the Evolution team's existence, six of its eight kids qualified for the United States' youth national team. Such success, and the innovation of the team's collectivist principle, ingratiated Vidulescu with American competition organizers; he was chosen to be a coach for the United States' team of youngstars at multiple World Youth Championships run by the UIAA, particularly in Scotland in 2004 and in China in 2005.[22]

---

22. Prior to traveling to China, Vidulescu held a three-day "Pre-Worlds" training camp for the members of the American youth team in Atlanta, Georgia. It was the first preparatory summit of its kind, but it is just as significant for the unplanned team-building that took place. Vidulescu and his wife were moving into a new house the same day that all the team members arrived in Atlanta. When the team's prearranged housing accommodations fell through, everyone ended up boarding at Vidulescu's new home. "My wife and I moved into the house around 4:00 PM, and the kids arrived at 5:00—luckily enough they helped us move all our furniture from the moving truck into the new house," Vidulescu recalls. "The air conditioner didn't work that first night, so we had about 20 kids and coaches staying in the house, spread out everywhere. Kyle [Clinkscales] was there, and he ended up going to Wal-Mart at 2:00 AM to buy fans for everyone because it was so hot. It was kind of a nightmare, but also it's something that everyone that was there will remember forever."

Videlescu and Clinkscales were two of the most respected competition climbing coaches in the United States; to complete the optimal coaching trifecta for Vail in 2008, USA Climbing chose another
competitor-turned-coach, Tyson Schoene, to act as an assistant.

Schoene's interest in competition climbing dated back to his
childhood. His father traveled to Europe frequently for conferences
and brought back European magazines—with coverage of World
Cup events—for Schoene to study; Schoene would later recall using
German and French translation dictionaries to decipher what the foreign magazines were saying about various competitions. That interest
in competition climbing was further fueled when the Sport Climbing
Championships series formed in the United States in the late 1980s.
Schoene explained his personal connection to American competition's history in an interview, stating, "I started to really get psyched
in the mid-late eighties when sport climbing came around. I remember going to a comp...I think in Seattle, it was one of the national
events with guys like Jim Karn and Chris Hill. I couldn't have been
more psyched. I went out and bought black tights [because] that's
what the top guys were wearing."

Schoene took part in climbing competitions throughout the early
1990s, having even participated in a youth portion of the longstanding bouldering contest at Mount Woodson at the beginning of the
decade. But he exited the competitive climbing circuit due to a scar-
city of competitions around his home in the Pacific Northwest after
a few years and opted to focus instead on snowboarding. In the early
2000s, however, he reemerged on the scene as the mastermind behind
a talented and successful climbing team at the Vertical World climbing gym in Seattle. The facility was significant for being one of the
country's oldest indoor climbing gyms and also had the distinction of
being one of the first to have its own climbing team. Schoene would

recall frequenting the gym—then still known as Vertical Club—as a kid, saying, "Rich Johnston and Dan Cauthorn, the owners of Vertical World, used to pay for me and a couple other guys' entry fees to comps. We would travel together and put Vertical Club stickers on things and wear the shirts. That, I believe, is when it all started with Team VC."

Under Schoene's guidance, Vertical World's team quickly grew to more than 50 young members, and the gym itself expanded to four separate locations around the state of Washington. In time, two of Schoene's young athletes, Sean Bailey and Drew Ruana, would progress through the Vertical World youth climbing program to become key stars on the national and international stage. But for the time being, the extensiveness of Vertical World's youth program made Schoene not only deftly qualified to fine-tune the upcoming talent and future generations of American competition climbers, but also to help head up the current youths on the national team as the summer of 2008 approached.

With the national team and its trio of coaches established in early 2008, the months following February's ABS championship passed in a blur. Spring brought idyllic climbing conditions in Colorado and other parts of the United States, so most climbers were left to enact their own training programs at outdoor crags and in local gyms. In some cases, the best preparation entailed not altering the formulas that had already proved effective. "I was just training and studying at [the University of Colorado Boulder]," Paul Robinson would say about his routine during the lead-up to the World Cup in Vail. "Nothing really out of the ordinary. I climbed a lot both inside and out and looked forward to the big event."

While the competitors trained with a pervasive calm, the climbing media eagerly latched onto the larger patriotic storyline that was playing out with each passing day. Magazine headlines heralded the onset of WORLD CUP FEVER. "Excitement is building as 20 of America's strongest competitors prepare to face off against challengers from across the globe (reigning Bouldering World Champion Kilian Fischhuber, David Lama, and Anna Stöhr, among them) and answer the question: how do we stack up?" posed *Urban Climber* in its June/July 2008 issue. At the onset of summer, the United States national team finally convened for a two-day training session at the Boulder Rock Club. The sessions mostly consisted of apprising the competitors of the logistics of international adult competitions and reviewing the IFSC's scoring system. "I never thought I was the coach. What I was—I was the wrangler," explains Vidulescu. "I had to keep all the people on the team together, make sure they knew what time isolation would be, make sure they knew what the rules would be, and make sure they knew what to do to prepare themselves. You can't call someone like that a coach. With the Evolution team, I was in charge of everything from training to dieting, whereas with the World Cup team, all these people were just kind of dropped in my lap."

Unconventional as the team might have been, the prestige leading up to the World Cup was the figurative maturation of American competition climbing. It marked the coming of age for an entire organizational structure. "Prior to 2008, adult competitors were kind of an afterthought," Clinkscales would later say. "Everything was based on the youth because that's where the money came from. 2008 was the moment where we were going, 'Okay, we must put energy and effort into the adult community too. We need to brand USA Climbing and make its events the biggest events in the country.'"

With members of the bouldering national team finally primed and looking to make history, the IFSC's World Cup event in Vail kicked off on June 6. With a couple days of preliminary Teva Mountain Games festivities having already taken place, the crowd that gathered around the bucolic grounds' freestanding artificial bouldering wall for the World Cup competition's formal start was primed for a big show.[23]

Some spectators set up tents on the expansive lawn while others clamored to stand at the front of the throng mere feet from the competitors. In many ways, the onlookers, gathering to witness American competition climbing history, harkened back to the crowd at the first Snowbird competition in 1988. The lively scene there, which had also been a mix of picnickers, photographers, and curious observers, had celebrated the momentous achievement of Jeff Lowe and Bob Carmichael, the ushers of international climbing's biggest American spectacle onto the side of the resort's Cliff Lodge.

In a way, the crowd at Vail exactly 20 years later celebrated the heritage of Snowbird too, as well as the heritage of all competitions that had followed it; the Teva Mountain Games' crowd was the zenith of the United States' storied competition past.

As the momentous World Cup event progressed under the cloud-filled Colorado sky, it was evident that the American competitors were as proficient on the boulders as the rest of the world's elite. Schoene, Videlescu, and Clinkscales had primed their national team for such a landmark experience. Multiple Americans coasted through the day's early rounds.

---

23. The climbing portion of 2008's Teva Mountain Games also featured a Citizen's Division that was open to the public and a Youth Division, both of which were separate from the World Cup proceedings.

However, if any Americans were going to do particularly well in the finals of the competition—or, better yet, place on the World Cup podium at the competition's end—it was going to be the result of a dogged, gripping contest. Also climbing well as the event cruised into its second day and the crowd on the lawn swelled were Canada's Sean McColl, one of the standouts from the ABS championship, Great Britain's Tyler Landman, and Italy's Gabriele Moroni in the men's division. They arose as the chief challengers to the American men who had withstood the competitive initial rounds: Chris Sharma, Daniel Woods, and the defending ABS champion, Paul Robinson.

The women's division was equally competitive and filled with international stars. Austria's Katharina Saurwein and Slovenia's Natalija Gros had appeared on World Cup podiums the previous year, and each appeared to be in top form on the current season's circuit. Austria's Anna Stöhr had won the previous stop on the 2008 World Cup circuit in Grindelwald just one week prior and seemed unwaveringly strong. But American women Alex Johnson, Alex Puccio, Tiffany Hensley, and Lisa Rands were holding steady. They stayed neck-and-neck with the international favorites as the early rounds ended and the finals were cast with a nationalistic glow. Suddenly a question started to flutter through the enthusiastic crowd: Might an American actually *win* the historic event?

To answer that question in the men's finals, Woods, Sharma, and Robinson would have to climb flawlessly on four dissimilar boulders. The common phrase "American style" had come to signify American boulderers' penchant for powerful movements of brute strength, often sustained throughout extended sequences, rather than the more graceful, balance-based "European style." Whatever phraseology was used, a diverse skillset would need to be utilized if any of the top American competitors were to beat the best from countries like France, Austria, Italy, and England that had great legacies of technical climbing.

The men's finals began with a steeply overhung boulder that necessitated steady progression up a left-hand arête. A heel hook and a big right-hand reach to a pink sloper, the penultimate hand-hold, proved arduous for every competitor. On the whole, competitors found more success on the second boulder, a dyno to a large donut-shaped pocket in a dihedral section of the wall. Daniel Woods, wearing a black and gray sleeveless jersey from The North Face (the official uniform of the United States team), stuck the dyno and bellowed loudly to the cheering crowd at the boulder's top. Italy's Moroni, adorned in blue, and France's Gérome Pouvreau, decked in his country's gray, reached the boulder's top as well and celebrated in more subdued fashion.

By the third boulder, the men's field had separated; Kilian Fischhuber, already a climbing legend in his native Austria, was clearly in the hunt for a possible win; Pouvreau was close on the scorecards, as was Great Britain's Landman. Sharma and Woods were climbing well, but the standout American for the day was proving to be Robinson. He made quick work of the snug finger pockets of the third boulder, unable to secure the final handhold but wowing the crowd with a lunging attempt. The excitement continued into every competitor's attempt on the last boulder. It featured an awkward outward-facing start that transitioned into a smattering of overhanging pockets. Fittingly, the upper section of the boulder featured a large ovular hold painted to look like the American flag. Fischhuber and Moroni were able to reach the top. Robinson, as the leading American to challenge for the win, came close but fell while reaching for a small, far-out crimp.

In the end, it was Fischhuber who won the men's competition, earning the gold medal with Moroni placing second. But as a suitable complement to the American setting, Robinson's performance, his first at the international level, was enough to earn third place—a bronze medal at Vail and a place on the World Cup podium.

If Robinson's third-place finish was a fitting result given the pervasive patriotism on the lawn at Vail, the result of the women's competition had the potential to be legendary and among the most celebrated showcases in the history of world competitions.

One of the American team favorites in the women's division, Lisa Rands, had already proved capable of greatness on the World Cup stage. She had famously won a bouldering World Cup event on June 26, 2002, in Lecco, Italy, thus becoming the first American woman to ever win such a title in the discipline. Puccio and Johnson were newer to international competition. In fact, Puccio's previous bouldering successes had happened almost exclusively in the United States, and Johnson, who also dabbled in rope climbing, had never before competed in a bouldering World Cup. Yet both women were as formidable as Rands, and the ABS championship had proved that they were each in top physical form.

The finals of the women's division kicked off with a straightforward first boulder. It required high foot placement and a balanced progression up a vertical face. Hensley set an optimistic tone for the United States' prospects with a quick initial send. Austria's Stöhr responded in kind, as did Johnson. The second women's boulder stylistically mirrored the arête progression from the opening boulder of the men's final round. Most women struggled on it, with Stöhr landing the top dyno and illustrating why she was considered to be one of the most exciting competitors on the European scene.

The third women's boulder featured a similar dynamic lunge near its top, and Johnson methodically began to separate herself from the rest of the field. She used her height to full advantage, precisely extending to handholds and maintaining composure that belied her relative inexperience at bouldering's most elite level.

Upon Johnson's reaching the top of the third boulder, a cool dusk settled over Vail and the realization hit that she was on target for a place on the podium. She could make history at the World Cup and provide a storybook ending to the United States' long and complicated competition narrative, but she would have to climb flawlessly on the fourth boulder in order to do so. Austria's Saurwein had reached the top of the third boulder as well and was also pursuing a high place in the standings. And Stöhr had several years of competition experience that had fine-tuned her nerves for such a suspenseful finish.

When the crowd's gaze turned to the fourth and final boulder, it was apparent just how heady the end of the competition would be. The boulder combined elements of previous boulders—snug finger pockets, a succession of right-hand taps up an arête, and an upper-section dyno onto a globular sloper.

Hensley and Puccio powered through the boulder's lower section of pockets as the crowd stood and cheered. Both competitors, however, struggled to latch the top dyno as the crowd collectively gasped in awe.

By this time, darkness had fallen over the lawn. The collection of spectators had grown to a fervent mass; some estimates put the turnout at 9,000 onlookers. And at the focal point of everyone was a lone spotlight, a flood of luminescence that encased the showdown between Johnson, Stöhr, and the other competitors who sought the gold medal.

Under the bright light, Stöhr approached the base of the wall and set up for her attempt on the final boulder. She scrunched her fingers inside its lower pocket handholds and used the arête to support a finishing lunge toward the top. Her left hand slapped the boulder's top sloper, but Stöhr couldn't secure a matching right hand before falling to the ground in a spectacular flail. The attempt confirmed that she would not win the gold medal, but the great effort throughout the competition had endeared Stöhr to the American crowd.

Johnson was able to similarly establish a secure position with a left-hand pocket and a right-hand arête for the boulder's conclusive dyno when it was her turn. She launched and latched one hand onto the finishing sloper. The crowd gasped in anticipation; the moment seemed to slow, Johnson was caught in legendary equipoise. In many ways, that quick demonstration of her grit and exertion denoted the development of the American team and the whole American competition infrastructure after so many years. One hard move in front of an adoring crowd epitomized it all.

Johnson fell to the ground just as Stöhr had, unable to match her hands at the boulder's top. Yet, an accomplishment that would have been unthinkable a few years before had officially been realized: an American had won a World Cup competition on American soil. Johnson, the eventual victor, lifted herself from the padded mat at the base of the artificial wall and the crowd applauded ravenously. Below Johnson's gold medal performance in the concluding results were Saurwein earning the silver medal and Stöhr earning the bronze medal.

"It was like a Cinderella story," says Vidulescu. "It was a phenomenal event, and no one—the athletes, the spectators, the people from USA Climbing, the people from IFSC—could have pictured such an outcome."

Equally as significant as Johnson's extraordinary victory in the women's division and Robinson's gutsy third-place finish in the men's division were the high standings of the other members of the United States' national team: Hensley, Woods, Puccio, Sharma, and Rands had all placed in the Top 10 of the respective men's and women's fields. "Everyone had showed up [from Europe] expecting it to be a beautiful location and a great new country to be in, but not really taking the American climbers into consideration," says Vidulescu. "It was almost like America had been, to a certain point, the underdogs—to the Europeans, at least."

Underlying the results was the fact that most of the Americans in the Vail World Cup had been nurtured under the contemporary American arrangement; they had trained in American gyms under the auspices of the American governing body, and they had been supported by a hearty American fan base. It was a multitiered system that now had proof of its own effectiveness, able to produce athletes of the highest competitive caliber.

With such depth, and a formal place in the annals of the IFSC's world-class competitions, the only direction that the American competition entity could expand was outward, targeting new markets and seizing expansion opportunities. Paralleling the enlargement was a new, intriguing question, less contingent on the efforts of individuals and more embracing of the fruitful climbing collective: Just how big could American competition climbing become?

CHAPTER 20

THE FUTURE IS NOW

T HE 2008 WORLD CUP provided a narrative of great athletic feats, particularly in the case of Alex Johnson. In retrospect during the
months that followed, however, the competition became a single
point in the larger tapestry of the United States' longitudinal youth
development. The American competition scene thus entered a new
phase with greater international clout and incorporated an even
wider young audience in the post-Vail period.

Amid an increased interest in climbing, in general, the ever-
growing network of gyms around the country continued to cultivate
a new generation of "kid crushers," as the United States' talented
youths were deemed.

Many of the top young competitors arose from areas of the
United States with sparse outdoor climbing options. Gyms and competition circuits in urban, farmland, and seaside regions increasingly
served as the sole developers of youth climbing aspirations, much as
they had in the early years of Scott Rennak's American Bouldering

Series (ABS). The Vail World Cup women's champion, Johnson, for example, hailed from Wisconsin, approximately 1,000 miles east of the most formidable American mountain topography. She had been first exposed to climbing via a portable climbing wall at the Wisconsin State Fair, and then honed her skills at a gym, Vertical Endeavors, in St. Paul, Minnesota. Her counterpart in many events' standings, Alex Puccio, was from Texas—and an alumna of Kyle Clinkscales' Team Texas. Meagan Martin, another competitor who had received accolades for placing high in competitions organized by the Junior Competition Climbing Association (JCCA) and the Professional Climbers Association (PCA) before entering the USA Climbing fray, hailed from the exceptionally mountainless suburbs of Orlando, Florida.

This abundance of competitors of all ages being trained at gyms in disparate regional pockets was quickly identified by USA Climbing as an American asset. Indeed, no other country in Europe or Asia possessed such gym depth or a roster of top youths that was spawned directly from it. To further emphasize the youth contingent, USA Climbing created a youth bouldering national championship that offset the adult-oriented ABS championship.

On an international scale, as momentous as the 2008 World Cup at Vail had been, it birthed new ambitions for American coaches and competitors related to having success at multiple international events rather than just one. "It wasn't until we started having our younger generation get hyped on World Cup that I started getting hyped," Tyson Schoene, who had acted in an assistant coaching capacity at the renowned World Cup at Vail, would say. "Winning one World Cup was cool. But placing top five at every event in a season was more my goal and mindset."

As competitions thrived for youths and adults alike, it became apparent that the gyms cultivating the United States' collective competition skillset were no longer the ideal venues for showcasing it. This was exemplified at the 2009 ABS championship, ultimately won by Daniel Woods in the men's division and Alex Johnson in the women's division, and hosted by The Spot in Boulder, Colorado. That competition, like previous ABS championships, was a raucous success with music, prize giveaways, and compelling routesetting, but it drew a massive throng of spectators—some of whom traveled hundreds of miles to attend, only to find standing-room-only viewing options at the finals. The Spot was widely regarded as one of the preeminent bouldering gyms in the entire world, yet it lacked the open floor space that was now necessary to accommodate a major bouldering event's audience. No other gym in the United States was particularly better suited to house a multitude of onlookers either, which prompted USA Climbing to conjure up a solution.

The burden of solving the spectating dilemma, which also befell smaller-scale competitions, was shouldered by Kynan Waggoner, who moved up USA Climbing's operational hierarchy to become, first, Operations Assistant and eventually Director of Operations. Waggoner's chief objective in the new role became the methodical improvement of indoor competitions' spectatorship, as he realized, "[USA Climbing] couldn't keep hosting these things in climbing gyms because we'd end up with parents that were really upset about flying their kids around the country and not being able to watch them compete."

Waggoner's initial solution was to repurpose the modular wall system from the 2008 Vail World Cup in a section of a chosen climbing gym that would allow for better visibility. This idea was put into practice at the ABS championship in 2010, held at a gym called

Sportrock in Alexandria, Virginia. Treadmills and other freestanding pieces of workout equipment were moved out of the gym's fitness area to create an easily viewable competition platform and a space for the freestanding competition wall.

Daniel Woods again won the men's division at the Sportrock event, and Alex Johnson took second place in the women's division behind winner Alex Puccio. However, the familiarity of the competitors on the ABS podium belied changes that were taking place in overall event presentation behind the scenes under Waggoner's direction. "This was really the start of us considering taking our bouldering national championships outside of climbing gyms," Waggoner would later reflect. "We had realized that it wasn't appropriate to do a bouldering World Cup in climbing gyms, but now we were faced with the fact that even at the youth level—and at our national level—we were seeing such success that we were turning spectators away and not providing a great competition experience. We needed to go someplace else that was set up to accommodate spectators in such a way."

A unique competition platform with a modular wall system was installed at the following year's ABS championship (won by Puccio in the women's division and Canadian Sean McColl in the men's division), although this would prove to be merely a preliminary phase of Waggoner's larger strategy to overhaul competition presentation. Similar to what Jeff Lowe had done for the North American Rockmaster Series of competitions 22 years earlier at the Community Theater in Berkeley and the Hec Edmundson Pavilion in Seattle, Waggoner envisioned competitions taking place in large municipal venues. Unlike Lowe's era, which had lacked a gym infrastructure to buttress the larger Rockmaster competitions, 2012 saw numerous gyms capable of supporting extensive local and regional circuits. But at the national level, Waggoner realized, championships would be best contested in multiuse community areas with greater expanses for observers, and optimal sightlines for parents and camera crews alike.

The first major USA Climbing competition under this improved viewing mission was the 2012 ABS championship, then branded as the culminating event of a Unified Bouldering Championship Pro Tour. The event was held at the Colorado Springs City Auditorium, a historic stone building that was known primarily for hosting concerts and school exhibitions. The auditorium's boxy layout proved ideal for presenting climbing in a decidedly theatrical manner, centering and spotlighting the competition's modular wall in front of a large grid of evenly spaced audience seats. The auditorium hosted the championship again the following season, with both Puccio and Woods reigning supreme each year in their respective divisions.

As Waggoner worked to improve climbing's literal and metaphoric visibility in new cities and markets, key personnel surrounding him at USA Climbing began to change. Anne-Worley Moelter, who had acted as the organization's chief executive officer for years, left the organization to start a gym, Movement Climbing and Fitness, in Boulder with her husband, Mike Moelter. The couple, along with Waggoner, had undeniably spearheaded USA Climbing's multiyear youth climbing focus and revived and revamped the adult sport climbing circuit. One of the most significant illustrations of their hard work paying off had been the hosting of an IFSC sport climbing World Cup at the Movement gym in 2011—the return of a sport climbing World Cup competition to the United States after a multi-decade absence. Bringing a sport climbing World Cup event back to the country was an epic achievement, as sport climbing was the discipline most deeply ingrained in competition climbing's global heritage.

But the departure of the Moelters from American competition climbing's governing body left a void, even though gyms around the country were still basking in the afterglow of world-class competitions and benefiting from a surging interest in indoor climbing.

USA Climbing's board of directors hired Keith Ferguson to be the organization's next CEO. Ferguson, a former sponsorship executive for the American professional bull riders' rodeo circuit and a former director of the United States Olympic Committee, stayed at the helm of USA Climbing for more than three years before being succeeded in the role of CEO by Mary-Claire Brennan. Like Ferguson, Brennan had served previously as a director of the United States Olympic Committee—a relevant credential as the International Federation of Sport Climbing (IFSC), USA Climbing's key sanctioning body, continued to vie for climbing's Olympics inclusion.

Upon Brennan's departure, Waggoner expressed interest to USA Climbing's board of directors to become the organization's new CEO. In many ways, Waggoner was the ideal candidate; his close ties to Anne-Worley and Mike Moelter, Chris Danielson, and other initial visionaries of the organization, as well as his experience shepherding the World Cup at the Teva Mountain Games, gave him prescient insight into growing the organization internally and externally. In addition, Waggoner had top-notch assistance from Krista Henehan, who had begun working for the organization as an event coordinator and project manager before directing USA Climbing's membership and marketing—and assuming Waggoner's previous role of director of operations.

Beginning his CEO tenure in June 2014, Waggoner continued to enact many of the initiatives that he had worked on in previous roles, including a targeted focus on youth competitors. The ABS

Youth National Championship in March 2014 featured a whopping 366 youth competitors, illustrating just how popular bouldering had become with American kids and teenagers at the time Waggoner took the reins.

In fact, bouldering remained a focal point under Waggoner's guidance, too, which deviated from the international norm. In Europe—and on the international circuit—lead climbing was still viewed as the preeminent competitive discipline. To Americans, however, bouldering was far and away the competition and recreational preference. This was largely a consequence of the uniquely American bouldering traditions of years past, particularly the ABS of Scott Rennak and the PCA of Mike Uchitel and Scott Mechler, as well as publications such as *Urban Climber, Bouldering,* and *DPM Magazine* that had promoted the youthful bouldering ethos.

Rather than force Americans to align with the international preference, Waggoner embraced the distinctiveness that the American bouldering craze offered. He chose to focus much of USA Climbing's subsequent efforts on it; USA Climbing hosted bouldering team training camps to prepare for future bouldering World Cup events, and a number of American gyms organized youth local and regional bouldering competitions while the national championships were still contested at municipal facilities such as the Monona Terrace in Madison, Wisconsin.

On September 1, 2015, USA Climbing's regional and divisional makeup was revamped with new geographic boundaries. The new boundaries separated a total of eight competition divisions and 16 competition regions around the United States. With the clearly defined regions—Cascadia, Mountain West, Midwest, Great Lakes, South Central, Capital, New England, and others—USA Climbing now had an official span of the entire country's youth scene with competition circuits in mind. "Over the next three years, USA Climbing will be closely monitoring the further growth of our membership and championship participation rates in order to restructure again, if necessary," read a USA Climbing press release about the altered boundaries. "The new structure will also allow the vast majority of our competitors to enjoy an 8-hour (or less) drive time to all competitions within their Region."

Amid such striation, there was a healthy bump in USA Climbing's membership—an 18 percent increase, most of which were kids. Waggoner made a point to homogenize American competitions at all levels. To Waggoner, it was less important to mirror the event formats of international federations, and more important to maintain the unique American heritage and stabilize the competition climbing experience in all states. "From the scoring format to the actual competition format itself, [USA Climbing] was seeing all kinds of different ideas being implemented at competition," Waggoner would later say. "I thought it would be best that we standardize as much as we could so that the competitor knew what to expect. They'd have a clearer understanding of how they were going to be scored, what their experience was going to be like."

In short order, the unique regional network adhered to a single set of regulations: the top 10 youth competitors in each category at any regional competition sanctioned by USA Climbing would earn invitations to a divisional championship; then the top six competitors in each category at a given divisional championship would receive invitations to the national championship. The standardized format was expected to increase the total number of young competitors by nearly 40 percent. It coincided with a new youth-themed marketing campaign by USA Climbing, which featured the slogan "Join the Movement." Complementing it all was the unveiling of a new USA

Climbing logo, adorned on everything from shirts and stickers to notebooks.

The success of USA Climbing's youth emphasis was evident in the fact that it continued to nurture world-class competitors. An unbroken streak of international achievements traced back to the 2008 World Cup at the Teva Mountain Games, but at the 2009 World Cup bouldering competition, again at Vail, Alex Puccio won the women's division and Daniel Woods placed second in the men's division. A headline at the time had proclaimed, AMERICANS SHINE AT VAIL WORLD CUP.

The following year, with Vail's festivities having become a celebrated mainstay on the annual bouldering circuit of the International Federation of Sport Climbing (IFSC), Woods won the men's division and Puccio placed fourth in the women's division.

The duo of Woods and Puccio, along with other Americans such as Alex Johnson, Carlo Traversi, Tiffany Hensley, and Angie Payne, would continue to place high in World Cup competitions in ensuing years.

In 2014, a 16-year-old American phenom named Megan Mascarenas finished in fourth place in the women's division at the Vail World Cup competition. The following year, Mascarenas finished in first place, and in 2016 she again won the competition, which had seen its Teva Mountain Games backdrop rebranded as the GoPro Mountain Games. Mascarenas' performance in the final round of competition at Vail in 2016 was regarded as "nearly perfect," as she successfully climbed to the top of all four boulders—three tops of which were reached on her initial attempts.

But the same year as Mascarenas' second consecutive victory at the Vail World Cup, she also won the women's discipline at the United States' Bouldering Open National Championship. The competition had shed its longstanding ABS moniker, but not its festive atmosphere. The winner in the men's division that year, 2016, was a young climber named Nathaniel Coleman, who was entering the adult circuit after a celebrated youth career. One recap of the performances of Mascarenas and Coleman at the event proclaimed, "Youngsters dethrone 9-time national champions Alex Puccio and Daniel Woods."

The 2016 Bouldering Open National Championship was also noteworthy for being livestreamed on YouTube with commentary by Brian Runnells and Chris Weidner. YouTube soon became a chief media vehicle for American competitions, with other popular events such as the Dark Horse competitions in New England and Oregon's annual Portland Boulder Rally also being streamed live. And a production company, Louder Than Eleven, established itself as the preeminent studio for filming and broadcasting the biggest championships in the United States. Some competitors, like Chris Sharma and Paul Robinson, started their own YouTube channels for presenting personalized content and new climbing projects. On the subject of running a YouTube channel, Robinson would say, "It definitely is not for everyone. It requires 10,000 times more work than Instagram, but for those that put the effort in, it is extremely rewarding. I love the community and just the overall vibe of You-Tube. I feel it has been very accepting and my subscribers really show their appreciation for my videos. I was always making videos and selling them for basically nothing to companies. They would market them poorly and more or less the video would die. I wanted to take all of this into my own hands. I don't mind if I don't make anything on my videos, but I want to have a place on YouTube where I have my own voice and I can show people that I am moti-vated and dedicated. I make videos on what I am passionate about, climbing and filmmaking. I also like to listen to what my subscribers are interested in as well."

In the age of YouTube subscriptions and Internet video sharing, any competition's visual presentation—and the presentation of climbing cinematography, in general—continued to owe a big tip of the hat to the vertical dolly and other mechanical innovations that Bob Carmichael developed almost three decades ago.

As livestreamed competitions became more common and young bouldering competitors like Coleman and Mascarenas garnered more headlines, a teenager from New York City named Ashima Shiraishi was hyped as a rock climbing wunderkind by the American media and touted as possibly the nation's next competition superstar. Coached by Obe Carrion, a mainstay on the PCA circuit from years past, Shiraishi was, at first, not even old enough to test her mettle on the adult circuit, but a large fan base immediately wondered how her competition career would progress. She eventually proved worthy of all the acclaim by claiming a victory in a Bouldering Open National Championship that saw thrilling back-and-forth climbing against Alex Johnson, by then acting as the savvy competition veteran. For all intents and purposes, this victory—youthful Shiraishi narrowly besting highly experienced Johnson—marked the torch being passed to a new generation that held its own promise and possibilities. Similar curiosity and anticipation mounted for another youngster on the competition scene named Kai Lightner. Still in high school when he started turning heads with his lanky frame and methodical climbing style, Lightner was labeled "Climbing's Boy Wonder" by one magazine after he won a slew of youth championships around the country. It was only a matter of time before Lightner, too, won a national title in the men's division—which he did in sport climbing the same weekend, and at the same competition, that Shiraishi also claimed victory in the women's division.

Young competitors who specialized in speed climbing such as John Brosler, Grace McKeehan, and Piper Kelly gained quick acclaim on the scene, too. Brosler even set a new American speed climbing record of 3.95 seconds on a 10-meter wall at a National Championship. And an annual Adaptive National Championship, organized by USA Climbing and fed by smaller-scale events, promptly rose to prominence and became the most significant climbing competition for adaptive and paraclimbers around the United States. A *Climbing* article by noted competitor and author Craig DeMartino quipped around this time that adaptive climbers were "taking the 'dis' out of disability with their boundary-pushing accomplishments."

Aside from large-scale climbing events in the United States that fed into the IFSC's World Cup configuration, the option for any ambitious organizer to bootstrap a new contest concept remained strong.

In 2013, Chris Sharma, Mike Call, and climbing wall manufacturer Walltopia collaborated to create the Psicobloc Masters Series, a deepwater soloing competition on a 55-foot wall over a 750,000-gallon pool. The event was inspired by a deepwater solo contest in Bilbao, Spain.

The United States' Psicobloc Masters occurred in conjunction with the summer's Outdoor Retailer tradeshow and was contested as a multiround elimination tournament. The inaugural competition, in Park City, Utah, brought competitors from various generations together. Although Sharma himself participated but lost in the quarterfinals, an exciting men's finals featured Daniel Woods climbing side-by-side with a bouldering standout from Tennessee named Jimmy Webb. The women's finals presented Sasha DiGiulian going head-to-head with Delaney Miller, both of whom were breakout American stars. The following year, 2014, Sean McColl and Claire Buhrfeind won the men's and women's division respectively. Webb and a French competitor, Charlotte Durif, were the winners in 2015, at an event marred by rain and lightning.

Following years' Psicobloc Masters saw clearer Western skies and new names added to the men's and women's winner's circle, such as Michaela Kiersch, Kyra Condie, Hannah Tolson, and Germany's Jan Hojer.

But Psicobloc Masters, which was also livestreamed on YouTube, was largely a showcase for professional climbers. A smaller-scale competition, the Pocatello Pump, in Idaho, which had been the brainchild of a college student named Peter Joyce in the early 1980s, continued to host climbers of all levels every year and raise funds for climbing organizations such as the Access Fund in the process. Competition legends such as Hans Florine had taken part in the Pocatello Pump in previous years, but so had countless amateurs and recreational climbers from around the southeastern Idaho region. The competition's longevity earned it the distinction of being the United States' longest-running climbing competition.

Other annual gatherings varied greatly in size and scope, only further attesting to climbing's popularity. For instance, a get-together in Fayetteville, West Virginia, called HomoClimbtastic purported to be "the world's largest queer-friendly climbing convention." Additionally, the Hueco Rock Rodeo in Hueco Tanks, Texas, continued to be held every winter over a three-day period. The contest was organized by the American Alpine Club, a direct tie-in with American competition climbing's very first overseeing entity. In time, the National Senior Games would include exhibition climbing competitions with various age divisions, including Over 50, Over 60, and

Over 75. The Boulder Field Masters, a competition series at a gym in Sacramento, California, would include multiple events over a six-month period—all boosted in reputation by a considerable total prize purse of $60,000. And a festival called Color the Crag at Horse Pens 40 in Alabama would support, encourage, and celebrate diversity in climbing. One occurrence that tied the modern competition scene to that of previous years perhaps more poetically than any others was a relaunching of the JCCA (as the Junior Competitive Climbing Association) by Kyle Clinkscales and routesetter Canon Huse in 2017. The impetus behind the organization's restart was to provide kids with a more recreational competition track than the national one offered by USA Climbing.

An addendum to the richness of competitions within the United States was an official announcement on August 3, 2016, that climbing had finally been approved for inclusion in the Olympics after a vote by the 130 members of the International Olympic Committee (IOC). The decision had its roots in a brainstorming conference held December 8–9, 2014, called the Olympic Agenda 2020. Climbing was thus scheduled to make its debut in the 2020 Olympic Games in Tokyo, Japan, alongside a host of other sports additions such as skateboarding and surfing. The President of the IOC, Thomas Bach, indicated that the package of new events was a calculated measure to draw in young viewers. A preceding Youth Olympics in Buenos Aires, Argentina, would also feature climbing.

For many competitors and event organizers in the United States and around the world, climbing's Olympics inclusion was long overdue. Its acceptance was a result of persistent efforts of the International Federation of Sport Climbing (IFSC), but the broader notion of climbing being an Olympic sport predated even the IFSC's existence. To support the Olympic journey of the United States' elite competitors, USA Climbing created a fundraising initiative called the Circle of Gold.

Climbing's Olympics inclusion was not without a degree of controversy and consternation, as the chosen Olympic format combines sport (difficulty) climbing, speed climbing, and bouldering into a single event—akin to three sequential sports making up a single triathlon. Yet for the 20 men and 20 women competitors who will vie for the gold medal over a four-day period of Olympic competition, the uncommon format is ancillary to the larger promise of prestige and competition climbing history.

In an illustrative extension of the Olympic excitement, USA Climbing moved its headquarters from Boulder to Salt Lake City, Utah, in 2018. Utah is also home to the American governing bodies of skiing, snowboarding, and speed skating, thus aligning USA Climbing geographically with several other sports that possess Olympics heritage. Patti Rube, the president of USA Climbing's board of directors, said of the relocation, "USA Climbing has worked closely with the Utah Sports Commission, Salt Lake City, and local business leaders over the past two years for our Bouldering National Championships with tremendous results. We are eager to continue and expand this partnership as we prepare for the 2020 Olympic Games." An Overall National Team formed and trained at an exclusive facility in Salt Lake City, too. The team comprised the eight Americans who were contending for Olympic qualification: Kyra Condie, Ashima Shiraishi, Brooke Raboutou, Margo Hayes, Zach Galla, Nathaniel Coleman, Sean Bailey, and Drew Ruana. Notably absent from the squad was Alex Puccio. Despite having won the Bouldering National Championship with a career-defining performance in 2018, Puccio chose to end her Olympic push prematurely out of disinterest in training for the Olympics' combined discipline format. Her recusal, announced to the public on her

Instagram account, was illustrative of the dramatic and unpredictable nature of American competition climbing under the Olympic banner.

Of those athletes who *were* on the Overall National Team, Raboutou, in particular, shined early and became the first-ever American climber to qualify for an Olympic Games. She earned her berth to the Tokyo 2020 Olympics via the "combined" discipline at the IFSC World Championships.

A more somber bookend to USA Climbing's relocation to Utah and subsequent Olympic preparations, however, was the passing of Jeff Lowe—a native of the state—in the same year. Lowe died on August 24, 2018, after a long battle with a neurodegenerative disorder. Although media outlets widely praised Lowe's ice climbing accomplishments in memoriam—even proclaiming him to be "widely regarded as the finest American alpinist of his generation," there was coverage given to his pioneering efforts to bring competition climbing to the American masses exactly three decades earlier. In many ways, the progress of USA Climbing, the vigor of the American competition scene, and Olympic esteem was Lowe's original vision, morphed significantly but nonetheless finally fully realized.

The guarantee of an Olympic presence was just one long-term goal finally achieved for the United States' competition enthusiasts. Another was the career opportunities for routesetters. Tim Steele would recall asking his Ohio employer, RockQuest, about the potential for advancement as a routesetter in the late 1990s, only to be told by the gym at the time that the options were limited. A little more than a decade later, largely due to the multilevel routesetting certification course of USA Climbing, routesetters could find far more lucrative options and a more accessible communal network. "The modern gyms are paying health care, and you have a salary, and people are obviously making a living off of it," Steele says of routesetting in the present day. "Back then, there weren't that many routesetters because it just wasn't a career-oriented thing."

Few Americans played as pivotal a role in routesetting's vocational development as Mike Pont. From ASCF and JCCA championships to World Cups, the X Games, and the Gorge Games, the events on Pont's resume represented the history of American competition climbing itself, and thus revealed the establishment a national heritage. So it was fitting that Pont took a break from routesetting after a nonstop, multidecade push, only to return to set routes at a gym near his home with an unwavering delight in the craft. "In my heart, I love making climbing moves and making them feel just right," Pont would explain of his lifelong devotion to—and pioneering work in—routesetting. "I can't really describe what 'just right' means, but I know when I feel it that a route is just the way I want it. And I love that with a wrench and five minutes, I can take that thing apart—it's like pop-up art. It's a thing that I can create, and I take it away; it's there and then it's gone. I love that."

Routesetting as a utilitarian art offered other opportunities as well. Beginning in 2017, a company of gyms in California, Touchstone Climbing, created an annual Woman Up festival. The first iteration was held at the Dogpatch Boulders gym in San Francisco, with the Cliffs of Id gym in Culver City hosting the event the following year. The multiday climbing festival was advertised as featuring an entire gym of boulders set by women routesetters, a women-only competition, and a routesetting clinic. The overarching aim was to inspire women to join the climbing industry, and the initial events drew hundreds of participants. Also appearing around the same time was SheSets, a website and database aimed at delivering content about routesetting for women through blog posts, videos, and symposiums. And an organization called Brown Girls Climb offered a wide range of services for—and related to—self-identified women of color in climbing gyms. In Colorado, a collective known as the Routesetting Institute served as a consortium for routesetters who would travel around the country to give educational symposiums. Among the educators were Sarah Filler, Jackie Hueftle, and Jeremy Ho, all renowned for their routesetting experience and expertise.

The network of climbing gyms sustaining routesetting as a craft and career around the United States continued to expand rapidly. *Climbing Business Journal*, a publication created by routesetter Mike Helt to serve, monitor, and promote the indoor aspect of the climbing industry, reported that 27 new climbing facilities opened in the United States in 2016. In 2017, 43 additional gyms opened. Some of these new gyms had direct ties to routesetting's past—such Gripstone Climbing in Prescott, Arizona, started by key historical figures Tony Yaniro and Derek Waggoner. Other new climbing gyms had novel business ideas. A Tennessee gym, Memphis Rox, opened with a financial model of having visitors pay only what they could afford; visitors to the gym were also given the option of doing volunteer work at the gym to earn a full membership. This was just one example of a larger industry movement to make gym climbing a recreation accessible and feasible to more people. Momentum Indoor Climbing in Salt Lake City encapsulated this concept in a 2017 advertising campaign with the catchline "Climbing Is for Everyone." Two years later, a non-profit, 1Climb, put climbing's universal appeal into practice by building climbing walls at Boys and Girls Clubs chapters across the United States.

With new gyms and facilities came a vibrant product industry. Companies such as eGrips, Rock Candy, Atomik, Teknik, Element, Metolius, VooDoo, So iLL, and Kilter (co-owned by Hueftle and Ian

Powell) frequently released new handhold and foothold designs and textures. Distributors such as Premium Holds and Volumes, which works with foreign companies 360 Holds, Cheeta, Squadra, and Simpl, made European handholds and footholds readily available in the United States.

Influential figures of routesetting's past continued to intertwine with the craft of shaping ever-more-modern holds around the United States. Louie Anderson and Kevin Branford connected with Las Vegas, Nevada–based Method Grips. Anderson even started his own hold company, Legacy Ascension, based out of the small town of Ten Sleep, Wyoming. In Boulder, Colorado, Scott Rennak founded Incredigrips, a brand of handholds and footholds that could be screwed onto any surface; such versatility nodded to the earliest imaginative spirit of the "glue-ups" on the stark pillars of a highway overpass. Rennak helped get Kilter off the ground from a business perspective, and he eventually assumed a leadership role at *Climbing Business Journal*.

One of Rennak's contemporaries, Chris Danielson, went from being instrumental in the development of USA Climbing's Routesetting Committee to working as the Administrator of USA Climbing's Clinic and Certification Program and chairing the organization's Rules Committee. He would also work on the Certification Committee of the Climbing Wall Association (CWA) and sit on the IFSC's Route Setter Commission. In addition to being a routesetter for myriad World Cup competitions, Danielson would work with gyms through his own sales and consulting business, Thread Climbing. In that, he would advise clients on gym start-up and wall design, as well as represent and distribute leading American, Canadian, and European climbing companies. Danielson thus became an even greater linchpin connecting the United States' business enterprises to the global competition infrastructure.

Elsewhere, Big Stone Publishing, the parent company of *Rock and Ice*, launched a new magazine, *Gym Climber*, in 2018, while *Climbing* magazine launched its own competition-themed website channel the same year. Fittingly, *Rock and Ice* and *Climbing* both frequently featured the professional photography of Jim Thornburg, long removed from his "glue-up" days but nonetheless continually connected to climbing innovation. Thornburg's counterpart in creating the "glue-ups," Scott Frye, remained in the climbing industry as a gym staffer and mentor to younger climbers.

Also innovative were American companies such as Cascade Specialty, started by Mike Palmer, and Futurist, founded by Timy Fairfield, which offered consulting services for custom climbing gym floor padding. Fairfield also co-founded and became the CEO of Chalk Cartel, a company that focused solely on climbing chalk. Fairfield's multiple entrepreneurial efforts, which also included being a presenter at the CWA's annual summit and a designer of climbing walls and climbing shoes, were expansions of his relationship with climbing as a longtime competitor.

Bobbi Bensman, who had one of the longest careers of any American competitor, applied the same competitive drive that had brought her numerous victories at Snowbird, ASCF National Championships, and Phoenix Bouldering Contest events over the years to business endeavors. She became a sales representative, first for The North Face and later for La Sportiva and Mammut. The jobs kept her continuously connected to the domestic and international competition circuit, traveling and working with sponsored climbers and occasionally competing in events herself at gyms around the United States.

As the gym industry grew and the competition experience at-large grew along with it, USA Climbing continued to evolve. A series of prestigious bouldering competitions for adults called the National Cup series launched in 2016 with Chris Danielson serving as its Technical Director. The first season kicked off with the Yank-N-Yard event at Stone Age Climbing Gym in Albuquerque, New Mexico, followed by additional bouldering events in San Diego, California; Birmingham, Alabama; and elsewhere. The National Cup series continuously benefited from sponsorship by The North Face and featured $10,000 contest winnings. Eventually the series even unveiled a new multizone scoring system.

Separate from the National Cup series was an American Combined Invitational. It featured sport climbing, speed climbing, and bouldering as joint disciplines, mirroring the Olympics' format. At the onset of the first Combined Invitational, USA Climbing entered into a multiyear agreement to televise and livestream subsequent American competitions on ESPN's many media platforms. The inaugural event featured commentary from Meagan Martin and ESPN play-by-play announcer Sam Farber—and attracted viewers who were devoted climbers as well as just casual sports fans.

Around the same time that the National Cup series was taking shape, Claudiu Vidulescu, the head coach of USA Climbing's national team for approximately a decade, was joined by another coach, Josh Larson. The two shared national team coaching duties until Larson, a former competitor, took over the role fully approximately one year later. Vidulescu, however, remained a fixture on the competition scene as the head coach of the team at Stone Summit in Atlanta, Georgia. Tyson Schoene, who stepped away from the national team spotlight in 2010, returned as one of the national team's assistant coaches in 2015 and remained in the role for subsequent years. "I had just gotten married in 2008, and my climbing was important to me, and [Vertical World] was winning championships as a team," Schoene says on his impetus for taking a hiatus when he did. "So I stepped away for a bit. I always intended to return, I just didn't know when."

By the time Schoene did return at Vidulescu's request, he found the American national team to be "more professional," and with even greater general parental support. A squad of other highly qualified assistant coaches formed over time as well and included Kim Mitchell, Meg Coyne, and Meghan McDonald. An orthopedic specialist named Zack DiCristino was brought on as the national team's physical therapist.

At the business level, Waggoner left his post as USA Climbing's CEO in July 2018, and in a statement, his successor, Marc Norman, said, "USA Climbing is a star in competition event organizing and is seeing tremendous growth in its membership and visibility."

Norman's statement was accurate, but perhaps the greatest effect of the United States' storied competition history at the time of Norman's appointment was less trackable than membership growth and gym data, and less flashy than a potential Olympics medal or event trophy. It was nonetheless ever-present in every climbing gym around the country, at every playground or college recreation facility that featured a climbing wall. Wherever there was someone climbing on artificial handholds or partaking in a structured contest, there were intangible possibilities. Those possibilities could be as personal or as professional as the climber chose, with an infrastructure and competition community now ready and willing to support one's climbing ambitions.

There were still lessons to be learned in competition climbing, as there had been ever since the initial grassroots bouldering contests in Southern California. There were lessons on dedication and determination, as well as winning and losing. There were teachings of sportsmanship and camaraderie that lasted longer than any victory celebration.

But in between those lessons, entwined with the ropes and the rigging, blending with the cheers of any given crowd, there was a remarkable story. It was a story of aspiration and ingenuity, of multiple decades and multiple dreamers, of men and women with purpose and precision to better the competition status quo. The incredible American competition narrative had endured highs and lows to reach an apex. It possessed a history of ups and downs and yet, somehow and some way, it had always remained vertical.

AFTERWORD

THE HISTORY OF AMERICAN COMPETITION CLIMBING follows a fascinating trajectory, but it does not neatly conclude. There are new competitions taking place each year, along with new national championships, and new opportunities for competitors regarding sponsorships, endorsements, and promotion. The history is still being written.

It can still be difficult to make a living as a professional climber; most must scrabble together a career out of competition prize money and sponsorship support from multiple brands. Such a vocational grind is usually hampered by injuries, given the physical demands of the sport in a contemporary context. The requisite travel can be grueling, as can the ongoing anxiety that competitions, by nature, cause. Competitors must also pay for coaches, trainers, and often occasional medical rehabilitation, none of which are cheap. USA Climbing does not receive any funding from the United States federal government, unlike the governing bodies of competition climbing in most other respective countries.

Yet, there are unique paths to be trod by American competitors amid the funding issue. Social media offers unique opportunities for an athlete's exposure and with that, competitions and their contestants have become a big part of the computer-mediated age. Some Americans—such as Alex Puccio—have used crowdfunding donation campaigns as a means of earning money to cover the requisite competition expenses. "Although I love the life I live and wouldn't trade it for anything being a professional climber has allowed me to live a very modest lifestyle at best," Puccio wrote in a post for her campaign. "I just can't afford to compete in the entire World Cup season all on my own anymore. That's why I am asking for support from you to help me achieve my dreams and represent my country to the best of my ability!" In 2019, speed climber Shae Kelly took a similar approach by starting a GoFundMe page prior to the Pan American Youth Championships.

One sympathizes with Kelly, Puccio, and other American competitors. In a way, it's a very exciting and unpredictable time for climbing promotion and marketing.

A noteworthy development in the career ambitions of climbers is the specificity of commitment that is required nowadays. In previous decades, climbers could oscillate between participating in numerous competitions indoors and climbing famous routes outdoors. Indeed, if one peruses the results of competitions throughout history, one will note that oftentimes the winners of competitions in a given year were also the ones climbing the hardest outdoor routes at the time. While such crossover still exists, it is less common. For the most part, elite climbers nowadays must choose whether they want to be primarily outdoor climbers or primarily competitors, because each specialty entails so much nuance at the elite level. Perhaps renowned climbing coach Kyle Clinkscales said it best: "Yes, you have to be strong to be an outdoor climber and a competition climber. But one is competing, and one is climbing. And there is a huge difference between the two."

The gym scene is ever-changing, too. Many gyms nowadays have cafes and bars in addition to climbing walls, as well as amenities like study rooms and yoga studios. Some gyms, massive in size, occasionally feature live music. Others sometimes host art fairs. Such diverse offerings complicate, in an intriguing way, what a climbing gym is, but they all expand a facility's importance in the lives of its members. The fancy industry term for this is "third place," meaning that a gym can be a space that people frequent when they are not at home or at their place of employment.

With more gyms will come more tangents to the ongoing trajectory. Routesetting is expanding in its nuance, with parkour, "comp-style," "skate-style," and other such designations now specifying certain acrobatic formulations and methodologies. Many of these styles are possible now due to the widespread usage of large volume holds on gym walls, as mentioned previously in this book (particularly in reference to Rene Keyzer-Andre building a volume for a competition at Miami University in 1991).

While ubiquitous in competitions all over the world, volumes as commercial commodities have noteworthy American roots too, tracing back to a Dallas, Texas–based company called Motavation Volumes that was started by hold shaper Jared Stains. Volumes have significantly influenced routesetting, and from an entertainment perspective, they have helped competitions become more visually interesting for spectators. The immense size and geometric shapes of most volumes necessitate full-body movement and hand-foot coordination from the competitors, which adds visible drama to any climb.

"The more people that you have in a crowd, the further back they stand, the less they can see and understand," said Clinkscales about the aesthetic change in routesetting. "So, putting crimps on a wall—when people stand 100 or 200 feet back—looks bad. Whereas if there is a gigantic volume that's bigger than the competitor's body, and there are some little crimps attached to it, it has this three-dimensional aspect literally and figuratively that resonates with the crowd."

Ironically, coupled with the rise of indoor climbing and climbing-as-entertainment, bolstered by elaborate gyms and several generations of young competitors and routesetters, has come an ethical consideration about outdoor stewardship. The innumerable gyms are staffed to accommodate the swell of new climbers, in terms of safety and training. The outdoor crags, however, are not. One question then becomes how the climbing community-at-large can safely and responsibly provide gym patrons (*indoor* climbers) with access to the *outdoor* climbing experience in a way that is not damaging or excessively burdensome to the rocks or the wilderness.

Not long ago, the Access Fund, one of the leading American organizations focused on the conservation of outdoor climbing areas, created an educational poster with this very issue of stewardship in mind. The poster, titled "Making the Transition from Gym to Crag," can be seen hanging on the walls of gyms around the country. That's a good start, but certainly more efforts will be needed as successive gym generations venture into the wild. It is beyond the scope of this book to propose solutions, but I urge the reader to consider the issue.

The truth is that it might take decades to quantifiably assess the impact of gym climbers—and the popularity of competition climbing—on the outdoors. So, once again, this is part of the story that cannot fully be concluded in this book. I hope it is an issue that another writer will feel passionate about and feel compelled to explore in essay or book form in the future.

There are other ways, perhaps more pleasant, in which the competition narrative is continuing. Consider the thousands of children who are currently enrolled in some sort of climbing team program at a gym, either as an after-school option as a replacement for school athletics. These children are being mentored by climbing coaches and introduced to role models who can have a positive impact that goes beyond the local, regional, divisional, and national competition circuit.

On a personal note, while writing this book, I took a job as a coach of a gym's youth climbing team, and I would not trade that experience for anything. I have talked to a number of coaches who hold their own position in similar high regard. It is a pleasure and a privilege to be a coach. In fact, I don't think I'm overstepping my bounds to assert that introducing others to the sport is one of life's true joys for any climber. And even if the kids that I coached never compete, the infrastructure that continues to support them— meaning the other coaches, the parents, and the gym itself—is a byproduct of the United States' competition metamorphoses of the past and present. What great accomplishments will these young kids add to the story in five years? In a decade?

I am reminded of something climber Beth Bennett told me when I interviewed her about her appearance in the 1979 film *First Ascent* and the American competition scene that launched less than a decade after that. "The comps really came into vogue after I had dropped out of the climbing scene," she said. "I never felt like participating. But I love seeing how kids get into the sport through teams nowadays—I think climbing is a great team sport. It offers such a cool venue for kids to be social, to have healthy adult mentoring, to have healthy friendships without girlfriend/boyfriend pressures. Being successful at something when you're a teenager is really a valuable experience. So I've flip-flopped, in terms of valuing competition in climbing."

I thus leave the reader with an ongoing history. There is a robust competition narrative that can still be added to—by researchers, by competitors, by coaches, by kids, and by fans. I hope this book has shown that competition climbing in its current form and the entire gym network are products and byproducts of people from all areas of the country and all walks of life; the history was constructed by down-to-earth people with creative ideas, by competitors with unwavering athletic determination, and by all sorts of individuals in between who simply wanted to take part because they loved climbing.

In other words, the competition scene was not constructed by inaccessible superiors or entities from afar. Like the best aspects of any sport, the competition community was—and continues to be— the outcome of resolute grassroots efforts that eventually caught on and were transformed into a singular phenomenon. And every time you enter a gym, grip a handhold, or watch an exciting competition in awe, you are part of it too. Part of that community and history; a participant in the captivating drama.

APPENDIX
Competition Results

___

Central Arizona Bouldering Contest

Camelback Mountain, Arizona
May 15, 1983

1. Chris Raypole
2. Scott Wade
3. Jim Zahn

Central Arizona Bouldering Contest

Beardsley Rockpile, Arizona
1984

Expert

1. Brian Sarni
2. Eric Johnson
3. Mike Cook
4. Darius Azin
5. Jason Sands
6. Jim Gaun
7. Chris Dunn
8. Lance Hughson
9. Dennis McMahon
10. Dow Davis

Novice

1. Debbie Marsino
2. Jeff Corbin

3. Steve Stull
4. Todd Applewhite
5. Steve Allen
6. John Rapp
7. Russ Thielman
8. John Aughimbaugh
9. Matt Lofdahl
10. George Thielman

Central Arizona Bouldering Contest

Camelback Mountain, Arizona
1985

Expert

1. Paul Davidson
2. Brad Smith
3. Brian Sarni
4. Tony Cosby
5. Eric Rhicard

Novice

1. Douglas Smith
2. Leo Garcia
3. Matt Lofdahl
4. Rick Percival
5. Rick Hlava

Central Arizona Bouldering Contest

Beardsley Rockpile, Arizona
1986

Expert

1. Paul Davidson
2. Chip Ruckgaber
3. Steve Smelser
4. Jason Sands
5. Bill Dockins

Novice

1. Tom Suriano
2. Dave Combest
3. Jim Duvall

Women

1. Kristin Drumheller
2. Mimi DeGravelle
3. Laurie Wheeler

Phoenix Bouldering Contest

Camelback Mountain, Arizona
1987

Expert

1. Ron Kauk
2. Chris Gore
3. Dariius Azin
4. Chris Raypole
5. Dave Schultz

Intermediate

1. Rick Hlava
2. Jeff McQueen
3. Curtis Fawley
4. Rob Jacobson
5. Jeff Wax

Novice

1. Eric Fedor
2. Heath Moss
3. Andy Vejnoska
4. Leonard Paup
5. Rob Rosebrough

Women

1. Bobbi Bensman
2. Andrea Azoff
3. Cyrena Goodrich
4. Libby Rohovit
5. Jeanie Haney

International Sport Climbing Championship

Snowbird, Utah
June 7–12, 1988

Men's

1. Patrick Edlinger
2. Jean-Baptiste Tribout
3. Marc Le Ménestrel
4. Martin Atkinson
5. Jason Stern
6. Christian Griffith
7. Scott Franklin
8. Alex Duboc (tie)
8. Geoff Weigand
10. Ron Kauk

Women's

1. Catherine Destivelle
2. Lynn Hill (tie)
2. Mari Gingery
4. Isabelle Patissier
5. Corrine LaBrune
6. Jennifer Cole
7. Pascuale Montse
8. Alison Osius
9. Rosie Andrews
10. Andrewa Eisenhut

Speed Climbing (winners only)

Men's: Jacky Godoffe
Women's: Catherine Destivelle

International Sport Climbing Championship

(North American Open & World Cup Final)
Snowbird, Utah
August 11–20, 1989

NORTH AMERICAN OPEN

Men's

1. Jim Karn
2. Merrill Bitter
3. Alex Lowe
4. Chris Hill
5. Jason Stern
6. Colin Lantz
7. Jordan Mills
8. Tray Mayr
9. Tedd Thompson
10. Hans Florine

Women's

1. Bobbi Bensman
2. Robyn Erbesfield
3. Shelley Presson
4. Melissa Quigley
5. Meg Hall
6. Aimee Barnes
7. Jessica Gladstone
8. Kristen Drumheller (tie)
8. Bird Lew (tie)
8. Shannon Wade (tie)

WORLD CUP FINAL

Men's

1. Didier Raboutou
2. Simon Nadin
3. Ron Kauk
4. Francois Lombard
5. Robert Cortijo
6. Andrej Marcicz
7. Jim Karn
8. Geoff Weigand
9. Yann Ghesquiers
10. Carlos Garcia

Women's

1. Nanette Raybaud
2. Lynn Hill
3. Catherine Destivelle
4. Robyn Erbesfield
5. Luisa Iovane
6. Corinne Labrune

North American Open ("Seattle Open")

Union Station
Seattle, Washington
October 11–12, 1989

Men's (lead)

1. Jim Karn
2. Dale Goddard
3. Chris Hill (tie)
3. Jason Stern
5. Peter Mayfield
6. Doug MacDonald

Women's (lead)

1. Bobbi Bensman
2. Akiko Ohiwa
3. Julie Leino
4. Melissa Quigley
5. Aimee Barnes
6. Georgia Phipps

North American Continental Championship

Event Center
The University of Colorado
Boulder, Colorado
December 1–3, 1989

Men's (lead)

1. Jim Karn
2. Dale Goddard
3. Pat Adams
4. Todd Skinner
5. Chris Hill
6. Scott Franklin
7. John Duran
8. Jim Sandford
9. Doug Englekirk
10. Scott Frye

Women's (lead)

1. Alison Osius
2. Bobbi Bensman
3. Melissa Quigley
4. Bird Lew
5. Shelley Presson
6. Susan Price
7. Shannon Wade
8. Carmel Schimmel

Berkeley Rockmaster

Berkeley Community Theater
Berkeley, California
March 17–18, 1990

Men's (lead)

1. Jim Karn
2. Colin Lantz
3. Will Gadd
4. Geoff Weigand
5. Jim Thornburg
6. Pat Adams
7. Hans Florine
8. Scott Frye
9. Tom Herbert
10. Max Dufford

Women's (lead)

1. Bobbi Bensman (tie in finals)
2. Alison Osius (tie in finals)
3. Laura Lonowski
4. Susan Price
5. Amy Irvine
6. Nancy Prichard
7. Shelley Presson
8. Lisa Rehms
9. Bird Lew
10. Aimee Barnes

Seattle Rockmaster

Hec Edmundson Pavillion
Seattle, Washington
April 21–22, 1990

Men's (lead)

1. Jim Karn
2. Dale Goddard
3. Jason Karn
4. Geoff Weigand
5. Hans Florine
6. Peter Mayfield
7. Tom Herbert
8. Drew Bedford
9. Ed Keller
10. Mike McCarron

Women's (lead)

1. Bobbi Bensman
2. Alison Osius
3. Shelley Presson
4. Melissa Quigley
5. Lisa Rehms
6. Jade Chun
7. Diane Russell
8. Shannon Wade
9. Julie Lieno
10. Laura Lonowski

Speed Climbing (winners only)

Men's Winner: Hans Florine
Women's Winner: Laura Lonowski

United States Championships

Snowbird, Utah
July 4–8, 1990

Men's

1. Dale Goddard
2. Will Gadd
3. Doug Englekirk

Men's finals was rained out; semi-final results became the finals results

Women's

1. Bobbi Bensman
2. Alison Osius
3. Diane Russell

Speed Climbing (winners only)

Men's: Hans Florine
Women's: Sally Bartunek

1990 World Cup

The William Randolph Hearst
Greek Theatre ("Greek Theater")
The University of
California–Berkeley
Berkeley, California
August 17–19, 1990

Men's

1. Simon Nadin
2. Francois LeGrand
3. Jindrich Hudecek
4. Jose Maria Gomez
5. Jim Karn
6. Thomas Fickert
7. Jerry Moffat
8. Jean-Baptiste Tribout
9. Ben Moon
10. Tony Ryan

Women's

1. Nanette Raybaud
2. Lynn Hill
3. Isabelle Patissier
4. Robyn Erbesfield
5. Alison Osius
6. Ana Ibanez
7. Luisa Iovane
8. Jennifer Cole
9. Isabelle Dorismond
10. Andrea Eisenhut

Speed Climbing (winners only)

Men's: Hans Florine
Women's: Isabelle Dorismond

Pumpfest in Paradise

Paradise Rock Gym
Denver, Colorado
January 26–27, 1991

Men's

1. Kurt Smith
2. Pat Adams
3. Jim Surrette

Women's

1. Jennifer Whaley
2. Elaine Chandler

San Diego Indoor Climbing Championship

San Diego County Fairgrounds
San Diego, California
February 9–10, 1991

Men's

1. Kelly Wilson
2. Kevin Wilson
3. Tom Herbert
4. Kurt Smith
5. Doug Englekirk
6. Boone Speed

Women's

1. Bobbi Bensman
2. Diane Russell
3. Jade Chun
4. Sylvia Mireles

1991 ASCF National Championship

CityRock Climbing Gym
Emeryville, California
June 7–9, 1991

Men's

1. Hans Florine
2. Jason Karn
3. Dale Goddard

Women's

1. Bobbi Bensman
2. Alison Osius
3. Diane Russell

Speed Climbing (winners only)

Men's: Hans Florine
Women's: Connie Koch

Snowbird Sport Climbing Championship (ASCF Regional)

Snowbird, Utah
July 5–7, 1991

Men's

1. Kurt Smith
2. Dale Goddard
3. Doug Englekirk
4. Hans Florine
5. Steve Schneider
6. Pat Adams
7. Dan Michael
8. Geoff Weigand
9. Tony Yaniro
10. Tim Wagner
11. John Mireles
12. Porter Jarrard

Women's

1. Bobbi Bensman
2. Alison Osius
3. Cathy Beloeil
4. Nancy Feagin
5. Bird Lew
6. Laura Lonowski
7. Diane Russell (tie)
7. Mindy Shulak
9. Deb Sleven

Speed Climbing (winners only)

Men's: Hans Florine
Women's: Sally Bartunek

"For Women Only" Sport Climbing Championship

The Sporting Club
Chicago, Illinois
July 14–15, 1991

Women's

1. Alison Osius
2. Bobbi Bensman
3. Diane Russell
4. Melissa Quigley
5. Shannon Wade
6. Nancy Feagin
7. Susan Price
8. Jade Chun
9. Laura Lonowski
10. Bird Lew
11. Sue Patenaude
12. Mia Axon (tie)
12. Mindy Shulak

Happy Climbers Competition

Healthworks Gym
Fort Collins, Colorado
November 9–10, 1991

Men's

1. George Squibb
2. Joe Desimone
3. Bruno Lanson
4. Hank Caylor
5. Alan Lester
6. Alan Nelson
7. Keith Lenard
8. John Colten
9. Rick Lince
10. Michael Johnson

Women's

1. Suzanne Paulson
2. Susan Wint
3. Jessica Zieve
4. Leslie Coon

Showdown at Paradise

Paradise Rock Gym
Denver, Colorado
November 23–24, 1991

Men's

1. George Squibb
2. Pat Adams
3. Jim Surrette
4. Christian Griffith
5. Mike Downing
6. Colin Lantz
7. Joe Desmone
8. Alan Lester
9. Gary Ryan
10. Kevin Gonzales

Women's

1. Mia Axon
2. Jennifer Whaley
3. Suzanne Paulson
4. Bettina Campos

Pre-Olympics

Chambéry, France
January 30–February 1, 1992

NORTH AMERICAN OPEN
Men's

1. Stefan Glowacz
2. Didier Raboutou
3. Stephan Furst
4. Yuji Hirayama
5. Fancois LeGrande
6. Fredric Nicole
7. Klaus Buchele

Women's

1. Susi Good
2. Isabelle Patissier
3. Robyn Erbesfield
4. Nanette Raybaud
5. Andrea Eisenhut
6. Luisa Iovane

1992 ASCF National Championship

CityRock Climbing Gym
Emeryville, California
August 26, 1992

Men's

1. Doug Englekirk
2. Jim Karn
3. Kurt Smith
4. Timy Fairfield
5. Scott Franklin
6. Andy Outis
7. Hank Caylor
8. Harrison Decker
9. Will Gadd
10. Seth Johnston

Women's

1. Alison Osius
2. Bobbi Bensman
3. Georgia Phipps
4. Kadi Johnston
5. Diane Russell
6. Melissa Quigley

Invitational Redpoint Competition

CityRock Gym
Emeryville, California
February 6, 1993

Men's

1. Doug Englekirk
2. Scott Franklin
2. Andy Outis (tie)
3. Hans Florine
4. Tom Richardson
5. Scott Frye
6. Christian Griffith
7. Tony Yaniro

Women's

1. Anne Smith
2. Diane Russell
3. Nancy Feagin
4. Georgia Phipps
5. Bird Lew

Mideast Indoor Climbing Competition (ASCF Regional)

Miami University
Oxford, Ohio
April 2–3, 1993

Men's

1. Ben Ditto
2. Rob Butsch
3. Greg Echelmeyer
4. Jeff Moll
5. Chris Zweig

Women's

1. Tiffany Levine
2. Dina Johnstone
3. Margarita Martinez
4. Barb Shelohzek
5. Jen Hackman

1993 ASCF National Championship

CityRock Climbing Gym
Emeryville, California
June 19–20, 1993

Men's

1. Jim Karn
2. Scott Franklin
3. Doug Englekirk
4. Christian Griffith
5. Kevin Gonzales
6. Rudy Hofmeister

Women's

1. Robyn Erbesfield
2. Tiffany Levine
3. Bobbi Bensman
4. Diane Russell
4. Shelley Presson (tie)
6. Suzanne Paulson

Speed Climbing (winners only)

Men's: Greg Lowe
Women's: Diane Russell

1994 ASCF Junior National Championship

Climb North
Pittsburgh, Pennsylvania
June 3–5, 1994

Men's/Boys' (winners only)

Age Division	Name
11 & Under	Dustin Link
12–13	Dave Hume
14–15	Jayson Hovarth
16–17	Aaron Chaney

Women's/Girls' (winners only)

Age Division	Name
13 & Under	Claire Lyon
14–15	Bonnie DeBrujin
16–17	Sarah Weiland

1994 ASCF National Championship

CityRock Climbing Gym
Emeryville, California
June 11–12, 1994

Men's

1. Scott Franklin
2. Jim Karn
3. Doug Englekirk
4. Steve Hong
5. Timy Fairfield
6. Jeff Cloud
7. George Squibb
8. Kevin Branford
9. John Cronin
10. Jordi Salas

Women's

1. Bobbi Bensman
2. Mia Axon
3. Georgia Phipps
4. Shelley Presson
5. Melissa Quigley
6. Susan Price
7. Lizz Grennard
8. Trish Houghtaling
9. Michelle Hurni
10. Diane Russell

Gay Games IV (Unity '94)

(First-ever climbing competition
at the Gay Games)
Inner Wall Climbing Gym
New Paltz, New York
June 23–24, 1994

Men's

1. Mountain Miller
2. Cliff Ketchum
3. John Skinner
4. Russell Clifton
5. Philip Judson
6. David McColgen

Women's

1. Diane Russell
2. Zachary Nataf
3. Elaine Lee
4. Shawna Cordell
5. Yvette Segal
6. Caroline Peck

Pacific Edge (ASCF Regional)

Pacific Edge Climbing Gym
Santa Cruz, California
August 26, 1994

Men's

1. Tom Richardson
2. Jason Campbell
3. Marcos Nunez
4. Ty Foose
5. Chris Sharma
6. Ian Powell
7. Jim Thornburg

Women's

1. Diane Russell
2. Suzanne Paulson
3. Michelle Locatelli
4. Susan Price
5. Georgia Phipps
6. Alexa Foose
7. Caroline Peck

The Bluegrass Climbing Classic (ASCF Regional)

Rocksport Gym
Louisville, KY
September 24–25, 1994

Men's

1. Jordi Salas
2. Ben Ditto
3. David Hume
4. Pascal Roberts
5. Kenny Matys
6. Tony Berlier
7. Sam Adams
8. Bob Bergman
9. Robert Marsh

Women's

1. Nadine Gagnon
2. Karen Rand
3. Zoe Panchen
4. Michelle Hale

Extreme Games

Newport, Rhode Island
June 24–July 1, 1995

Men's (Difficulty)

1. Ian Vickers
2. Arnaud Petit
3. Francois Petit

Women's (Difficulty)

1. Robyn Erbesfield
2. Elena Ovchinnikova
3. Mia Axon

Speed Climbing (winners only)

Men's: Hans Florine
Women's: Elena Ovchinnikova

1995 ASCF Junior National Championship

SolidRock Gym
San Diego, California
August 12–13, 1995

Men's/Boys' (winners only)

Age Division	Name
11 & Under	Chris Lindner
12–13	Jay Weber
14–15	Chris Sharma
16–17	Tommy Caldwell

Women's/Girls' (winners only)

Age Division	Name
11 & Under	Chelsea Raymond
12–13	Shena Sturman
14–15	Katie Brown
16–17	Nancy McCullough

1995 ASCF National Championship

Mission Cliffs Gym
San Francisco, California
August 19–20, 1995

Men's

1. Chris Sharma
2. David Hume
3. Steve Hong
4. Doug Englekirk
5. Timy Fairfield
6. Jason Campbell
7. Jeff Webb
8. Tommy Caldwell
9. Kevin Branford
10. Wil Catlin

Women's

1. Robyn Erbesfield
2. Elena Ovchinnikova
3. Mia Axon
4. Katie Brown
5. Natalie Richer
6. Bobbin Bensman
7. Shelley Presson
8. Tiffany Levine
9. Michelle Locatelli
10. Trish Beerman

1996 ASCF Junior National Championship

Vertical World
Seattle, Washington
August 24–25, 1996

Men's/Boys' (winners only)

Age Division	Name
11 & Under	Landon Little
12–13	Jason Helig
14–15	Chris Sharma
16–17	Kevin Branford

Women's/Girls' (winners only)

Age Division	Name
11 & Under	Kate Johnson
12–13	Seren Rubens
14–15	Shena Sturman
16–17	Beth Rodden

1996 Continental Sport Climbing Championships

Pacific National Exhibition
Vancouver, British Columbia,
Canada
August 30–September 1, 1996

Men's

1. Chris Sharma
2. Tommy Caldwell
3. Doug Englekirk
4. Steve Hong
5. Kevin Branford
6. Jason Campell
7. Seth Mason
8. David Hume

Women's

1. Mia Axon
2. Tiffany Levine
3. Jola Sandford
4. Kathryn Embacher
5. Beth Rodden
6. Michelle Locatelli

Speed Climbing (winners only)

Men's Winner: Chris Bloch
Women's Winner: Michelle Hurni

JCCA Mid-Atlantic Championships

Philadelphia Rock Gym
Oaks, Pennsylvania
July 16, 1997

Men's/Boys' (winners only)

Age Division	Name
11 & Under	Ryan Flynn
12–13	Robert D'Anastasio
14–15	Nate Gold
16–17	Ian Rooney
18–19	Jason Lance

Women's/Girls' (winners only)

Age Division	Name
11 & Under	Nicolette Raleigh
12–13	Ellen Houle
14–15	Nina Rodriguez
16–17	Whitney Hemingway-Duffy

South Texas Heat

San Antonio Rock Gym
San Antonio, Texas
September 20, 1997

Men's

1. Kenmar Smith
2. Zach Sokoloski
3. Ray Kinnaird

Women's

1. Marcia Ethridge
2. Misty Eberhart
3. Rene Hurt

Hound Ears Bouldering Competition

Boone, North Carolina
October 4, 1997

Men's

1. Andrew Taylor
2. Bob Otto
3. Ashley Overton

Women's

1. Lisa Semple
2. Gina Vess
3. Ashley Overton

Alamosa Crux Open

Adams State University
Alamosa, Colorado
October 15, 1997

Men's

1. Sky Lopez
2. Brent Edelen
3. Nathaniel Walker

Women's

1. Rynn Nicols
2. Megan Emmons
3. Christen Clayton

Rock Rodeo

Hueco Tanks, Texas
February 28, 1998

Men's

1. Nick Yosbein
2. Michael Ontiveros
3. Kurt Speir

Women's

1. Kristin Dockstader
2. Lisa Hathaway
3. Marieke Neethliny

The event also featured a "Super Expert" division, won by Doug Ayers; Chris Grijalva placed second, and Elliot Bloch placed third.

1998 ASCF National Championship

Rock'n & Jam'n
Thornton, Colorado
April 25–26, 1998

Men's

1. Chris Sharma
2. Tommy Caldwell
3. Steve Hong
4. Vadim Vinokur
5. Paul Preuss
6. David Hume
7. Jason Campbell
8. Aaron Shamy
9. Michael Doyle
10. Josh Heiney

Women's

1. Katie Brown
2. Elena Ovchinnikova
3. Shena Sturman
4. Beth Rodden
5. Michelle Hurni
6. Jola Sanford
7. Bobbi Bensman

Gym Rat Jamboree

Peak Performers Gym
Jacksonville, Florida
May 9, 1998

Men's

1. John Davidson
2. Greg Ganbelta
3. Robert Terem

Women's

1. Janine Marello
2. Lindy
3. Christy Swofford

Hound Ears Bouldering Competition

Boone, North Carolina
October 3, 1998

Men's

1. Scott Freeman
2. Robert Otto
3. Dean Melton

Women's

1. Gina Vess
2. Lisa Semple
3. Amy Clark

Fall Rock Rodeo

Miami University
Oxford, Ohio
October 10, 1998

Men's

1. James Pruden
2. Trevor Sutherland
3. Frank Cleveland

Women's

1. Lynette Miller
2. Maureen Kunz
3. Sierra Schnerder

1998 Touchstone/JCCA Junior Invitational

Mission Cliffs Gym
San Francisco, California
October 17, 1998

Men's/Boys' (winners only)

Age Division	Name
11 & Under	Scott Cory
12–13	Ethan Pringle
14–15	Robert D'Anastasio
16–17	Aaron Shamy
18–19	Dan Gable

Women's/Girls' (winners only)

Age Division	Name
11 & Under	Samantha Jang-Stewart
12–13	Josie Spagnolo
14–15	Barbara Schranz
16–17	Shena Sturman
18–19	Beth Rodden

Pump-Kin Pull-Down

Rock'n & Jam'n
Thornton, Colorado
October 31, 1998

Men's

1. Kevin Branford
2. Tommy Caldwell
3. Paul Preuss

Women's

1. Pam Winberg
2. Michelle Hurni
3. Angele Liegeois Sjong

Hold On or Go Home 2

Vertical Endeavors
Columbus, Ohio
November 7, 1998

Men's

1. Jeff Lehmkuhl
2. James Pruden
3. Brian Moone

Women's

1. Roxanna Brock
2. Rebecca Noyes
3. Maureen Kunz

Touchstone Invitational

Mission Cliffs Gym
San Francisco, California
November 14, 1998

Men's

1. Tommy Caldwell
2. Aaron Shamy
3. Vadim Vinokur
4. Jason Campbell
5. Chris Bloch

Women's

1. Katie Brown
2. Elena Ovchinnikova
3. Shena Sturman
4. Beth Rodden
5. Heather Collins

Cranksgiving Climbing Competition

Vertical Relief Rock Gym
Flagstaff, Arizona
November 22, 1998

Men's

1. Joe Czerwinski
2. Brian Benson
3. Keith Hickey

Women's

1. Sadie Landram
2. Rayne Demoulin
3. Regina Richer

Top Gun Competition

Adventure Sports Rock Gym
Logan, Utah
January 23, 1999

Men's (bouldering)

1. Jordan Davis*
2. Mike West
3. Jared Campbell

Women's (bouldering)

1. Amanda Congelose
2. Maggie Karren
3. Tam Laycock

*Davis also won a lead competition at the event.

Midwest Bouldering Tour Championship

Climb Time
Cincinnati, Ohio
May 15, 1999

Men's (Invitational)

1. James Pruden
2. Brian Moone
3. Jeff Lehmkuhl
4. Frank Cleveland
5. Eric Bauman
6. Jason Martin
7. Paul Emanovsky
8. Steve Kaufmann

Women's (Invitational)

1. Lauren Lee
2. Tori Allen
3. April Hensley
4. Liz Gieseke
5. Vanessa Parras
6. Jill Messer

Eastern Bouldering Series Championship

Climb Time
Cincinnati, Ohio
March 25, 2000

Men's

1. Jeremy Mariette
2. Doug Ayers
3. G.P. Salvo
4. James Pruden
5. Adian Miller
6. Andy Raether
7. Eric Greulich
8. Brandon Mallak
9. Jeremy Peetrovich
10. Dan Chancelor

Women's

1. Lynette Miller
2. Tori Allen
3. Angie Payne
4. Sara Garland
5. K.C. Fischer
6. Andrea Dissenger
7. Jennifer Orman

Kids'

1. Alex Brock
2. Clark Allen
3. Paul Robinson
4. Patrick Wyatt
5. Greg Kerzhner
6. Mike Kerzhner
7. Conrad Kirby
8. Grady Bagwell
9. Elia Burkardt
10. Tyler O'Connor

Subaru Gorge Games

Bouldering Competition
Hood River, Oregon
July 13–14, 2000

Men's

1. Nels Rosaasen
2. Chris Sharma
3. Eric Scully
4. Jason Kehl
5. Rob D'Anastasio
6. Jeff Lehmkul
7. John Stack
8. Matt Goreham

Women's

1. Lisa Rands
2. Claire Murphy
3. Marea Palmer
4. Pam Wimberg
5. Zoe Kozub
6. Seren Rubens
7. Melissa Griffith
8. Katie Brown

Bring the Ruckus

The Front Climbing Club
Salt Lake City, Utah
August 13, 2000

Men's

1. Chris Sharma
2. Dave Graham
3. Francois Legrand
4. Jared Roth
5. Obe Carrion

Women's

1. Liv Sansoz
2. Claire Murphy
3. Maureen Kunz
4. Yikiko Maeshima
5. Marea Palmer

American Bouldering Series Championship ("ABS 1")

Climb Time
Cincinnati, Ohio
March 17, 2001

Men's

1. John Stack
2. Joel Brady
3. Doug Ayers
4. Obe Carrion
5. Jody Miall
6. Brandon Mallak
7. Galen Mitchell
8. Ben Montgomery
9. G.P. Salvo
10. Matt Bosley

Women's

1. Tori Allen
2. Lisa Rands
3. Angie Payne
4. Pam Winberg
5. Andrea Wilkins
6. Charlotte Jouett
7. Elizabeth Hardwick
8. Lynette Miller
9. Renata Dziak

The Pusher Open

The Front Climbing Club
Salt Lake City, Utah
August 18–19, 2001

Men's

1. Chris Sharma
2. Malcolm Smith
3. Stephane Julien
4. Jérôme Meyer
5. Joel Brady

Women's

1. Myriam Motteau
2. Liv Sansoz
3. Lisa Rands
4. Tori Allen
5. Angie Payne

The Cordless Benefit

The Front Climbing Club
Salt Lake City, Utah
October 2001

Men's

1. Jérôme Meyer
2. Christian Core
3. John Stack

Women's

1. Lisa Rands
2. Tori Allen
3. Brandi Mulligan

Second American Bouldering Series Championship ("ABS 2")

Boulder Rock Club
Boulder, Colorado
March 30, 2002

Men's

1. Obe Carrion
2. John Stack
3. Mike Audridge
4. Joel Brady
5. Adam Stack
6. Brian Capps
7. Nate Gold
8. Josh Heiney
9. Chad Gilbert
10. Tommy Caldwell
11. Will LeMaire
12. Matt Bosley

Women's

1. Tori Allen
2. Lisa Rands
3. Lauren Lee
4. Angie Payne
5. Natasha Barnes
6. Brandi Mulligan
7. Emily Harrington
8. Dana Johns
9. Alexandra Holkova
10. Alex Johnson
11. Pauline Hsieh
12. Nikki Whelan

Professional Climber's Association Boulder Brawl

The Spot Bouldering Gym
Boulder, Colorado
December 14, 2002

Men's

1. Chris Sharma
2. Jérôme Meyer
3. Nels Rosaasen

Women's

1. Jolie Matkowski
2. Emily Harrington
3. Portia Menlove

Third American Bouldering Series Championship ("ABS 3")

Berkeley Ironworks
Berkeley, California
March 22, 2003

Men's

1. Tom Durant
2. Vadim Vinokur
3. Chad Gilbert
4. Chris Bloch
5. Leif Palmer-Burns
6. Ethan Pringle
7. Matt Segal
8. Brian Capps
9. Tyson Atwell
10. Ken Dick
11. Craig Gilbert
12. Steven Lapen

Women's (Open)

1. Alex Johnson
2. Lizzy Asher
3. Emily Harington
4. Natasha Barnes
5. Rebeckah Berry
6. Laura Griffiths
7. Mykael Ann McGinley
8. Corinne Kohlen
9. Sydney McNair
10. Anja Presson
11. Laura Beckerich
12. Autumn Duke

2004 Professional Climbers Association Tour Championship

The Spot Bouldering Gym
Boulder, Colorado
May 13–15, 2004

Men's

1. David Hume
2. Daniel Woods
3. Ethan Pringle
4. Steven Jeffery
5. Luke Parady
6. John Goicoechea
7. Keita Mogaki
8. Rob D'Anastasio
9. Simon Villenueve
10. Obe Carrion

Women's (Open)

1. Angie Payne
2. Alex Johnson
3. Lizzy Asher
4. Portia Menlove
5. Natasha Barnes
6. Mykael Ann McGinley
7. Adrienne Drolet
8. Sharlotte Jouett
9. Ally Dorey
10. Zoe Kozub

SendFest

The Front Climbing Club
Salt Lake City, Utah
August 12–13, 2005

Men's (Pro)

1. Chris Sharma
2. Keita Mogaki
3. Zeb Engberg
4. Sean McColl
5. Matt Bosley
6. Chris Lindner
7. Paul Robinson (tie)
7. Daniel Woods
9. Steven Jeffrey
10. Vasya Vorotnikov
11. Ethan Pringle
12. Rob D'Anastasio

Women's (Pro)

1. Tomoko Ogawa
2. Emily Harrington
3. Natasha Barnes
4. Lizzy Asher
5. Alex Johnson
6. Ally Dorey
7. Rebeckah Berry
8. Alex Puccio
9. Portia Menlove
10. Jody Hansen
11. Lani Adamson
12. Yuko Sakakibara

Organic/So iLL Vedauwoo Bouldering Competition

Vedauwoo, Wyoming
October 1, 2005

(Mixed field)

1. Daniel Woods
2. BJ Tilden
3. Chuck Fryberger
4. Johnny Goicoechea

The Gravity Brawl (Mammut Bouldering Championship)

New Jersey Rock Gym
Fairfield, New Jersey
March 2–3, 2007

Men's

1. Paul Robinson
2. Daniel Woods
3. Vasya Vorotnikov

Women's

1. Lizzy Asher
2. Kate Reese
3. Sasha DiGiulian

2008 American Bouldering Series Championship ("ABS 9")

The Spot Bouldering Gym
Boulder, Colorado
February 14–16, 2008

Men's

1. Paul Robinson
2. Chris Sharma
3. Sean McColl
4. Mark Hobson
5. Tyler Haack
6. Keita Mogaki
7. Kyle Owen
8. Ryan Olson
9. Kazuma Watanabe
10. Robert D'Anastasio

Women's

1. Alex Puccio
2. Alex Johnson
3. Paige Claassen
4. Lizzy Asher
5. Tiffany Hensley
6. Lisa Rands
7. Akiyo Noguchi
8. Angie Payne
9. Kate McGinnis
10. Charlotte Jouett

2008 Bouldering World Cup (Teva Mountain Games)

Vail, Colorado
June 6–7, 2008

Men's

1. Kilian Fischhuber
2. Gabriele Moroni
3. Paul Robinson
4. Gérome Pouvreau
5. Daniel Woods
6. Tyler Landman
7. Remo Sommer
8. Chris Sharma
9. David Lama
10. Sean McColl

Women's

1. Alex Johnson
2. Katharina Saurwein
3. Anna Stöhr
4. Tiffany Hensley
5. Vera Zijlstra
6. Alex Puccio
7. Natalija Gros
8. Chloé Graftiaux
9. Lisa Rands
10. Silvie Rajfova

2009 Bouldering World Cup (Teva Mountain Games)

Vail, Colorado
June 5–6, 2009

Men's

1. Jonas Baumann
2. Daniel Woods
3. Kilian Fischhuber
4. Paul Robinson
5. Kyle Owen
6. Rustam Gelmanov
7. Guillaume Glairon Mondet
8. Tsukuru Hori
9. Gabriele Moroni
10. Loic Gaidioz

Women's

1. Alex Puccio
2. Alex Johnson
3. Akiyo Noguchi
4. Anna Stöhr
5. Jain Kim
6. Natalija Gros
7. Maud Ansade
8. Tiffany Hensley
9. Chloé Graftiaux
10. Therese Johansen

Psicobloc Masters Series

Utah Olympic Park
Park City, Utah
August 2, 2013

Men's Finals

Jimmy Webb*
Daniel Woods

*indicates winner

Men's Semifinals

Jimmy Webb*
Jon Cardwell

Daniel Woods*
Matty Hong

Men's Quarterfinals

Jimmy Webb*
Vasya Vorotnikov

John Cardwell*
Carlo Traversi

Daniel Woods*
Nalle Hukkataival

Matty Hong*
Chris Sharma

Women's Finals

Sasha DiGiulian*
Delaney Miller

Women's Semifinals

Sasha DiGiulian*
Vikki Weldon

Delaney Miller*
Mcagan Martin

Women's Quarterfinals

Sasha DiGiulian*
Nina Williams

Delaney Miller*
Angie Payne

Meagan Martin*
JC Hunter

Vikki Weldon*
Andrea Szekely

2013 Bouldering National Championship ("ABS 14")

City Auditorium
Colorado Springs,
Colorado
February 22–23, 2014

Men's (Open)

1. Daniel Woods
3. Ian Dory
4. Vasya Vorotnikov
5. Carlo Traversi
6. Garrett Gregor
7. Peter Dixon

Women's (Open)

1. Alex Puccio
2. Andrea Szekely
3. Isabelle Faus
4. Megan Mascarenas
5. Angie Payne
6. Alex Johnson
7. Lisa Chulich

Psicobloc Masters Series

Utah Olympic Park
Park City, Utah
August 8, 2014

Men's Finals

Sean McColl*
Daniel Woods

*indicates winner

Men's Semifinals

Sean McColl*
Chris Sharma

Daniel Woods*
Carlo Traversi

Men's Quarterfinals

Sean McColl*
Jimmy Webb

Chris Sharma*
Jon Cardwell

Daniel Woods*
Matty Hong

Carlo Traversi*
Klemen Bečan

Women's Finals

Claire Buhrfeind*
Delaney Miller

Women's Semifinals

Claire Buhrfeind*
Alex Puccio

Delaney Miller*
Grace McKeehan

Women's Quarterfinals

Claire Buhrfeind*
Michaela Kiersch

Alex Puccio*
Ashima Shiraishi

Delaney Miller*
Sasha DiGiulian

Grace McKeehan*
Kyra Condie

2015 Bouldering National Championship ("ABS 16")

Monona Terrace
Madison, Wisconsin
February 5–6, 2015

Men's

1. Mohammad Jafari Mahmodabadi
2. Daniel Woods*
3. Michael O'Rourke
4. Josh Larson
5. Nathaniel Coleman
6. Austin Geiman
7. Rob D'Anastasio

*Woods was deemed the national champion because Mohammad Jafari Mahmodabadi was not a United States citizen.

Women's

1. Alex Puccio
2. Alex Johnson
3. Angie Payne
4. Megan Mascarenas
5. Kyra Condie
6. Grace McKeehan

Bouldering Open National Championship

Monona Terrace
Madison, Wisconsin
January 29–30, 2016

Men's

1. Nathaniel Coleman
2. Jimmy Webb
3. Carlo Traversi
4. Daniel Woods
5. Tyler Landman
6. Kai Lightner
7. Mohammad Jafari Mahmodabadi

Women's

1. Megan Mascarenas
2. Alex Puccio
3. Claire Buhrfeind
4. Michaela Kiersch
5. Meagan Martin
6. Sierra Blair-Coyle
7. Krya Condie

Sport Climbing Open National Championship

Central Rock
Boston, Massachusetts
March 18–19, 2016

Men's

1. Sean Bailey
2. Kai Lightner
3. Ben Isaac Tresco
4. Elan Jonas Mcrae
5. Drew Ruana
6. Carlo Traversi

Women's

1. Margo Hayes
2. Grace McKeehan
3. Michaela Kiersch
4. Claire Buhrfeind
5. Kyra Condie

Speed Climbing (winners only)

Men's: Libor Hroza
Women's: Claire Buhrfeind

Bouldering Open National Championship

Salt Palace Convention Center
Salt Lake City, Utah
February 3–5, 2017

Men's

1. Nathaniel Coleman
2. Kai Lightner
3. Alexey Rubtsov
4. Sean Bailey
5. Shawn Raboutou
6. Nicholas Milburn
7. Andy Lamb
8. Tyler Landman
9. Alex Waterhouse

Women's

1. Alex Puccio
2. Ashima Shiraishi
3. Brooke Raboutou
4. Michaela Kiersch
5. Kyra Condie
6. Megan Mascarenas
7. Margo Hayes
8. Grace McKeehan
9. Lily Canavan

Sport Climbing Open National Championship

Movement Climbing and Fitness
Denver, Colorado
March 11–12, 2017

Men's

1. Kai Lightner
2. Jesse Grupper
3. Drew Ruana
4. Noah Ridge
5. Shane Messer
6. Bobby Taft-Pittman
7. Josh Levin
8. Vasya Vorotnikov
9. Austin Geiman
10. Solomon Barth
11. Joey Catama

Women's

1. Ashima Shiraishi
2. Margo Hayes
3. Brooke Raboutou
4. Kyra Condie
5. Michaela Kiersch
6. Claire Buhrfeind
7. Julia Talbot
8. Melina Costanza
9. Natalia Grossman
10. Meagan Martin
11. Juliet Hammer

Speed Climbing (winners only)

Men's: John Brosler
Women's: Claire Buhrfeind

Bouldering Open National Championship

Salt Palace Convention Center
Salt Lake City, Utah
February 2–3, 2018

Men's

1. Nathaniel Coleman
2. Sean Bailey
3. Drew Ruana
4. Matt Fultz
5. Zach Galla
6. Carlo Traversi

Women's

1. Alex Puccio
2. Ashima Shiraishi
3. Brooke Raboutou
4. Claire Buhrfeind
5. Margo Hayes
6. Meagan Martin

Sport Climbing Open National Championship

Mesa Rim Climbing and Fitness
Reno, Nevada
March 17–18, 2018

Men's

1. Sean Bailey
2. Drew Ruana
3. Solomon Barth
4. Josh Levin
5. Noah Ridge
6. Zach Galla
7. Dalton Bunker
8. Nathaniel Coleman

Women's

1. Claire Buhrfeind
2. Michaela Kiersch
3. Alex Puccio
4. Margo Hayes
5. Brooke Raboutou
6. Delaney Miller
7. Kyra Condie
8. Sophia Kwon

Speed Climbing (winners only)

Men's: John Brosler
Women's: Claire Buhrfeind

Combined Invitational

Momentum Indoor Climbing
Salt Lake City, Utah
January 18–20, 2019

Men's

1. Zach Galla
2. Nathaniel Coleman
3. Sean Bailey
4. Colin Duffy
5. Drew Ruana
6. Kai Lightner
7. John Brosler
8. Josh Levin

Women's

1. Kyra Condie
2. Brooke Raboutou
3. Natalia Grossman
4. Ashima Shiraishi
5. Margo Hayes
6. Piper Kelly
7. Sienna Kopf
8. Claire Buhrfeind

Bouldering Open National Championship

Deschutes County Fairgrounds
Redmond, Oregon
February 1–2, 2019

Men's

1. Sean Bailey
2. Nathaniel Coleman
3. Drew Ruana
4. Zach Galla
5. Dylan Barks
6. Matty Hong

Women's

1. Ashima Shiraishi
2. Alex Johnson
3. Margo Hayes
4. Claire Buhrfeind
5. Brooke Raboutou
6. Sienna Kopf

Sport Climbing Open National Championship

Sportrock Climbing Centers
Alexandria, Virgnia
March 8–9, 2019

Men's

1. Jesse Grupper
2. Zander Waller
3. Solomon Barth
4. Sean Bailey
5. Dylan Barks
6. Drew Ruana
7. Charlie Osborne
8. Matty Hong

Women's

1. Margo Hayes
2. Ashima Shiraishi
3. Katherine Lamb
4. Kyra Condie
5. Michaela Kiersch
6. Lauren Bair
7. Emma Palmer
8. Claire Buhrfeind

Speed Climbing (winners only)

Men's: John Brosler
Women's: Emma Hunt

ACKNOWLEDGMENTS

THANK YOU TO JOSH WILLIAMS, Michelle Bruton, Sam Ofman, Jen DePoorter, Preston Pisellini, Tom Galvin, and the whole crew at Triumph Books for believing in this project and contributing countless hours to its completion. Also, thank you to Anne Dubuisson for seeing promise in this book when it was still just a Word document without a home.

This book would not have happened if not for the willingness of many people to talk, share memories, and inform me of a fascinating history that had otherwise gone largely undocumented. I will arrange my gratitude according to the various eras of the history, although in many cases there is considerable overlap.

First, there is very little formal documentation and reportage on the bouldering contests that were held in Southern California in the late 1970s and early 1980s. Thus, I am grateful to Lynne Leichtfuss, Kevin Powell, Doug Munoz, Ron Amick, Randy Vogel, Maria Cranor, Tom Jones, and Ron Gomez; they regaled me with stories of—and insight into—a magical time and place in climbing's past.

Jim Waugh was kind enough to provide me with an extensive oral history of his Phoenix Bouldering Contest and the many other areas of the history to which he contributed greatly. It was a joy every time I talked with him. Similarly, I was fortunate to talk to both Jim Thornburg and Scott Frye about their "glue-ups," and I am appreciative of the details and memories they relayed to me.

I had the pleasure of corresponding with Jeff Lowe prior to his passing, when this book was still in its early research phases; I'll never forget that Jeff thanked me in advance for writing the book and expressed happiness that the full competition story was finally going to be told. It is my hope that Jeff would be proud of how the book turned out.

Exposure in the mass media was a catalyst for competition climbing's initial American boom. To that point, I must be effusive in thanks to Bob Carmichael for taking the time to talk on a number of occasions. It was some early correspondence with Bob that gave me the conviction to turn my journalistic curiosity into a long-term book project. Thank you also to Beth Bennett for giving me insight into various climbing and film projects. Also, I am grateful to David Michaels and Kevin Donald for their willingness to explain various production aspects of climbing, sports, film, and television around the late 1980s and early 1990s. Dan Goodwin was also a significant resource for useful content about that era.

For decades, Roy McClenahan has done yeoman's work to preserve information about Jeff Lowe's competitions. Without the materials that Roy has saved over the years (including journal entries, charts, statistics, measurements, and photographs), there would be an unfillable void in the history. If I had to guess, I would say that Roy and I exchanged a thousand emails throughout the course of this book's research—and I enjoyed every bit of that correspondence.

Roy deserves a genuine thank you for the preservation he has done, as well as his kindness in sharing it with me.

Regarding those competitions of the late 1980s and early 1990s, I would also like to thank Steve Gabel, Paul Sibley, Rex Wilson, Chris Noble, Sasha Montagu, Isabelle Patissier, Beth Wald, Deanne Gray Said, Susan X. Billings, Malcolm Daly, and Guy Kenny. They shared stories and anecdotes, aided in the clarification of details, and conveyed both the mania and the magic of the endeavors.

The ASCF lasted for years, and many people contributed to its success. First, thank you to Ralph Erenzo and Peter Darmi for informing me of the organization's formation, early efforts, and evolution. The information that I gathered from Ralph and Peter was vital. Thank you also to Peter Mayfield for conversing with me about the founding of CityRock and the competitions held there. And, I am appreciative of the openness of Hans Florine, Kurt Smith, Bobbi Bensman, and Alison Osius—for sharing memories and perceptions from the competitor's point of view. Timy Fairfield was also kind enough to speak on a number of occasions and I am forever grateful for his acumen and expertise.

In regard to the routesetting of the ASCF years, I am indebted to Mike Pont, Rene Keyzer-Andre, and Kevin Branford for giving me foundational data as well as incredible amounts of useful nuance.

Deepest thanks are also owed to Chris Danielson, Ted Welser, and Tim Steele, who vividly transported me back to the magical days of Miami University's early competition scene and provided essential details about the development of routesetting in the 1990s and 2000s. Tim maintained—and shared—many routesetting documents (and photographs) from the past that were instrumental in providing particulars, corroborating details, and pinpointing important historical dates—particularly related to the American League of Forerunners.

And to cap all that off, I am grateful for the correspondence of Jackie Hueftle; she was kind enough to set me on the right track in seeking out many pivotal routesetters of the history.

My key contact for much of the foundational JCCA history was Jeanne Fernandez-McShane. I am thankful not only for her guidance, but for her willingness to share other JCCA friends and contacts too. In particular, thank you to Zoe Mark, Scott Rider, Kate McShane Urban, Molly Beard, and Emily Varisco. I extend a heartfelt thanks to Sasha Akalski for sharing memories of the Extreme Games. Ivor Delafield was also forthcoming with an insider take on that event.

I had the fortune of talking with some of the most instrumental and influential people of the post-JCCA American competition scene. Scott Rennak captivated me with the full story of how the ABS was formed, and I am forever thankful for his correspondence. Kynan Waggoner also supported this book from the get-go—and I could not have asked for a kinder and more knowledgeable source. I am thankful for the time that Anne-Worley Moelter spent explaining the inner workings of the American competition scene of the early 2000s. In addition, I am grateful for the mentorship and knowledge of Mike Helt. I'd also like to thank Clark Shelk, Mike Call, Zoe Johnston, and Louie Anderson for filling in various gaps in the research.

When it comes to the coaches and competitors of USA Climbing's infancy, it was an honor to gain insight from Claudiu Vidulescu, Tyson Schoene, Kyle Clinkscales, and Paul Robinson. I'm indebted to the recollections and wisdom they each provided. Thank you also to Steve Woods for documenting the period with photos and allowing me to include some of those historical images in this book. And thanks to Jessi Haynes for the constant coaching mentorship.

There are other friends, colleagues, and contacts that I would like to formally acknowledge: Kevin Corrigan at *Climbing*, Francis

Sanzaro at *Gym Climber* and *Rock and Ice*, Joe Robinson at *Climbing Business Journal*, Eddie Fowke at *The Circuit Climbing*, and Tyler Norton at *Plastic Weekly*. I am grateful for the work they have all done to promote competition climbing—and the fact that they have supported or complemented my work in that same sphere. Also, thank you to Scott Yorko and Stefanie Kamm for the hospitality during some of this book's research. Thank you always to my dear friends Dan Kojetin and Soo-yeon Sung. Thank you to the whole Hoosier Heights crew, and to Steve Schwortz—a true friend and industry mentor. And I'd like to express my appreciation for the work and generosity of Daniel Gajda, Josh Horsley, Juliane Fritz, Andrea Laue, Greg Mionske, Colton Marsala, Grant Kates, Jeff Wagenheim, Kelly Feilke, Zach Brinchi, Meg Coyne, and Wes Shih and the other kind folks at Sender One. Very special thank yous are due to Robyn Erbesfield-Raboutou and Brooke Raboutou for all they did to help this book during their incredibly busy schedules.

Finally, love and gratitude are forever due to Bill and Vicki Burgman, to my brother, Will Burgman, and to the rest of my family. Love and gratitude are due as well to Zooey Ahn for her boundless support.

If there is anyone who was omitted from this list, it was purely by mischance and accident, and my appreciation and captivation are nonetheless ever-present.

BIBLIOGRAPHY

I interviewed a great number of people for this project—many of them more than once—during a period of time that began in 2016 and continued through early 2019. Generally, the direct quotes in this book are sourced from those interviews unless otherwise noted or attributed. Here is a listing of individuals whose interviews and correspondence proved particularly useful: Sasha Akalski, Ron Amick, Louie Anderson, Molly Beard, Beth Bennett, Bobbi Bensman, Susan X. Billings, Kevin Branford, Bob Carmichael, Kyle Clinkscales, Malcolm Daly, Chris Danielson, Peter Darmi, Ivor Delafield, Kevin Donald, Ralph Erenzo, Timy Fairfield, Jeanne Fernandez-McShane, Hans Florine, Scott Frye, Steve Gabel, Ron Gomez, Dan Goodwin, Mike Helt, Jackie Hueftle, Zoe Johnston, Tom Jones, Guy Kenny, Rene Keyzer-Andre, Lynne Leichtfuss, Zoe Mark, Peter Mayfield, Roy McClenahan, Kate McShane Urban, David Michaels, Anne-Worley Moelter, Doug Munoz, Alison Osius, Isabelle Patissier, Mike Pont, Kevin Powell, Scott Rennak, Scott Rider, Paul Robinson, Deanne Gray Said, Tyson Schoene, Clark Shelk, Paul Sibley, Kurt Smith, Tim Steele, Jim Thornburg, Emily Varisco, Claudiu Vidulescu, Randy Vogel, Kynan Waggoner, Jim Waugh, Ted Welser, Rex Wilson, Steve Woods.

Competition results were sourced primarily from *Climbing*, *Rock and Ice*, and *Urban Climber*. In some cases, results were informed by additional data provided by Scott Rennak, Jim Waugh, and Steve Woods.

Wire Services

Associated Press

Periodicals

The Baltimore Sun
Chicago Tribune
Climbing
Deseret News
The Guardian
Gym Climber
Los Angeles Times
Men's Journal
Mountain
The New York Times
Outside
Rock and Ice
Sport Climbing
Sports Illustrated
Urban Climber
USA Climbing Annual

Websites

blisterreview.com
browngirlsclimb.com
climbing.com
climbingbusinessjournal.com
climbingwallindustry.org
climbstoneage.com
espnpressroom.com
gripped.com
homoclimbtastic.com

ifsc-climbing.org

joerockheads.com

miamioh.edu

pusher.world

rockandice.com

time.com

usaclimbing.org

usaclimbing.rallyme.com

verveclimbing.com

voodooclimbing.com

wcpo.com

youtube.com

Writers

Dave Angle

Conrad Anker

Thomas K. Arnold

Todd Balf

Drew Bedford

Michael Benge

Bobbi Bensman

Charles Bentley

Todd Berlier

George Bracksieck

Baptiste Briand

Corey Buhay

Matt Burbach

Neil Cannon

Janet Coolum

Kevin Corrigan

Mikaela Curaza

Craig DeMartino

Steve Dieckhoff

Shelley Downing
Mark Eller
Ralph Erenzo
Hans Florine
Will Gadd
Debbie Gawrych
Joe Glickman
Stefan Glowacz
Dale Goddard
Nicole Graiff
Joseph Hooper
Amy Irvine
Jeff Jackson
William Oscar Johnson
Steve Keenan
George Keenen
Kurt Kragthorpe
Ally Kramer
Gary Langer
Scott Leonard
Alan Lester
Michael Levy
Dougald MacDonald
Clark Man
Jim McCarthy
Marjorie McCloy
John Mireles
Ed Mistarka
Veronique Mistiaen
Alison Osius
Mike Papciak
Ian Parnell
Dave Pegg
Kate Pickert

Matt Pincus
Nancy Prichard
Stephen Regenold
Scott Rennak
Scott Rider
Joe Robinson
Rob Robinson
Justin Roth
Gail Rothschild
Matt Samet
Richard Sandomir
Steve Schneider
Susan E.B. Schwartz
Robert Semple
Lee Sheftel
Kiesha Simpson
Bennett Slavsky
Tim Sprinkle
Matt Stanley
Tim Steele
Dave Struthers
Ramsay Thomas
Jim Thornburg
Sasha Turrentine
Craig Vetter
Jorge Visser
Megan Walsh
Geoff Weigand
Janet Wells
Marlene Werner
Tony Yaniro
Wills Young

Video

Break on Through (1972)
Cliffhanger, TriStar Pictures (1993)
Dosage, Big UP Productions (2001)
Fall Line, Sports Imagery Inc. Productions (1981)
First Ascent, Sports Imagery/George Schlatter Productions (1979)
Outside the Arena, Sports Imagery Inc. Productions (1976)
Painted Spider, Spire Productions (1992)
Star Trek V: The Final Frontier, Paramount Pictures (1989)
West Coast Pimp, Soma Entertainment (2000)

Television

CBS Sports Presents. "International Sport Climbing Championship." CBS (1989)

Advertisements, Flyers, Pamphlets, Programs

The 1986 California Bouldering Championship and 1st Annual Stone Masters Freeclimbing Competition (1986)
"The 1990 United States Championships." *Sport Climbing Championships* (1990)
The American Sport Climbers Federation Membership Packet (1996)
ASCF News (1997)
"Beyond Snowbird." *The American Alpine Club* (1988)
Climb to the Top of the Rock (Undated)
Course Setting Clinic (1999)
Junior News: The Newsletter of the JCCA (1997)
Steele, Tim. *Tim's Routesetting Sermon* (Undated)

Books

Darmi, Peter. *The Sport Climbing Competition Handbook* (Revised Edition). Chockstone Press (1992)
Erbesfield, Robyn and Steve Boga. *Sport Climb with Robyn Erbesfield*. Stockpole Books (1997)

Hill, Lynn with Greg Child. *Climb Free*. W.W. Norton and Company (2002)

Rennak, Scott. A*merican Bouldering Series Organizer Handbook* (Fourth Edition). (2003)

Roper, Steve. *Camp 4*. Mountaineers Books (1998)

Sherman, John. *Stone Crusade*. The AAC Press (1994)

Woolum, Janet. *Outstanding Women Athletes Who Influenced American Sports* (Second Edition). Oryx Press (1998)

ABOUT THE AUTHOR

JOHN BURGMAN'S PREVIOUS BOOKS are *Why We Climb: A Dirtbag's Quest for Vertical Reason* (2015) and *Island Solitaire* (2018). He is a former editor at *Outdoor Life*, a former Fulbright grant recipient, and a graduate of New York University's MFA program. His work has appeared online and in print at *Esquire, Trail Runner, Portland Review, Gym Climber, Boundary Waters Journal, The Rumpus,* and elsewhere. He often reports on competition climbing for magazines such as *Climbing* and *Climbing Business Journal*. He is a frequent guest on the popular climbing podcast *Plastic Weekly*.